THE CHEAP BASTARD'S® GUIDE TO

Seattle

HELP US KEEP THIS GUIDE UP TO DATE

We would love to hear from you concerning your experiences with this guide and how you feel it could be improved and kept up to date. Please send your comments and suggestions to:

editorial@globepequot.com

Thanks for your input, and happy travels!

CHEAP BASTARD'S® SERIES

THE CHEAP BASTARD'S® GUIDE TO

Seattle

Secrets of Living the Good Life—For Less!

First Edition

David **Volk**

gpp®
travel

Guilford, Connecticut
An imprint of Globe Pequot Press

All the information in this guidebook is subject to change. We recommend that you call ahead to obtain current information before traveling.

To buy books in quantity for corporate use
or incentives, call **(800) 962–0973**
or e-mail **premiums@GlobePequot.com.**

Text design by Sheryl P. Kober

Library of Congress Cataloging-in-Publication Data is available on file.

ISBN: 978-0-7627-6036-7

Printed in the United States of America
10 9 8 7 6 5 4 3 2 1

To Cindy, Hana, and Nathan,
the reasons I get out of bed every morning
and the ones who inspire me to do what I do . . .
even on those rare occasions when I wish I didn't.

CONTENTS

ABOUT THE AUTHOR

David Volk is an award-winning humor writer and the author of *The Tribe Has Spoken: Life Lessons From Reality TV*. He has written for national and regional publications including *Seattle Magazine, Alaska Airlines, AAA Journey,* and *Koi World*. He has called Seattle home for more than 20 years. When he isn't writing, he can be found searching for urban adventures, odd experiences, and kitschy places to take his family and for locals to take out-of-towners.

He has a serious side, but often has trouble locating it.

Volk also writes humorous rants on his Web site, www.davidvolk.com. Contact him via the Web site to join the rant list.

ACKNOWLEDGMENTS

It not only takes a village to raise a child, it also takes one to write a book like this. Especially in 90 days. It's late and my deadline is fast approaching, but I wanted to say thanks to some of the key people who made this book possible. I couldn't have done this without the help of my wife who served as my editor and also watched our kids after a full day of work when I switched hats from being Mr. Mom to Writer Dad. I also greatly appreciate the patience of my kids who rarely saw me on weekends for the first three months of the year. Although they are just old enough to know I'm writing a book, they're far too young to know the title. Then there's my mother-in-law, Rita Katz, who came in once a week to watch the kids so I would have a little extra time to man the phones during business hours. Neighbor Kathie Jordan and Julia Snyder also provided similar help.

Part of the blame or credit also goes to Annika Hipple who got me into this mess in the first place when she gave Globe Pequot Editor Kevin Sirois my name after she turned the project down herself.

I owe an extra special thanks to the folks at the University of Washington's Experimental Education Unit. Although I'm thankful for the 90 minutes of work time having my kids in the program gave me on Tuesdays and Thursdays, I'm even more grateful for the difference the EEU has made in their lives. The school specializes in working with young children with all sorts of developmental issues at a time in their lives when it can have the greatest impact. In less than a year we have watched our children blossom in ways we never expected. If you happen to have a few spare dollars and are looking for a worthy cause, your money will be well spent here.

I also can't forget my researchers in the field and many Facebook friends who turned me on to places I might have missed. The crew includes brother-in-law extraordinaire Andrew Hess and his wife Julie Katz, Charyn Pfeuffer of the Global Citizen Project, Carrie Wachob, Scotti Andrews, Greg Berkman, Donna Blankinship, Amanda Castleman, Jay Coskey, Kevin Coskey, Elizabeth Davis, Sara Eizen at Nest, Debi Robson Vans Evers, Nick Fraser, Michelle Goodman, Carol Gown, Valerie Hockens, Jane Hodges, Leah Kaminsky, Renee Katz, Larissa Sapegin Long, Laura Machia, Julie Mains, Diane Mapes, Dottie Martin, Nicole Meoli, Ginny Morey, Heija Nunn, Alison Peacock, Eric Radman, Virginia Smyth, Irene Sveti, Grant Thornley, M. Susan Wilson, and the ever-amusing Bret Fetzer.

I also appreciate the advice provided by Tony Berman at Berman Entertainment and Technology Law (BEAT-LAW) in San Francisco.

Finally, I'd like to thank chef Gordon Ramsey. I've never met the man or eaten at one of his restaurants, but I somehow managed to watch the entire run of *Hell's Kitchen* while I was working the phones and sitting on hold during the research phase of the book. I don't know why, but it somehow allowed me to retain my sanity while trying to meet an insane deadline. Or maybe seeing how difficult a boss Ramsey was made me appreciate my editor even more.

INTRODUCTION

My name is David Volk and I'm a freelance writer. Not many people know this, but freelance is from the Latin for "unemployed"—"free" meaning "no pay," and "Lance" meaning "a guy."

I wasn't always a freelance writer, though. I became a freelancer for the same reason that many other people do. I was let go. Laid off. Made redundant. Pushed out of the nest. Asked to take a hike. Ordered to move on. Edged out. Given the heave ho. Told to hit the road.

And it was one of the best things that ever happened to me.

Even in the best of times, newspaper reporting isn't the most lucrative field and these times aren't even close. Fortunately, my time in newspapering taught me how to be thrifty. At my first job, for example, the afternoon daily I worked at had just changed from a weekly pay schedule to twice monthly the day I started and I had to wait three weeks to get paid. So, I survived on pot pies and spaghetti sandwiches the last few days of the pay period. My new co-workers stared in dumbfound shock, but I actually thought it was pretty doggone funny.

Of course, I was younger then, I could eat just about anything, I lived in a less expensive city, and I hadn't yet learned the ways of the cheap bastard.

Once I became a freelance writer, though, my skills moved to a whole new level. It was no longer about squeezing a penny so tight it would make Abraham Lincoln cry. Instead, it became all about quality of life. Sure, I couldn't eat at a fancy restaurant, but I could occasionally splurge and get a huge meal at a University District restaurant for a pittance. Of course, plays at the Seattle Rep were out of my reach, but a monthly late night fringe theater cabaret for $1.95 was just my speed. While I couldn't see blockbuster movies the night they came out, I could see them at a second run cinema for $2.

Then, I became a volunteer usher at the Seattle International Film Festival and learned a glorious new word: free. When I learned that I could see the movie I volunteered at for free and earn a comp ticket for another movie it seemed like the clouds parted, the sun came out, and the angels began singing.

And a cheap bastard was born.

Suddenly, expensive Seattle became a much more affordable town and there were new opportunities everywhere I looked. I could see expensive plays, eat out, watch blockbuster movies before they were released, take dance lessons, visit my favorite museums, and see live music for free or almost nothing.

This guidebook will show you how to become a cheap bastard, too, in a good way. *The Cheap Bastard's Guide to Seattle* is your secret weapon to improving the quality of your life in the Emerald City because it shows you how to do many of the things you already pay to do, for free. It covers everything from the obvious, like the Outdoor Sculpture Garden and the Ballard Locks, to opportunities you never even knew existed like summer weekend concerts at the Locks. It shows you places you've overlooked and the secret strategies to do things you didn't know you could afford.

The best part is, it will make the memory even sweeter and truly make getting there more than half the fun. Sure, you could just go to the box office and buy tickets to see a ballet . . . or you could go behind the scenes to see the show come together. Of course, you could call up Ticketmaster and purchase theater tickets . . . or you could become an usher and maybe seat a few famous folk along the way while seeing the same play for free. Doing it the cheap bastard way will allow you to do more than just talk with your friends about the newest big, blockbuster movie everyone's seen, it might just give you the opportunity to impress them by telling them what the star said about his role or the director said about her experience.

Did you ever want to sail Lake Union, but thought it would cost too much? The Center for Wooden Boats offers a free public sail of Lake Union aboard a classic sailing ship every Sunday. Wish you could have attended the live performance of *A Prairie Home Companion* the last time it was in town, but couldn't afford a ticket? If you lived life the cheap bastard way, you could have gotten in for free. All you had to do was volunteer with the local National Public Radio affiliate hosting the show.

At this point it's only right to mention that "Cheap Bastard" is a tongue-in-cheek phrase. While I wear the title with pride, that doesn't mean I believe in being stingy for its own sake or being rude to get a deal. All of the methods I suggest are legal, moral, ethical, and a heck of a lot of fun. And none of them involve negotiating, haggling, or figuratively beating someone over the head just to save a few cents. But they all involve finding ways to beat the system and enjoying yourself along the way.

The book contains three kinds of listings to help you do just that. There are truly free opportunities, those that are free with a catch, and the ridiculously cheap. Truly free items require little additional effort on your part other than calling, making a reservation, or just showing up, such as visiting the Boeing Assembly Plant or touring the Communications Museum. Free with a catch listings require a little more effort whether it be volunteering as an usher to see a play or helping set up before a show to see a dance performance. As the name suggests, ridiculously cheap items do require you to dip into your wallet, but the financial impact is so light you barely feel it . . . unless you decide to pinch yourself to make sure you heard right.

As with anything free or cheap, there may be a few provisos along the way. For example, some free outdoor movies have suggested donations and some bars that offer free entertainment may have a minimum drink purchase. In addition, some performing groups prefer only to use volunteers who are willing to make a season-long commitment instead of a person who only wants to help out at one performance. In such cases I've added the phrase "The Catch" to a listing and then explain other conditions you'll need to know about before you go.

I've done my best to sniff out and hunt down every free opportunity in the Seattle area, but it's important to remember that things change. All of the information was accurate at press time, but it's always best to check before you go, especially with free events. Places close, prices change, events that were once free suddenly add fees, comedy and open mic nights come and go, and in the current economic climate programs disappear when government funding dries up. That's why I've added as much contact information as possible so you can call ahead, check the Web site, or even stop by just to make sure it's all still current. After all, we may be cheap bastards, but we aren't stupid.

SECTION 1:
Entertainment in Seattle

THEATER:
FREE SPEECH

"If you really want to help the American theater, don't be an actress, dahling. Be an audience."

—TALLULAH BANKHEAD

If it's true that "All the World's a stage, and all the men and women merely players," why the heck do plays cost so much? I mean, if all of us are actors, how come we don't get some sort of professional discount? True, we don't have union cards, but I don't see why that should stop us, especially since there's so much to see in the Emerald City. Mainstream, fringe, ethnic, youth, community, and even clown theater are among the many options available all year long.

Until we can convince box office managers that we're with the cast, however, we'll have to find other ways to get in free. Or at least avoid paying retail. Here are a few ways that work well.

THE **RISE** OF **THE** HOUSE **USHER** (WITH **APOLOGIES** TO **EDGAR** ALLEN **POE)**

Today's usher is a man (or woman) of many contrasts. Although he may seem to lead a carefree existence, happily tearing tickets, passing out programs, answering patrons' questions, and showing people to their seats, he's got a lot on his mind. These days there are times when he likely finds himself concerned about a variety of issues. "Am I getting the right crowd count?" "Am I prepared to help out in case of an emergency?" "Do I need to report the guy using the laptop during the play to the house manager?" and, even more importantly, "Will I get the seat I want or will I end up standing?"

We're kidding, of course, but only partly so. Although ushering is one of the best ways to see a show for free, there's a bit more to it than showing up at your favorite theater on the day of a performance holding a "Will Work for Plays" sign.

The best way to start is by contacting the theater of your choice and beginning the actual volunteering process, which is far less painful than it sounds. Prospective ushers typically fill out an application and wait for a response. The larger the theater is, though, the more formal the process and the longer the wait. A Contemporary Theater, for example, requires prospective ushers to e-mail a request for information about ushering. Intiman Theater not only wants people to call before the start of the theater season, it also wants them to pick their performance dates shortly after. At the opposite end of the spectrum, if you want to volunteer at Annex Theater all you have to do is call.

Some companies also require volunteers to attend usher training. The sessions aren't long or involved, but they do explain the job's responsibilities. While some are shocked to learn there are actual responsibilities, they aren't terribly onerous. You just have to know how to interact with the public and tear ticket stubs so the company knows exactly how many people are attending a particular performance. Also, you will need to be trained what to do in the event of an emergency, in case there's a need to evacuate the building. Apparently, running around screaming like a girl is not the appropriate response . . . even if you're a girl given to screaming.

Once you've made it through those hoops, you're ready to work. And once the work is done, there's a play. As long as there's an empty seat for you to sit in. Fortunately, there are usually enough no-shows that there are some pretty good seats left over.

One last note: While some smaller companies are grateful for any help even if it's only for one show, larger theaters prefer people who are willing to volunteer on an ongoing basis over those who want to usher just so they can see one particular show. As with any job, the longer you hang around and the more seniority you gain, the better your choices.

A Contemporary Theatre
700 Union St.
(206) 292-7660
www.acttheatre.org
Ushers per performance: 4 to 12

As the name suggests, ACT focuses on new plays that push the envelope. Originally founded as a fringe theater, ACT now attracts what could be described as a better dressed, less pierced crowd. That doesn't mean it isn't above doing edgy stuff. Years later, I'm still scratching my head over a play where a man leaves his wife because he's fallen in love with a goat. The building has four performance spaces ranging from a small cabaret to a large theater in the round, so the number of ushers needed can vary wildly. To get on the usher list, you must send usher coordinator Christine Jew an e-mail requesting ushering information at cjew@acttheater.org. ACT also typically offers two Pay What You Can performances per play. The theater also offers day-of-show rush tickets and discounts for people under 25.

The Great Pay What You Can Debate

There appear to be two schools of thought on Pay What You Can really means. While administrators at some companies feel that PWYC shows allow people who couldn't otherwise afford it to attend live theater, others say they believe some in the theatergoing public are abusing the special shows by attending those performances when they could easily pay for a regular ticket. It's easy to tell where the company falls on the issue by looking at how they charge for the shows. All theaters that offer them know they won't break even on the show, but some actually post a suggested donation.

Olympia's Harlequin Productions just leaves a box in the lobby and asks audience members to put in whatever they want to. The amounts are usually pretty small, but someone once left a $100 bill.

"Pay what you can is what it is," artistic director Scot Whitney says. "What's it worth to you? What can you pay? We don't set any guidelines. They're such fun performances. Often they're our best audiences. I would rather have some people take advantage of it than be a hard-ass. Who am I to judge what people can pay?"

At the same time, A Contemporary Theater has a suggested minimum donation of $5 and Taproot Theater Company charges $10. All of which prompts us to wonder, is it really Pay What You Can if someone is telling you how much to pay?

See Appendix D: PWYC Performances on page 251 for details on a variety of theaters that offer additional discounts.

Annex Theatre

1100 East Pike St.
(206) 728-0933
www.annextheatre.org
Volunteers per performance: 3

One of Seattle's oldest surviving fringe theater companies, Annex's regular shows focus on new works and what it calls "radical reinterpretations of classic scripts . . . and non-linear wild-ass spectacles." It also hosts "Spin the Bottle," a late night variety show on the first Friday of the month. Annex's performance space is so small there's no need for ushers, but it does need a volunteer to run the box office each show. There's no waiting list to sign up. Just call the main number to volunteer. Most shows have Pay What You Can performances during the second week of a play's run. Students get in for $5 to any show.

Artattack Theater Ensemble

1715 East Olive Way
(206) 905-9835
http://artattacktheater.com
Volunteers per performance: 2

A relative newcomer to the city's fringe scene, Artattack has an intimate theater with 50 seats arranged in one row, putting the audience in the middle of the action. It doesn't use ushers, but does need volunteers in its concession stand and box office. Both get a free pass to see the show during their volunteer shift. There's usually one Pay What You Can performance per play.

ArtsWest

4711 California Ave. Southwest
(206) 938-0963
www.artswest.org
Ushers per performance: 6

The theater may be popular with West Seattleites, but many folks who don't live in this out-of-the-way neighborhood haven't heard of it. That's good news because it's easier to get tickets, but bad news for ArtsWest because it means fewer patrons, but more people are discovering it. It still has a long usher list, so there will likely be some jockeying for popular performances. Ushers can see performances free, but they must complete usher training before they can work their first shift. To volunteer, call or e-mail volunteer coordinator Mary Leatherman (206-938-0963, maryl@artswest.org) or go to the Web site, fill out the form, and mail it in or drop it by. The company usually holds a Pay What You Can preview the night before a show opens. Suggested donation is $5. Theater buffs under 25 pay $10 and seniors get a 10 percent discount.

Burien Little Theatre
Burien Community Center
Intersection of 4th Avenue Southwest and Southwest 146th Street
Burien
(206) 242-5180
www.burienlittletheatre.org
Ushers per performance: 2

It isn't in the heart of Seattle's theater-going world, but BLT offers professionally produced shows throughout the year. All volunteers get a free show ticket including people who work in props, costumes, and set design. Sign up to usher at BLT's Web site. You might not get the exact date you want, but it will be close.

Driftwood Players
950 Main St.
Edmonds
(425) 774-9600
www.driftwoodplayers.com
Volunteers per performance: 6

Edmonds 53-year-old community theater group is still going strong with a variety of presentations including Main Stage shows, Alternative Stage productions, Special Presentations, and periodic edgier Late Night shows. Driftwood generally uses six volunteers per performance (including one or two concession workers) who can stay and see the evening's show. Dress rehearsals aren't publicized, but are open to the public. Its occasional First Draft program allows patrons to sit in on a reading of a work in progress and ask questions after the performance. First Draft admission is free. Late Night shows are $5.

Ear to the Ground Theatre
(206) 390-7207
www.eartothegroundtheatre.org
Ushers per performance: 6

If theater companies had theme songs, "Send in the Clowns" might work for this group. But not the bad kind of clown like the scary Steven King clowns or the goofy guy you'd hire to perform at your three-year-old's birthday party. Instead, they prefer theatrical style clowning. Think commedia dell'arte or corporeal mime . . . We're not sure what that is either, but this fringe company's work is heavily physical and is so dedicated to showcasing theatrical clowning that its biggest production over the last two years has been a clown show. To volunteer, e-mail eartothegroundtheatre@yahoo.com.

Eclectic Theater Company
1214 10th Ave.
(206) 679-3271
www.eclectictheatercompany.org
Volunteers per performance: 3

Originally named the Green Theatre, the company that once focused on eco-friendly productions now focuses on helping local artists present "new, contemporary, and re-envisioned classics for all audiences." ETC allows front of house volunteers at Odd Duck Studio to see the show they're working for free. To volunteer, e-mail info@eclectictheatercompany.org. The organization typically needs three volunteers a night or two a night when Odd Duck is hosting a guest show. Pay What You Can Previews are the Thursday before opening night and dress rehearsals are free. Students, seniors, military, veterans, union members, and Cornish College of the Arts alumni get in for $10.

Edmonds Center for the Arts
410 Fourth Ave. North
Edmonds
(425) 275-4485
www.ec4arts.org
Ushers per performance: varies

The Edmonds Center doesn't do plays, but it does use volunteers as ushers, concession workers, and in administration. It may not be the fastest way to see a free show, however, because it uses a system where you accrue volunteer hours, then cash them in for tickets to future performances. On average, it takes 20 hours of work to earn a free ticket. Most shows are concerts. To volunteer, e-mail volunteer@ec4arts.org.

5th Avenue Theatre
1308 Fifth Ave.
(206) 625-1900
www.5thavenue.org
Volunteers per performance: varies

Originally built as a Vaudeville-era theater, the Imperial Chinese–influenced 5th Avenue easily makes staring at the architecture as entertaining as the live musical productions that echo through its halls. There are dragons here, a bas relief of the Forbidden City there, a pair of Fu Dogs presiding over it all, and, for all we know, there could be angels in the architecture. Many of the shows are either touring Broadway musicals or bound for Broadway. There's no volunteer ushering, but there are many volunteer options including data entry, event staffing, and other administrative tasks. Would-be workers who e-mail the 5th Avenue to volunteer receive notice of opportunities as they come up. Volunteers earn one credit per hour worked and need four credits to see select performances of certain shows. Day of show tickets are available to patrons under 25 for $20.

Ghostlight Theatricals
2220 Northwest Market St.
www.ghostlighttheatricals.org
Ushers per performance: 1

It's hard to say whether it's the result of a desire to increase audience participation or just plain indecision, but for the last four years in February, this company has held "The Battle of the Bards," in which it presents scenes from three plays in an evening, then has audience members vote on which should be featured in its upcoming season. Ghostlight generally needs an usher and someone to work the box office each show. It also has PWYC performances on Thursdays. The company's Web site also lists opportunities for cheap tickets and other PWYC performances. To volunteer, contact info@ghostlighttheatricals.org.

Harlequin Productions
202 4th Ave. East
Olympia
(360) 786-0151
www.harlequinproductions.org
Ushers per performance: 6 to 8 ushers

If you're willing to go a little bit further for your entertainment, this company in the state capital is worth a look. Unlike most theater troupes, Harlequin's theatrical season lasts a full year. No summer break for these folks. And its works run the gamut from musicals and classics to new works. Ushers can see the show they work for free. To get on the usher list, go to the Web site's volunteer page and fill out an application. PWYC performances are matinees on the second Saturday of a show's run. Rush tickets sell for $12 to $20.

Intiman Theatre

201 Mercer St.
(206) 269-1900
www.intiman.org
Ushers per performance: 14

The Catch: You not only have to volunteer before the start of the season, you also have to schedule your shifts far in advance.

Seattle Center–based Intiman is one of the big dogs in the area's mainstream theater scene. The name is Swedish for "intimate" and the performance space is just that, relatively speaking. It's just you and 445 of your closest friends. Volunteer ushers can see shows for free, but there's a catch: would-be volunteers have to express interest in ushering before the start of the season, which begins in March, and they have to schedule their shifts in advance. To volunteer, e-mail volunteers@intiman.org. Preview performance tickets are available and there are also PWYC shows. People 25 and under can get tickets for $10. Standby and rush tickets are released 15 minutes before a show and cost $20. Intiman also has a free program called Spotlight Supper that takes patrons behind the scenes of a production before previews and allows them to watch a rehearsal in progress while they learn more about the show. Dates for Spotlight Suppers and PWYC performances are on the Web site.

Jet City Improv

The Historic University Theater
5510 University Way Northeast
(206) 352-8291
www.jetcityimprov.com
Ushers per performance: 3

The Catch: All prospective volunteers must complete a training course and the company doesn't take people who plan to volunteer only once.

The Etiquette of Ushering

As we've already mentioned, there's a little more to ushering then meets the eye.

It's an easy job and the reward is great, but there are a few things you should remember:

- **Dress nicely:** Formalwear isn't necessary, but usher coordinators say your clothes should be in good condition. It's hard to go wrong in black pants and a nice white shirt. Avoid sloppy clothes or anything that's too revealing.
- **Be polite:** You're dealing with the public, so you should be on your best behavior, even if they aren't. As one volunteer coordinator put it, "You need to be civil to the public, even if the public is inebriated."
- **Be prepared for any task: You never know what you'll end up doing.** ArtsWest wants its volunteers to be able to calm the audience in the event of an earthquake or other emergency. At the same time, Harlequin asks one usher to stand at the front of the theater during intermission to make sure people don't walk onto the stage and start picking up props. It may sound strange, but artistic director Scot Whitney doesn't think so. "You'd be surprised" what people do, he said.

Every city has at least one improv theater group; this is one of ours. The troupe is made up of the same fun-loving people who are known for a production called "Twisted Flicks," which runs the last weekend of the month. Improvisors turn the sound down on a B movie and dub it live based on audience suggestions. In addition to its regular improvisational comedy competitions, the organization also produces a loosely scripted improv show and a more adult-themed midnight show on Saturday nights called Funbucket. Volunteers can see shows for free. To volunteer, go to the Web site and fill out a volunteer form.

Kirkland Performance Center

350 Kirkland Ave.
Kirkland
(425) 828-0422
www.kpcenter.org
Ushers per performance: varies

Originally built as a home for the Village Theatre, the 13-row, 402-seat center now hosts a wide variety of performances. It's possible to see an Indian
jazz show one night and a classical guitar concert the next. Although the
system for volunteering may be in flux, patrons who volunteer to usher or
work concessions can watch the performance they attend. At present, the
best way to express interest is to go to the Web site and fill out the sign up
form. There are occasional PWYC performances, which are advertised on the
Center's Web site, via e-mail, and through Seattle Comp Tickets on Facebook.

Macha Monkey

Freehold Studios
2222 2nd Ave. #200
(206) 860-2970
www.machamonkey.org
Volunteers per performance: 1 to 2

Fearless. Funny. Female. Helen Reddy, eat your heart out. Yes, we know it's
a dated reference, but all the productions here are new works with strong
female voices. Ushering is the best option to get a free ticket to main stage
shows. To volunteer, send an e-mail to info@machamonkey.org. Macha also
does a cabaret show. Patrons who show up dressed in the theme of the cabaret get in for $5.

New Century Theatre Company

1122 East Pike St.
www.newcenturytheatrecompany.org
Ushers per performance: varies depending on theater space

Imagine the drama scene's version of the Justice League of America and you
get the picture: A group of established Seattle actors banding together to
save humanity . . . er . . . the humanities. Okay, we're exaggerating, but
after seeing several medium size theater companies shutter, these folks got
together to create the city's first new professional theater company in more

than a decade. Their mission: present edgier work and newer plays that just aren't being performed in Seattle and bring fresh, modern perspective to older plays. New Century currently produces its plays at A Contemporary Theatre. The first preview of a run is a PWYC performance.

Northshore Performing Arts Center
18125 92nd Ave. Northeast
Bothell
(425) 408-7997
npacf.org
Ushers per performance: 6 to 10

The Catch: You have to pay $20 for the privilege of volunteering.

The NPAC is an eastern suburb community theater that offers a wide range of family entertainment from concerts to Broadway shows. The Northshore Theatre Guild provides most of the center's volunteers and the only way to get on the usher list is to join the guild for $20. Ushers can see the performances at which they volunteer. To find out more about volunteering, go to the Web site and fill out a guild signup form.

Our American Theater Company
Theater Off Jackson for main stage and other locations
(206) 937-0205
www.ouramericantheater.org
Volunteers per performance: 2

Our American Theater says its mission is to bring life to the voices of American theater ranging from the overlooked and unsung to the classic and the new. All of the company's productions are PWYC to ensure that no one who wants to see a play will be turned away. When the company does a full production, theater lovers can volunteer to usher and stay to see the show for free. It also does two-night staged readings with the first night at Theatre Off Jackson and the second at another venue. Previous venues have included ArtsWest and the Bathhouse Theatre. To volunteer, e-mail info@ouramerican theater.org.

Phoenix Theatre Edmonds

9673 Firdale Ave.
Edmonds
(206) 533-2000
www.phoenixtheatreedmonds.com
Ushers per performance: 1

Rising from the ashes of the Edge of the World Theater, the Phoenix focuses on humorous productions to dramatize our common humanity and to help foster a love of the magic of live theater. PWYC performances are held on the Thursday before opening night of a production. The in-residence improv group, Breakout Improv, also performs two shows a night once a month for $8.

Pork Filled Players

www.porkfilled.com
Ushers per performance: 1 to 2

Even if you're Jewish, it's still okay to see the Pork Filled Players. The only problem is this sketch comedy group is so funny that they could have you eating out of their hands. And we're still waiting for a ruling from the rabbis on that one. They may not be hungry, but they are homeless. The gypsy company puts on a show wherever it can find a performance space. The players do a racy, four-letter-word-laden late night cabaret once every two or three months and less risqué prime time presentations a couple of times a year. The group welcomes ushers.

Printer's Devil Theater

(206) 860-7163
www.printersdevil.org
Ushers per performance: 1 to 2

This nomadic theater company is always looking for ushers. It also offers PWYC performances the first two Thursdays of a production's run. And it's got a really great name.

ReAct

(206) 364-3283
www.reacttheatre.org
Ushers per performance: 1 to 6, depending on venue

ReAct Theater specializes in doing classic plays with non-traditional casts to increase awareness of the arts and humanitarian causes. There's not much of a waiting list, so would-be greeters and seaters will likely get their pick of performances, or at least something relatively close. All they have to do is e-mail react@reacttheatre.org. There are also one or two PWYC performances per main stage show. It's best to call the theater to find out more about when those shows are scheduled.

Redwood Theatre
Redmond Municipal Campus
8703 160th Northeast
Redmond
(425) 522-3730
www.redwoodtheatre.org
Ushers per performance: 2

A community theater in the heart of Microsoft country, Redwood is always looking for volunteers and would likely gladly add some Microsoft workers to its volunteer roles. The question is, do Microsofties even get time off for good behavior? The best way to sign up is to contact the theater through its Web site. Redwood has a PWYC performance on the first Sunday of a show's run.

Seattle Children's Theatre
Seattle Center
201 Thomas St.
(206) 441-3322
www.sct.org
Ushers per performance: varies

When it comes to volunteering, local theaters don't get any more accommodating than this one. To begin with, the volunteer coordinator takes requests and tries her best to meet them. First she finds out what play a prospective usher wants to see. If there's still space available, she'll then do her best to find a spot that matches the day they want to see the play. Of course, it is possible to schedule a shift as soon as the season is announced, but she has found slots for kids who call just days before the show they wanted to catch. Usher tasks aren't terribly taxing. They involve taking tickets, passing out programs, making sure no one's taking food into the theater, and watching the stage to make sure no one tries to climb up . . .

which, come to think of it, isn't all that different from ushering at a regular adult theater. In fact, the only thing that's different is that ushers here can be as young as eight years old (as long as the worker is accompanied by an adult). The only challenge for a first-time usher is getting there on time. Of course, the usher's family has to be equally accommodating. If it's a young volunteer's first shift, they must show up 90 minutes early to go through an orientation session. There is one other bargain to be had if ushering is too much of a hassle, though. Rush tickets are available for Friday performances and go on sale at 6 p.m. for a 7 p.m. performance. There are only 10 tickets available and they sell for $10 a piece. Teen Tix members can see SCT plays for $5. To volunteer, contact the volunteer coordinator.

Seattle Repertory Theatre

155 Mercer St. (Northwest Corner of Seattle Center)
(206) 443-2222
www.seattlerep.org
Ushers per performance: 4 to 5

Theater just doesn't get any more mainstream in the Emerald City than the Seattle Rep. The fare leans toward Broadway hits and classic comedies with a smattering of new drama thrown in for good measure. It has two performance spaces, with the Bagley Wright serving as the company's main stage and the Leo K. its more intimate auditorium. The Rep uses volunteer ushers in Leo K and allows them to stay and see the show if seats are available. If there's no seating, volunteers are given a voucher to see a performance later in the run. To volunteer, call (206) 443-2210 or e-mail lance.park@seattlerep.org. Keep in mind, there's a pool of 200 volunteers and there was a waiting list at press time. The Bagley Wright has PWYC previews the Tuesday before opening night. Tickets go on sale at noon and the theater asks a minimum donation of $1, cash only. Patrons 25 and under pay $12 for best seat available. Rush tickets are $22 and are released 30 minutes before the start of show. Teen Tix are available for $5.

Seattle Shakespeare Company

Center House Theater
Seattle Center
www.seattleshakespeare.org
(206) 733-8228
Volunteers per performance: 4 to 5

Don't let the name fool you. Shakespeare isn't the only thing this company does. It presents classical plays all year round with additional help during the summer from its sister company, Wooden O Summer Outdoor Theater. Ushers and other volunteers can see the show if seats are available. Pay What You Will performances are held early in a show's run, usually on a Tuesday or Wednesday. Rush tickets are available to a group called Groundlings for $10 on the day of show. You can become a groundling by applying at the box office. Membership is free.

Seattle Theatre Group
(206) 682-1414
www.stgpresents.org

Paramount Theatre
911 Pine St.
Ushers per performance: 18 to 25

Moore Theatre
1932 Second Ave.
Ushers per performance: 6 to 8

The volunteer ushering situation at two of the city's most beautiful turn-of-the-twentieth-century theaters is a bit like the punch line of a good news, bad news joke. The good news is that the Seattle Theatre Group does use volunteers. The bad news is that the backlog of applications is so long that the organization suspended accepting new applicants until the current logjam has been resolved. Some student rush tickets are available for some of the traveling Broadway productions. The best way to find out when volunteer opportunities will reopen and which shows offer rush tickets is to sign up for eNews at www.stgpresents.org.

Second Story Repertory
16587 Northeast 74th St.
Redmond
(425) 881-6777
www.secondstoryrep.org
Ushers per performance: 2

A shopping center isn't the likeliest location for live theater, but these are the Eastside suburbs we're talking about . . . where shopping *is* entertainment. So, Second Story Rep has found a home on the second story of Redmond

Town Center between an Aeropostale shop and a Borders bookstore. Now, if the company could just convince shoppers it isn't a movie theater. That's the next building over. Small ensemble musicals are Second Story's specialty and the company splits its productions between main stage shows and productions for children. Ushers can stay and see the show, but they are asked to do some light work before and after the performance. Fortunately, the tasks don't include dusting or windows, just a little tidying up here and there. There's a PWYC preview the Thursday night before opening night.

SiS Productions
Richard Hugo House
1634 11th Ave.
(206) 323-9443
www.sis-productions.org
Ushers per performance: 2

All SiS plays focus on Asian-American women as well as Asian-American themes and issues. The company strives to have members of its target group involved in all aspects of production. While ushering is a good way to see a free performance, it isn't the only way. You can also volunteer to build sets, hang lights, or do any of a variety of other necessary tasks. SiS has no usher waiting list, so it should be relatively easy to see the performance you want. The company also participates in the Teen Tix program, which allows patrons 19 and under to buy rush tickets for $5. There is also a PWYC dress rehearsal with a $5 suggested donation, but it's only advertised on the company's listserv and Facebook.

Sound Theatre Company
3830 31st Avenue West
(206) 856-5520
www.soundtheatrecompany.org
Ushers per performance: 2

Sound Theater features works that focus on language and music, often with a political bent. The company typically announces what shifts are available via e-mails to volunteers. To volunteer, contact info@soundtheatre company.org. PWYC performances are held almost every Thursday night during a play's run.

Stone Soup Theatre

4035 Stone Way North
(206) 633-1883
www.stonesouptheatre.org
Ushers per performance: 2 to 3

Stone Soup is a small community theater that also offers drama programs for children. All Thursday evening performances are PWYC and the final dress rehearsal is also PWYC. The company also offers several two-for-one deals per production to people on its mailing list. To volunteer, call the company.

Taproot Theatre Company

204 North 85th St.
(206) 781-9705
www.taproottheatre.org

Taproot's mission is to "create theatre that explores the beauty and questions of life while bringing hope to our search for meaning." Taproot volunteers do get free tickets, but the company says most of its dedicated corps of volunteers aren't in it for the perks. To volunteer, call the volunteer hotline at (206) 529-3655 or e-mail volunteer@taproottheatre.org. Patrons 25 and under can get tickets for $10. There is one PWYC performance per production with a minimum suggested donation of $10. Students and seniors get $4 off the $20 to $35 ticket price.

Theater Schmeater

1500 Summit Ave.
(206) 324-5801
www.schmeater.org
Volunteers per performance: 1

Submitted for your approval, a fringe theater company that has risen to prominence on its faithful to the original script, if somewhat campy, revivals of episodes of the old television show, *The Twilight Zone*. Even Schmee's Rod Sterling look-alike manages to be spot-on while still being just this side of over-the-top. Schmee's classic theater and edgy original productions are all presented out of a subterranean garage on Capitol Hill. Volunteering is easy and all volunteers get to see the show they work on for free. Ushers take tickets and run the concession stand. To volunteer, go to the Web site and fill out the online form. All Thursday performances are PWYC and some dress rehearsals are open to the public. Anyone under 18 can attend a production for free. The company also does a Free Classic in the Park production every summer.

Twelfth Night Productions
Youngstown Cultural Arts Center
4408 Delridge Ave. Southwest
www.twelfthnightproductions.org
Ushers per performance: varies

What started as a summer drama camp program has grown into a West Seattle–based production company that does a play each summer and an annual production of *Amahl and the Night Visitors*. To volunteer, contact info@twelfthnightproductions.org. Twelfth Night offers free tickets to ushers and people who work the concession stand during performances.

UPAC Theatre Group
United Evangelical Free Church basement
1420 Northwest 80th St.
(206) 375-5057
www.upactheatergroup.org
Ushers per performance: 2 to 4

Admittedly, the name UPAC may sound more like a mailing and packing service than a community theater group, but it's a heck of a lot better than United Performing Arts Company. Despite staging its plays in a church basement, the Ballard neighborhood group is not affiliated with any religious organization. It performs a main stage show in August and a one-act play in the spring. Ushers must agree to work at least three main stage shows and can see the show free on their second shift. They are also invited to the dress rehearsal. To volunteer, download an application from the Web site and return it via regular mail or e-mail. The main stage show has a PWYC performance the first Thursday of the run and a two-for-one matinee for seniors on the second Saturday of the play's run. There are no discounts for the one act, but admission is only $10.

Village Theatre

www.villagetheatre.org

303 Front St. North
Issaquah
(425) 392-2202

Everett Performing Arts Center
Everett
(425) 257-8600

The Catch: There's a waiting list for usher openings.

While some theater companies rely on the kindness of strangers to provide a performance space, Village Theatre is lucky enough to have two homes to call its own—one in Everett, the other in the eastern suburb of Issaquah. When one production wraps up in Issaquah, it often goes to Everett. The company's focus may be on musicals, but it also produces non-musicals as well. Most plays are suitable for the entire family. The theater also produces its own original musicals. Ushers may be able to see the shows they work for free, subject to seating availability. Rush tickets are available to students and members of the military 30 minutes before curtain.

WARP (Writers and Actors—Reading and Performing)
Odd Duck Theatre
1214 10th Ave.
(206) 229-7919
www.warptheater.org
Volunteers per performance: varies

This odd hybrid cuts out the middleman between the aspiring playwright and potential audience by presenting free readings of original scripts to anyone who will listen every Tuesday. It's more than just a critique group, though, as some of the scripts are incorporated into the shows WARP produces several times a year. Tickets to the plays are $10 at the door, but volunteers are admitted free and tech volunteers who work the entire run will get two comp admissions. WARP has a two-for-one special for people who buy advance tickets from WARP members. Students and seniors pay $5. To volunteer, e-mail warp@warptheatre.org.

Washington Ensemble Theater

608 19th Ave. East
(206) 325-5105
www.washingtonensemble.org
Volunteers per performance: 1

The Catch: Since the house manager handles money, the company prefers to establish an ongoing relationship with a volunteer rather than using someone only once.

Given that WET's has 49 seats with festival seating, there's no need for ushers. The company does use volunteer house managers, however, who get one free ticket per house management shift. There are PWYC previews each Thursday before a show opens. To volunteer, e-mail admin@washington ensemble.org.

Youth Theatre Northwest

8805 Southeast 40th St.
Mercer Island
(206) 232-4145
www.youththeatre.org.
Ushers per performance: 2 to 3

The Catch: Background check required for people who plan to usher on a regular basis.

YTN produces 12 shows a year for kids that are performed by kids of all ages. Although its main volunteers are the parents of children performing in the shows, the company does round out the ranks of its ushers with people from the community and does have one-day volunteer opportunities. People who are interested in volunteer ushering on a regular basis, however, require a background check because the job involves regular contact with children. To volunteer, contact the theater. YTN does offer some half off and two-for-one ticket deals through its e-mail list.

OTHER **CHEAPIES**

Backwards Ensemble Theatre Company
323 13th Ave. East, #3
(206) 920-8057
www.backwardscompany.org

Producing quirky, original plays is the specialty of the company, which was
founded by four grads from Cornish College of the Arts. Audience members
25 and younger are eligible for Pay What You Can prices and there's a new
playwrights' series on the second Sunday of every month at 15th Avenue
Coffee & Tea on a Pay What You Can as You Leave basis. Half price ticketing
is available through Goldstar.

Balagan Theatre
1117 East Pike St.
(206) 718-3245
www.balagantheatre.org

No ushering or discounts for volunteering here, but Balagan does have a Pay
What You Can performance the Monday before the closing weekend of each
of its productions. Night owls can also take advantage of "Schmorgasborg," a
free late night cabaret that starts at 11 p.m. on the second Saturday of each
month. So, even if it's bad, it's well worth the price. Like most smorgasbords
of yesteryear, however, you can usually find something good, even if you
have to plumb the depths of the salad bar to get it. Arrive early if you want
a seat.

Young Americans Theater
(206) 617-4002

YATC may not offer free tickets for ushers or volunteers; it is worth mentioning for two reasons. The production company is run by teens and it participates in the TeenTix program.

ALWAYS **FREE**

Seattle Outdoor Theater Festival
Volunteer Park
1247 15th Ave. East
www.greenstage.org/sotf

Much more successful than the Winter Outdoor Theater Festival, the summer celebration of the lively arts is held at Volunteer Park and features at least 10 performances over two days. So, you can pack a lunch, dinner, and evening snack and a blanket and watch to your heart's content or until your butt grows numb from all that sitting. The players include such outdoor regulars as Wooden O Theatre, GreenStage, and Theatre Schmeater as well as such dabblers as Open Circle Theatre and improvisation group Wing It Productions. If you miss the show you wanted to see, don't despair. The event is usually a launching point for the season and most of the shows will be performed again in parks throughout the area.

GreenStage
Venues vary; for information, check the Web site
(206) 748-1551
www.greenstage.org

There really is no better place to put on a play than a park when your mission is to "inspire audiences to engage with live theater as part of their recreation." And GreenStage has been doing just that with its productions of classic theater for the last 20 years. The company describes its productions as "fun and family oriented," but may have pushed it a bit with 2009's presentation of *Titus Andronicus*, in which, its Facebook page gleefully proclaimed, "4 gallons of stage blood spilled so far, 5 people walked out because of blood and violence, 1 passed out in his seat." Of course, it was *Titus* and it was a special Halloween-oriented production. At least you can't say they didn't stay faithful to the original.

Wooden O Summer Outdoor Theater
Locations vary
(206) 733-8228
www.seattleshakespeare.org/WoodenO/index.asp

The local company known for presenting Shakespeare in parks throughout Seattle and King County may have merged with the Seattle Shakespeare Company in 2008, but the show goes on to much critical acclaim. In 2009, Wooden O did 18 performances of *Taming of the Shrew* and 15 performances of *Richard III* in 13 parks stretching from Lynnwood and Issaquah to SeaTac and Bonney Lake. There really is no more civilized way to spend a weekend night than a picnic dinner under the stars surrounded by theater-goers of all ages trying to figure out what it was that someone just said in Shakespearean English.

DRAMA **DEALS:** DISCOUNT **TICKETS** AND **MORE**

Goldstar.com

The Catch: Tickets are half price, but there is a service charge from $2.50 to $9.

It may not offer the same personal touch as the once and former reduced price ticket kiosks run by Ticket/Ticket, but Goldstar does have one major advantage over its brick and mortar predecessor. You don't have to wait until the day of show to buy tickets. Now you can get tickets far enough ahead that you might actually have time to hire a baby-sitter and have a full night out complete with dinner using the money you saved. You do have to become a member, but it's free and it gives you the ability to buy tickets for everything from plays and concerts to sporting events and other diversions. The site does have a service charge, but it also gives helpful pointers including what to wear, how to get to the venue, and where to find parking.

Seattle Opera
Seattle Center
McCaw Hall
321 Mercer St.
(206) 389-7600
www.seattleopera.org

National Night of Free Theater

Of course, there is one night a year when you don't have to volunteer to see a free play, but even that requires a little bit of work if you want the best seats. Or, you can just stay at home, register online, and make do with whatever's left.

In Seattle, the National Night of Free Theater falls on the Thursday of Live Theater week, which occurs in mid-October. There's a bit of fudge factor built in, though, because not all companies have Thursday night performances. In that case, the free night is usually the show closest to Free Theater night. That doesn't mean that you can just waltz into any theater in the city for free, however. No, you still have to follow procedures.

The best way to get a free ticket is to attend a kick-off event at the start of the week when all of the tickets are up for grabs. The catch is that each company has a limited number of free seats and the best ones go first. In 2009, for example, much-loved local dinner cabaret Teatro Zinzanni offered less than a dozen tickets and they were snapped up immediately. The 100 free tickets offered by 5th Avenue Theatre also went quickly. There's more to the event than just standing in line, though. Each participating theater has a booth and many offer special deals that aren't available the rest of the season. In addition, there is a wide variety of activities designed to foster interest in the arts in general as well as specific upcoming productions.

If you can't make it to the in-person event, you can always visit Theater Puget Sound's Live Theater Week Web site the day after the gathering, then register and choose among the many tickets that are still left.

There are two other catches to this seeming free-for-all. Since you can't be in more than one theater at the same time (which seems so unfair), you're limited to one pair of free tickets. In addition, since the event is designed to encourage people to try something new, theater patrons are supposed to pick a theater company they've never visited before. Fortunately, there's no Department of Drama Security to enforce the rule or even a no-buy list, so you're on your honor.

What's that I hear? It's the fat lady singing about your chances of volunteering and staying to see a show for free. The opera doesn't use volunteer ushers and the people who do volunteer there don't get free passes to performances, either, but there are still so many ways to see shows at a discount that they fill a whole page on the opera's web site. For starters, there are a select number of tickets on the second balcony that sell for $25 a show. There are also rush tickets for students ($20) and seniors ($30) available at 5:30 p.m. for evening shows and noon for afternoon shows. Standing room tickets are available for Wednesday and Friday shows for $12 on the day of show. Teen Tix are available for $5. While being a volunteer doesn't get you any special consideration at the box office for regular shows, you may be able to get tickets to certain dress rehearsals for free.

Teen Tix
www.seattlecenter.com/teentix

One of the best bargains in town for kids 13 to 18, Seattle Center's Teen Tix program is designed to foster interest in the arts by giving teens inexpensive access to cultural and creative experiences all over town. Besides encouraging students to get more involved in the arts, Teen Tix also has the advantage of building up future audiences. Tix holders can buy $5 same day tickets to a variety of cultural organizations and events ranging from exhibits at the Seattle Art Museum to the Seattle Symphony (depending on availability). The service even has a blog that tells members which tickets are available each week and gives audience etiquette tips as well as directions and maps. Membership is free and available through the Seattle Center Web site.

MUSIC:
OF FREE I SING

"Talking about music is like dancing about architecture."

— STEVE MARTIN

As a local comedian once said, the great thing about Seattle is that you can go to a garage sale and get a grunge band. Grunge may have come and gone, but the Emerald City continues to be a hotbed for music of all types, whether it's serious groups like The Presidents of the United States of America and Death Cab for Cutie or whimsical ones like the Sedentary Sousa Band, a group that plays marching music sitting down. After months of rain and darkness, the abundance of summer festivals in our few sunny months alone is enough to guarantee a steady stream of free music throughout the summer. And that doesn't even count lunchtime concerts, farmers' markets, restaurants, coffeehouses, and your next-door neighbor's son's garage band.

For more on Seattle's music scene, see Appendix E: Additional Seattle Music Festivals on page 254.

JAZZ/**BLUES**/WORLD

Agua Verde Café and Paddle Club
1303 Northeast Boat St.
(206) 545-8570
www.aguaverde.com

The music at this restaurant/kayak rental place may be hit and miss because there's no regular schedule, but the food certainly isn't. Most days during the summer folks are lined up out the door waiting for the affordable Baja-inspired Mexican food and a spot on the patio overlooking the Ship Canal. There are even times when the restaurant sets up a stage in a park next door where artists play, but there's no predictable monthly schedule. Fortunately, there's no cover charge, so you can either show up and be surprised or you can call ahead and ask. There are worse things than sitting on a quiet patio looking out at the water and watching boats go by on a warm summer evening.

Amore Restaurant
2301 Fifth Ave.
(206) 770-0606
www.tasteofamore.com

The Catch: Two-drink minimum.

The Belltown restaurant's theater lounge plays host to a wide range of entertainment including karaoke, a monthly comedy night, and even movie nights, but music is the mainstay. The emphasis is on jazz from 9:30 p.m. to 12:30 a.m. Friday and Saturday nights, but it gives a nod to its Italian heritage with opera two Sunday nights each month.

Barca

1510 11th Ave.
(206) 325-8263
www.barcaseattle.com

If only the fourth letter in the name were a hard "c" and not a soft one and you were a regular, you'd be a Barca lounger. Sadly, that's not the case. Capitol Hill bar/art gallery Barca only has live music one night a month, but it's a good one. The Clark Gibson Trio performs the second Thursday of every month, but the bar hopes soon to make the group's appearances a weekly event.

Bilbao Tapas Bar and Restaurant

4500 9th Ave. Northeast
(206) 547-5034
www.bilbaorestaurant.com

There's never a cover charge for performances at Bilbao in the University District. Flamenco music plays Thursday night and Latin music on Friday and Saturday. All shows begin at 8 p.m.

The Capitol Club

414 East Pine St.
(206) 325-2149
www.thecapitolclub.net

The Catch: There's a two-item minimum.

Although the tapestries and little touches throughout give a feel of Morocco, the bar's only regular live music is flamenco from Morocco's neighbor to the north. If you're a real fan of the music, you may want to stick around to see if the students of Eric and Encarnacion from Children of the Revolution, and any flamenco artists who happen by, head downstairs and have a *juerga*—an after-show party. The show starts at 9ish on Tuesdays. There's also belly dancing on the first Thursday of the month, but the music isn't live.

Don't Forget to Tip Your Player

Free is a great price, especially when it comes to music, but don't forget that the people who are up on the stage playing their hearts out for you need to make a living, too. Sure, many aspiring musicians take the free gigs just for the exposure, but they wouldn't mind a little cash to help out, even if it just covers the cost of gas or a repair for the van that broke down two blocks away from the venue so they had to carry all their equipment on their backs. One of the nice things about putting the money in a performer's hat or instrument case is that they get to keep all of the proceeds. That isn't the case when you have to buy tickets later on. Then, everyone gets a cut including ticket sellers, club owners, and managers long before the musician sees any of the money.

We're not saying you have to reach into your wallet and give until it hurts or even pay the equivalent of a cover charge, although we're sure the artist wouldn't mind. But if enough people gave a dollar or two, it could make a difference in the artist's bottom line without affecting yours.

Faire Gallery Café-Bar

1351 East Olive Way
(206) 652-0781
www.fairegallerycafe.com

There aren't many bars with a mission—unless you count getting drunk or forgetting—but Faire Gallery is one of them. It's all about art and its main reason for being is to serve as a place where artists of all stripes get together. It describes itself as a combination art gallery and lounge where artists and the community can get involved in the artistic experience. There are art exhibits, music shows, performance art, and a weekly jazz show every Sunday from 9 p.m. to midnight or later.

Fu Kun Wu

5410 Ballard Ave. Northwest
(206) 706-7807
www.fukunwu.com

Located at the back of Thai-ku restaurant in Seattle's Norwegian-influenced Ballard neighborhood, small Fu Kun Wu has a different vibe from the eatery downstairs. Where Thai-ku is all dark wood tables surrounded by brick, Fu Kun Wu is designed to feel like an Asian apothecary. While I can't say I've ever been in an herbalist's shop, the herb drawers on the walls and the Asian tchotchkes on the wall make it easy to imagine that this is what one would be like if you added a bar with bar stools on a side wall, then plopped a jazz combo in the middle of it. The smell of Thai food might seem a little incongruous until you realize that the king of Thailand is a jazz artist. The herb-infused drinks are decidedly modern with one of the most popular being the oolong tea martini. The jazz starts at 8:30 p.m. on Wednesday and Thursday and goes until midnight.

Grand Cru Wine Shop and Bar
1020 108th Ave. Northeast
Bellevue
(425) 455-4278
www.grandcru-winebar.com

In its first year of business, Grand Cru seemed to be willing to do whatever it needed to do to gain a foothold in the Bellevue market. Dollar taco nights on Mondays, $5 tapas on Friday nights, and Dinner on Us on Wednesday and Saturday where a two-course dinner was on the house excluding tax, gratuity, and beverages. Jazz guitarist Michael Powers plays every other Tuesday night from 7 to 10 p.m. with another jazz artist on alternating Tuesdays. Flamenco artist Andre Feriante plays on Saturdays from 7 to 10 p.m. How long the Dinner on Us special will last is anybody's guess, but the free flamenco is expected to stay.

Hidmo Eritrean Cuisine
2000 South Jackson St.
(206) 329-1534
www.hidmo.org

Most reviews say the food and service are so-so, but the music gets high ratings. The focus is on Africa and the African diaspora and includes many styles ranging from traditional to contemporary music and it goes from 8 to 10 p.m. every Sunday.

The restaurant also occasionally features other shows including a first Saturday showcase by women performers. All ages are welcome, no cover.

Hiroshi Jazz and Sushi

2501 Eastlake Ave.
(206) 726-4966
www.hiroshis.com

Did you ever wonder if hot jazz makes sushi go bad? Well, neither have we, but the mix of jumpin' jazz and Japanese cuisine appear to go together quite well, thank you. And it's a good thing, too, considering that the strip mall restaurant calls its weekly live music offering "Jazz and Sushi Fridays." You don't have to order sushi, of course. There are other dishes, but free jazz comes on the side from 7:30 to 10 p.m.

Lucid Seattle

5241 University Way Northeast
(206) 402-3042
www.lucidseattle.com

One of the great Seattle mysteries is why University Way Northeast, the main drag through Seattle's University District, is commonly referred to as the Ave when it doesn't even have the word "avenue" in its name. Much of the street is filled with cheap restaurants, inexpensive shops, and stores for students. A hidden treasure, Lucid is located on the street's far northern reach where businesses thin out, giving way to apartments and mixed use buildings. It's steadily gained a following among jazz lovers and those who stumble across it. The club is open Wednesday through Saturday with free live music most nights, but closed for private parties Sunday through Tuesday. It also has an extensive cocktail menu with reworked classics and a bartender who makes his own syrups and infusions.

New Orleans Creole Restaurant

114 First Ave. South
(206) 622-2563
www.neworleanscreolerestaurant.com

The Catch: $8 cover charge on Saturdays. Friday shows are free.

Dixieland, zydeco, and jazz serve as tasty aural side dishes to this Pioneer Square eatery's Cajun and Creole dishes. The music is free most weeknights, but the cover can shoot up to $8 on Saturdays when the club features blues artists.

Seattle Mobile Espresso

13000 Linden Ave. North
(206) 420-4719
www.seattlemobileespresso.com

The Catch: There is a $5 suggested donation for the musicians and a suggested $5 minimum purchase.

This coffeehouse, which strives to be all things to all people in its community, hosts live jazz from 5:30 to 7:30 p.m. the first and third Sunday of every month and an open mic night on alternating Sundays. Although the band has no set schedule, Silent Blues, a group with a father and three sons, plays blues without words one Friday a month. The owner suggests a $5 donation for the musicians and a minimum $5 purchase, but says the rule is not rigidly enforced.

Serafina Osteria

2043 Eastlake Ave. East
(206) 323-0807
www.serafinaseattle.com

The Catch: You don't have to buy dinner, but it does guarantee a better seat if you're there to see the band.

Serafina is a neighborhood Italian restaurant, but it is loved city-wide despite the occasional parking difficulties. The osteria repeatedly shows up on ratings of the city's top eateries for its food, but it gets equally high praise for being one of the area's best date spots. Add a jazz combo and the occasional torch singer, and you have the makings of a beautiful evening on a Friday or Saturday night. Who knows? The romance might continue through to Serafina's Sunday Jazz Brunch from 11 to 1:30 p.m. There's music on the first Wednesday of the month from 8 to 10 p.m. Fridays and Saturdays 9 p.m. to midnight. It's free, but keep in mind that the stage is at the back of the dining room and the room is open to diners only until the waitlist has been seated around 10 p.m.

Waterfront Seafood Grill

2801 Alaskan Way, Pier 70
(206) 956-9171
www.waterfrontpier70.com

You might not be able to see the much-vaunted view of Elliott Bay through the floor-to-ceiling windows when you sit at the bar of one of the waterfront's most expensive restaurants, but you get what you pay for. If you manage to get one of the barstools, however, you may have a nice view of the Space Needle while you listen to Ben Fleck play soft jazz on the piano. The music starts at 6 p.m., but given the fact that it's meant to be background music, you might not notice.

ECLECTIC/**ROCK**/FOLK/ **COUNTRY**/BLUEGRASS

611 Supreme
611 East Pine St.
(206) 328-0292
www.611supreme.com

At first glance, crepes and bluegrass music might seem like an odd mix. Now that the restaurant has expanded its menu to include French wine and traditional bistro food like pâté and salad Niçoise, however . . . it's still a pretty strange combination. The owner says the band's specialty is bluegrass, but adds that the combo is pretty versatile. So, you can enjoy a taste of another country with the sounds of this one every Tuesday night from 8 to 11 p.m.

Central Club
124 Kirkland Ave.
Kirkland
(425) 827-0808
www.centralkirkland.com

No matter whether you call it a dive bar or a hole in the wall, it's a holdout against the upscaling of Kirkland. Given its history dating back to the city's early years, you might even call it a classic Kirkland place. There's free music on Wednesday and Sunday nights. Wednesday nights have an old school rock and roll feel while Sundays are more bluesy. The music plays from 8:30 to midnight on Sunday and 9:30 p.m. to 1 a.m. on Wednesday.

Conor Byrne

5140 Ballard Ave. West
(206) 784-3640
www.conorbyrnepub.com

There's just something about Ballard's old industrial district along Ballard Avenue that makes it a great spot for live music joints. There's the Tractor, the Sunset (which both have cover charges for all shows), and this place. An Irish pub that recently added food service, the CB offers a mix of styles throughout the week including alt country, rockabilly, western swing, and Irish, of course. No cover Sunday through Wednesday. Open mic night on Sunday, old time social on Tuesdays, and not-so-musical pub trivia on Wednesday nights. Covers range from $5 to $8, so even on nights when you have to pay to get in, it's still relatively cheap.

Couth Buzzard Books and Espresso Buono

8310 Greenwood Ave. North
(206) 436-2960
www.buonobuzzard.com

This well-loved Greenwood bookstore has seen difficult times in recent years, changing hands, closing, and then re-opening, but it may have finally found the right mix in its current incarnation by adding espresso and becoming a community gathering place. It features open mic nights every Wednesday, Celtic jams every other Saturday afternoon, and an occasional cabaret on a Saturday night every few months. For more details see the Web site calendar. Open mic goes from 7:30 to 9:30 p.m.

Crossroads Mall

Northeast 8th and 156th Avenue Northeast
Bellevue
(425) 644-1111
www.crossroadsbellevue.com

The same people who brought you Third Place Books helped rescue this mall from obscurity by taking it over and making it the center of its community with no end of entertainment and diversions every week including classes, community events, and hobbyist gatherings. The first Thursday of the month is open mic night while other Thursdays are singer-songwriter showcases. There's also a Big Band Dance the first Saturday of each month.

The music on Friday and Saturday nights can cover the waterfront from jazz and Cajun to big band or reggae and beyond. Weeknight shows go from 6 to 8:30 p.m. Weekend shows run from 7 to 9:30 p.m. All shows are free.

Fado Irish Pub
801 First Ave.
(206) 264-2700
www.fadoirishpub.com

Sure, Fado is part of a 14-bar chain with locations around the country, but the food is good and it doesn't have the cookie cutter feel of a TGI Fridays or an Applebee's. Sometimes you want the authentic, slightly dodgy Irish pub experience, sometimes you don't. This is a pleasant alternative with many nooks and crannies to hide out in where no one will be able to find you but the wait staff. The bands may play covers on Friday and Saturday, but at least Fado doesn't charge one. There's also an Irish session where a group of musicians gather to play traditional Irish music with harp, fiddle, and guitar. It's open to all ages and starts at 4 p.m. every Sunday. There's no cover and weekend shows run from 10 p.m. to 1 a.m.

Forecasters Pub
14300 Northeast 145th St.
Woodinville
(425) 483-3232
www.redhook.com

If you like Redhook ales, you'll love this place. It is one of Redhook's brew-pubs, after all. Set among some of the area's best-known wineries, it's a perfect fit. Bands play from 9 to 11:30 p.m. every Friday and Saturday. There's no cover charge.

Georgia's Greek Restaurant and Deli
323 Northwest 85th
(206) 783-1228
www.georgiasgreekrestaurant.com

Greek food just goes down better with a side of ethnic music regardless of whether it's Macedonian, Serbian, Albanian, or Balkan. And did we mention the belly dancing? Music is free and starts at 7 p.m. on Saturday.

Gypsy Café and Pub
3510 Stone Way North
(206) 632-0647
www.gypsycafeseattle.com

A funky cafe with comfortable couches and a hodgepodge mix of furniture, the Gypsy Café and Pub is popular with workers in the area during the day, and folks in the neighborhood at night. During the summer months boaters also like it because of its proximity to Lake Union. There's music on Friday and Saturday from 8 to around 11 p.m. Instead of emphasizing a particular style of music, the café favors local bands. As a result, it features an eclectic mix of blues, bluegrass, gypsy jazz, classic rock, and cover bands. There's an open mic night on the first Thursday of the month.

Jewel Box Café
321 Northeast Thornton Place
(206) 432-9341
www.jewelboxcafe.net

This little coffeehouse is the type of place you find and think, "How come I didn't know this was here?" The answer is easy enough. It's in the courtyard of a relatively new mixed-use housing development across from Northgate Mall. If listings on Yelp and other rating Web sites are any indication, most people find it when they're headed to a movie at the 14-plex movie theater across the courtyard. It's a cute place with lots of wood, a fireplace, and a menu that includes all the coffee drinks you'd find other places plus crepes, sandwiches, wine, beer and, a rarity for coffeehouses, bubble tea. And it often has live music one night each weekend. Check the Web site or call before you go.

John Howie Steak
The Bravern Bellevue
11111 Northeast 8th St.
Bellevue
(425) 440-0880
www.johnhowiesteak.com

If people who live in glass houses shouldn't throw stones, what shouldn't people who play glass pianos do? You might not find the answer at John Howie Steak's piano bar in Bellevue's high-end mall, the Bravern, but if you take up a seat at the showpiece, you'll get to see the piano work while you dine. And isn't that the mark of a high quality musical experience, after all? Live piano music starts at 7 p.m. and ends at 11 during the week (around midnight on Friday and Saturday) and begins at 6 p.m. on Sunday and ends around 9 p.m.

Kells Irish Restaurant & Pub
Pike Place Market
1916 Post Alley
(206) 728-1916
www.kellsirish.com

The Catch: There is a cover charge on Friday and Saturday, but only if you get there after 9 p.m.

Nestled in the bottom of a historic building in the Pike Place Market, the scene is decidedly more lively now than it was in its early days when it served as a local mortuary. People may quibble about the quality of the service and the food, but all seem to agree on the quality of the music. Not too surprisingly, it's almost all Irish or Irish-themed (think classic rock done in an Irish style). Go figure. Music during the week is free. If you get there early enough on weekend nights, you won't have to pay, either. The cover charge goes into effect at 9 p.m.

Laughing Ladies Cafe
17551 15th Ave. Northeast
Shoreline
(206) 362-2026
www.laughingladiescafe.com

Seattle has seen coffee cafes with all sorts of themes from S&M to science fiction, but this could well be the first comedy-themed café. When the ladies aren't laughing, they are often grooving on everything from blues and folk to jazz and Scandinavian music on Friday and Saturday nights as well as some Sunday afternoons. Night shows begin at 7:30 p.m.; Sunday shows start at 3 p.m. Check the Web site for more details.

Le Pichet
Pike Place Market
1933 1st Ave.
(206) 256-1499
www.lepichetseattle.com

It may seem odd for a traditional French bistro to feature folk, bluegrass, and alt country, but it makes perfect sense to the owners. The inspiration comes from their days when they were culinary students in Paris who couldn't afford to enjoy live music because the city's nightspots were so expensive. All that changed when they discovered that many of the cafes and bars at a local flea market all had free live music on Sunday. The tradition lives on in Seattle with their "Music Free for the People" series. French music is their preference, but they present any style of music that they feel is under-represented in Seattle. The music starts shortly after the lunch crowd dissipates at 2:30 and goes until 4:30 p.m. No purchase is required, but it couldn't hurt to order lunch or snacks if you're so inclined. And don't forget to tip the musicians.

Little Red Hen

7115 Woodlawn Ave. Northeast
(206) 522-1168
www.littleredhen.com

The Catch: It's not free, but it's cheap and there are free dance lessons.

Seattle may not seem the likeliest locale for a country bar, especially around Greenlake, a park known to attract politically correct power walkers and people who want to talk about their relationships, but the Little Red Hen has been holding its own for years. Although the name of the restaurant/bar is painted larger than life on the back outside wall, it's a safe bet that most non-country music fans don't even know it's there. There's a small cover after 8 p.m. Thursday through Sunday, generally around $3 to $5, but there are free dance lessons on Sunday nights before the dance starts. There are also line dancing lessons on Monday and regular lessons on Tuesday nights and no cover charge.

Mandolin Café

3923 South 12th St.
Tacoma
(253) 761-3482
www.themandolincafe.com

A coffeehouse that serves wine and beer along with baked goods and comfort food, the Mandolin welcomes a wide range of musical styles. One night it might be big band/swing, the next folk, and jazz the night after that. A recent night even featured boogie blues piano, electro, and indie pop on the same bill. There's never a cover charge Monday through Thursday, but there are occasional covers on weekends. Sunday is open mic night. It prides itself on presenting artists you haven't heard of yet, but eventually will.

Murphy's Pub
1928 North 45th
(206) 634-2110
www.murphyseattle.com

One of Seattle's first Irish pubs, the 30-year-old Wallingford neighborhood spot has plenty of nice touches—a hearth, stained glass, a dart court, and great microbrews and ales. Drop by Monday at 8 p.m. to hear Irish bands (and enjoy Irish drink specials) or take in Wednesday's open mic night.

The Ould Triangle
9736 Greenwood Ave.
(206) 706-7798

Considering that one of Seattle's claims to fame is its Nordic heritage, it sure has a heck of a lot of Irish bars. This one has acoustic and mellow rock music on Friday and Saturday and a jam session on Sunday, all free. There's also an open mic night on Wednesday. And for you billiard fans, pool is free all day Sunday.

Pan Pacific Hotel
2125 Terry Ave.
(206) 264-8111
www.panpacific.com

The high end hotel's lobby bar features the sounds of the ubiquitous flamenco artist Andre Feriante on Friday from 8 to 11 p.m. No cover.

Paragon Restaurant and Bar
2125 Queen Anne Ave. North
(206) 283-4548
www.paragonseattle.com

A neighborhood eatery where the crowd changes with the clock, this Queen Anne fixture offers a mixture of rock, acoustic, soul, R&B, and just a little bit of funk. It's also a cozy restaurant with everything from steaks and burgers to fancier dishes, wooden booths, and a big fireplace. On Tuesday, the band Fiasco puts on a mini rock show. On Wednesday, the two guitar players in Two Brothers take requests. Thursday is soul night. There's no music on Monday and there are DJs on Friday. The rest of the time it's a mix of R&B, soul, and a little bit of blues and rock. And there's never a cover charge.

Pies and Pints
1215 Northeast 65th St.
(206) 524-7082
www.piesandpints.com

Australian-style savory pot pies are the signature dish at this friendly neighborhood pub just north of the University District. There are other items including fish, soups, and salads, but let's face it, if you really wanted to eat healthy, you would have gone round the corner to Whole Paycheck. The music goes from 8 to 11 p.m. on Sunday and Wednesday. The Seattle Folk Review holds down Sunday nights. Calling regular Wednesday night band, Slim Pickins, a country/blues band doesn't do them justice. After all, "You Are My Sunshine" and "I'm the Sheik of Araby" aren't exactly country tunes. One of the waitresses simply calls it "happy music."

Ristorante Picolinos
6415 32nd Ave. Northwest
(206) 781-8000
www.ristorantepicolinos.com

I still wonder what reaction the Norwegian fishermen who settled Ballard would have if they heard world music pouring out of an Italian restaurant in their old stomping ground. It's not that it would keep me from visiting, mind you. I just stay up late at night wondering about these things. There's live entertainment most nights—usually either a pianist, guitarist, or accordion player—and it's always free. The tunes usually start between 6 and 7 p.m.

Salty's
www.saltys.com

Salty's on Alki, 1936 Harbor Ave. Southwest, Seattle; (206) 937-1600
Salty's at Redondo, 28201 Redondo Beach Drive South, Des Moines; (253) 946-0636

A West Seattle institution with a beautiful view of the Seattle skyline, Salty's is so well-known for its beautiful seafood brunch buffet with light piano accompaniment that most people don't even think of it as a live music venue. Heck, if it weren't for the piano being so close to the buffet, some are so food-focused, they might not even realize the piano music is live. The café bar features live boogie woogie music from Casey MacGill's Blue 4 Trio on Friday from 7 to 10 p.m. The Redondo location has pop music on Friday and Saturday from 8 to 10 p.m. There's also live music at the Columbia River location, but the three hour drive to Portland may be a bit further than most people are willing to go.

Smokin' Pete's Barbecue
1918 Northwest 65th
(206) 783-0454
www.smokinpetesbbq.com

One of the best things about the live music here is the time of the weekly Thursday night show. While most of the bands at bars in live-music friendly Ballard don't get started until 9 or 10, the music starts here at 6:30 p.m. So, you can take in a show without having to stay out late, which is especially nice for reformed singles who are now raising families of their own. The offerings include blues, bluegrass, jazz, and alternative music. It's so family-friendly that a middle school jazz band plays there twice a year.

SoulFood Books and Cafe
15748 Redmond Way
Redmond
(425) 881-5309
www.soulfoodbooks.com

Take one look at SoulFood's monthly calendar and you'll quickly realize that it's a New Age bookstore, but if you look closely, you'll see live music hidden among such offerings as tarot readings, drum circles, and Reiki workshops. There's an open mic night on the first Saturday of the month as well as music on most Fridays and Saturdays as well as the occasional Wednesday. What's on offer ranges from experimental jazz and folk all the way to a heavy metal guitarist. The café's only requirement is that "you must play the truth," which is why it recently rejected a band made up of bragging fisherman. Okay, I made that up. The best way to see if the music is to your liking is to go to the Web site, select "Soul Tribe Streaming," and listen to a few recent shows.

Singing for Supper (and Breakfast and Lunch)

The street musicians at the Pike Place Market are a motley crew and they embrace almost every musical style under the sun. One has a piano that he rolls out to street corners. There's also a gospel group that always seems to be perched at Starbucks and there's a continuing cast of thousands scratching out a living an hour at a time.

While we can't tell you who they all are or even where they came from, we can tell you how they get there. Every busker has to pay a $30 annual fee to get a permit to perform, which is valid until April 14 of the following year.

Once buskers have badges, they are free to perform at one of 14 locations throughout the market designated by a circle on the sidewalk. They can't hog the spot, though. Their performance time at each spot is limited to one hour if another performer is waiting. The circles also have a stenciled number in them to indicate how many performers can play in the spot at the same time. If the stenciled number is pink no performances are allowed after 7 p.m. Other locations allow playing from 9 a.m. to 9 p.m. Monday through Saturday and from 10 a.m. to 7 p.m. on Sunday.

Oddly enough, the market will only issue four permits to balloon artists each year. There appears to be no limit on the number of clowns, however, which seems wrong, somehow.

If you're up for a musical tour of the market, here's where to look for free live music in its natural setting:

St. Clouds

1131 34th Ave.
(206) 726-1522
www.stclouds.com

The Olive Garden may say "when you're here, you're family," but St. Clouds really means it. The restaurant is active in its community and supports a variety of local causes. Bands play in the small bar, but the music can be heard throughout the restaurant from 9 to 11:30 p.m. Friday and Saturday and 8:30 to 11 p.m. on Monday. People who want to enjoy dinner and music

- Under the clock at the entrance to the market (no performers allowed on Saturday all year or on Friday from May 1 to August 31).
- The corner of Pine Street and Pike Place near Cinnamon Works.
- The entry to the North Arcade from the Desimone Bridge (except on Saturday).
- In the courtyard between the Post Alley Building and the Sanitary Market near Copacabana.
- Near Left Bank Books and the flower shop at the corner of First Avenue and Pike Place.
- The corner of First Avenue and Pike Street.
- Next to the metal staircase at the southern end of the Triangle Building just south of Greek Delicacies.
- South of Virginia Street and First Avenue in the First Avenue Courtyard.
- At the bottom of the stairs from the Soames-Dunn courtyard to Post Alley.
- West of the information stand on the sidewalk between Pike Street and lower Post Alley.
- On the First Lower Level near the exit to the Pike Place Hill Climb.
- Next to Local Color at the corner of Pike Place and Stewart Street.
- On Pike Place near the second home of the original Starbucks.
- On the sidewalk in front of the Pike Place Grocery.

can reserve a small table in the bar for an intimate evening. The music runs the gamut from jazz and folk to Latin and blues. There's no cover and the bar seats 20 plus 15 standing.

Stir

Bellevue Place
10500 Northeast 8th St.
Bellevue
(425) 646-7847
www.stirmartinibar.com

Situated on the same floor as the hotel lobby of the Bellevue Hyatt, Stir describes itself as having an indoor-urban-lodge feel with modern twists including Lucite ceiling beams that change colors. Try putting that in your rural lodge and see how far it gets you. There's live music Thursday through Saturday and no cover charge.

Third Place Books

Lake Forest Park Town Centre
17171 Bothell Way Northeast
Lake Forest Park
(206) 366-3333
www.thirdplacebooks.com

It would be easy to think of Third Place Books as just a bookstore with a food court, but that's just part of its charm. The store offers something for just about everyone whether it's mah jong on Monday, childrens' story hour on Wednesday, writers' workshops on Thursday, frequent author readings throughout the week, or live music on Friday and Saturday. The large common area that serves as a community gathering place (and also a dining room for the store's five restaurants) converts to a dance floor for folks who feel the rhythm in the soles of their feet, but you don't have to dance if you don't want to. You can just sit back, tap your feet, and enjoy swing, jazz, blues, or whatever style happens to be playing the evening you're there. The music goes from 7:30 to 9:30 p.m. and it's open to all ages. There's also a separate area where kids can dance so that they won't be in the way of the serious dancers.

Thirteen Coins

www.13coins.com

125 Boren Ave. North, Seattle; (206) 682-2513
18000 International Blvd., Seatac; (206) 243-9500
There aren't many classic Seattle places left anymore, but this is one of them—a 24-hour watering hole where counter seating is preferred over booths because of the show the cooks put on in the kitchen. The food isn't cheap, but the music in the lounge is free on Friday and Saturday nights and starts at 9:30 p.m. There's also a location near Seattle Tacoma International Airport with music on Wednesday and Thursday starting at 7:30 and Friday and Saturday at 8:30. Much of the music at the Seattle location is request

play and Jimmy Buffett is high on the listener list. We're not sure why, but we hear there have been many lost shakers of salt.

Triple Door Lounge Musiquarium
Downstairs from Wild Ginger Restaurant
216 Union St.
(206) 838-4333
www.thetripledoor.net

Dominated by a 1,900-gallon glass aquarium, the Musiquarium at the Triple Door isn't just a place to hang out while waiting for the main stage show to start. There is a happy hour, of course, and a *Wine Spectator* Grand Award– winning selection of wines, but it also offers a wide range of music and entertainment in its own right every night, all of it free. Monday is open mic night, and Afro-centric music is the focus on Thursday night with live performances one week followed by DJs the next. There are two live performances on Friday with one during happy hour and the second at 9:30. The mix includes jazz, R&B, and rock while Saturday is always funk night focusing on bands that do experimental funk and jazz. Sunday is salsa night with a rotating cast of salsa and rhumba music.

Uncle Ned's Acoustic Jam Session
Fremont Abbey Arts Center
4272 Fremont Ave. North
(206) 414-8325
www.fremontabbey.org

You can either hang out and enjoy the scene or bring an instrument and join in the fun the third Sunday of every month from noon to 2 p.m. The mix includes folk, blues, and bluegrass. There's also free music at the Abbey during the Fremont Art Walk from 6 to 9 p.m. on the first Friday of the month.

Victrola Coffee
411 15th Ave. East
(206) 325-6520
www.victrolacoffee.com

This popular neighborhood cafe not only features live music several times a month, during its Summer Music Series it also offers specials on drinks and food during the shows. The styles range from jazz and Americana to folk and singer-songwriter. For more information, check the calendar on Victrola's Web site.

Wayward Coffeehouse
8570 Greenwood Ave. North
(206) 706-3240
www.waywardcoffee.com

Klingon love ballads, anyone? This Greenwood cafe may have a sci-fi/fantasy theme, but the music doesn't. At least, not usually. Most Friday and Saturday night performances lean toward jazz, folk, and acoustic rock, but there is the occasional filk artist (folk song with a science fiction/fantasy theme). And in case you were wondering, these aren't the droids you're looking for.

Wilde Rover Irish Pub and Restaurant
111 Central Way
Kirkland
(425) 822-8940
www.wilderover.com

This popular Kirkland bar features music every night of the week except pub trivia night on Wednesday. Musical styles include Irish bands, classic rock, and R&B. There's a $5 cover charge on Friday and Saturday, but you can avoid it by showing up before 9 p.m.

CLASSICAL

Frye Art Museum
704 Terry Ave.
(206) 622-9250
www.fryemuseum.org

An organization called the Ladies Musical Club may sound like a quaint cultural society from the late 1800s, but the group and the Seattle Classical Guitar Society organize concerts at this hidden gem of an art museum on First Hill. As the organizations' names would suggest, the concerts feature classical music. Although there's a concert every month, it's best to check the schedule on the Web site's music page to get concert dates. The concerts are free, but tickets are required. It's best to arrive at least an hour before the event because the 142-seat auditorium fills quickly. There are also other free concerts and recitals throughout the year; check the Web site regularly for more details.

Seattle Symphony Community Concerts
Various locations
(206) 215-4700
www.seattlesymphony.org/symphony/community/engagement/

No, the symphony hasn't started giving away free tickets yet, but it does a small number of free concerts throughout the community to bring music to the masses who might not otherwise experience orchestral music live. Most of the performances are in January, but the symphony also does a lunchtime concert at City Hall in spring. If you prefer the ambience of Benaroya Hall, you can also attend one of the free recitals performed on the 4,490-pipe Watjen Concert Organ. The performances occur about six times a year, start at 12:30 p.m. on select Mondays, and last a half hour. For dates of the recitals, check the Web site at www.seattlesymphony.org/benaroya/tour.

In a Class by Itself
A cathedral might not seem like the ideal place for a romantic date night, but over the last 50 years the Compline service at St. Mark's Cathedral, 1245 10th Ave. East, has become the church equivalent of a hot ticket. That doesn't mean that the Episcopal church on Capitol Hill is turning people away just yet. Instead, the formal service chanted by a men's choir in a darkened cathedral every Sunday night has quietly grown to a point where it now attracts 500 people week in and week out with much of the audience being in its teens and early 20s. If you can't make it to the St. Mark's, you can still get the idea by turning down the lights in your home, tuning in KING-FM (98.1) or www.king.org at 9:30 p.m., and listening that way. The service only lasts half an hour and is occasionally followed by a free organ demonstration, which you can only hear if you're at St. Mark's.

SUMMER **CONCERTS**

Concerts at the Mural
Seattle Center
http://seattlecenter.com

The Seattle Center and public alternative rock station KEXP join forces in August to present five concerts. Four two-hour shows feature three indy rock bands and begin on Friday nights at 6 p.m. The fifth is a full day barbecue that runs from 2 to 9 p.m. and includes seven bands. The shows are free, but the barbecue will cost you.

Downtown Bellevue's Live at Lunch Series
Various locations
Bellevue
(425) 453-1223
www.bellevuedowntown.org

Who says there's no culture on the Eastside? Well, Seattleites mostly. The Live at Lunch series of mid-week concerts proves that local business folk know how to rock, or tap their wing tips somewhat rhythmically. At least during the day when they probably should be in their offices, but who's counting? The 2009 schedule was jazz heavy, but also included country, flamenco, and a number of cover bands. The season begins in July and runs through September with shows held from noon to 1:30 p.m. on Tuesday, Wednesday, and Thursday. The Thursday concert is always at the Bellevue Galleria, but other performances are held at office buildings throughout downtown.

Hempfest
Seattle waterfront from Myrtle Edwards Park north to Elliott Bay Park
(206) 781-5734
www.hempfest.org

Part political gathering, part weekend-long concert, Hempfest's goal is to spread the word about hemp and advocate the legalization of marijuana. Shhh . . . shhhh . . . shhhh . . . Hey, man, does anybody have some Visine?

Kent Summer Concert Series
Locations vary
Kent
(253) 856-5050

Depending on your tastes, you could see as many as three free concerts a week in this south-end city during the summer. On Tuesdays, there's an out-to-lunch style concert from noon to 1 p.m. at Kent Station (417 Ramsay) that's a perfect afternoon break for employees of the Regional Justice Center, local office workers, shoppers, and people who just happen to have the time off. Wednesday concerts also start at noon at Townsquare Plaza (2nd Avenue and Harrison Street), but are for the school-aged set and feature children's entertainers. Thursday evening concerts at Lake Meridian Park (14800 Southeast 272nd St.) go from 7 to 8:30 p.m. and cover a wide variety of musical styles ranging from blues and jazz to world pop. The season runs from July to August and all shows are free.

Kidd Valley Summer Concert Series
Gene Coulon Memorial Beach Park
1201 Lake Washington Blvd.
Renton
(425) 430-6700
http://rentonwa.gov/living/default.aspx?id=74

Driving I-405 is never fun, but at least these concerts make the trip worthwhile and end in a nice family outing in the middle of the week. The Wednesday night series starts in early July and ends in mid-August with a variety of musical styles including everything from Celtic and steel drums to polka and rock and roll. The bands play in front of the Kidd Valley burger stand. Blankets and picnics are welcome, but, sadly, dogs are not.

Mostly Music in the Park
Mercerdale Park
77th Southeast and Southeast 32nd
Mercer Island
(206) 236-3545

Mostly Music is Mercer Island's summer concert series, which runs from July to August and usually includes nine shows. All performances are on Sunday and Thursday at 7 p.m. and last 90 minutes and take place under the Veteran's Pergola.

Northwest Folklife

Seattle Center
(206) 684-7300
www.nwfolklife.org

The Seattle Center becomes one giant folk music concert on Memorial Day weekend as folksters from all over gather to take in traditional American music as well as styles that most people have never even heard of. Hungarian Tanchaz. Pirate Pub. Tribal and fusion bellydance. Apparently, Balkan Bridge Dance has absolutely nothing to do with trumps and tricks. Who knew? Although there is an extensive schedule of concerts, some of the best music can be heard outside the venues where impromptu jam sessions come and go. Although there are scattered events held throughout town earlier in the month including the University District Street Fair, Folklife marks the true start of the summer festival season in Seattle.

Out to Lunch Concert Series

Various locations
Downtown
(206) 623-0340
www.downtownseattle.com

Now in its 31st year, the Downtown Seattle Association–sponsored series runs between Memorial Day and Labor Day with performances from noon to 1:30 p.m. on Wednesday and Friday. There's a different venue for every performance and the venues range from Pioneer Square all the way north to Denny Park, helping to ensure that workers from all over downtown will have the chance to see a performance near their office. Although the styles have included jazz, rock, pop, country, and even a stab at opera, the DSA refers to it as "just fun summer music."

Seattle Chamber Music Society

Benaroya Hall, 200 University St., Seattle
The Overlake School, 20301 Northeast 108th St., Redmond
(206) 283-8710
www.seattlechambermusic.org

For six weeks every summer, the society presents family chamber music concerts in just the right setting for kids and adults. The shows are performed inside, but the music is piped outside so families can enjoy the music without worrying that their squirmy kids might distract culture vultures. For many years, the shows were split between Lakeside School in North Seattle and the Overlake School in Redmond where the park-like settings made for an enjoyable, easily accessible experience. In 2010, the Lakeside shows moved to downtown Seattle's Benaroya Hall. A 7 p.m. recital is free and open to the public and is piped outside. The 8 p.m. concerts are not free, but the music is still piped to listeners outside the hall. The venue change means that families will likely have to deal with parking hassles on their way to the event and a less park-like setting, even if the music will be piped to the Garden of Remembrance on the side of the building. There will still be two weeks of concerts at the more park-like setting at the Overlake School in Redmond. Some of the rehearsals held during the Summer Festival are also free and open to the public.

Seattle Peace Concerts
Locations vary
(206) 465-9077
www.seapeace.org/events.html

Now entering its third decade, this Seattle institution brings together local musicians and large crowds in local parks for six hours on Sundays through-out the summer to benefit Northwest Harvest, a non-profit that helps feed those in need. The concerts are family friendly and include a wide range of musical styles.

Seattle Presents
Seattle City Hall
600 4th Ave.
(206) 684-7171
www.seattle.gov/seattlepresents

A perfect little getaway in the middle of the day for office workers who want to escape the grind, these concerts are held in City Hall's lobby at noon on the first and third Thursdays of the month throughout the year, except in July and August when the shows move outdoors and are held every Thursday. The series focuses on home-grown talent and includes a variety of musical styles. Check the Web site to find out what bands are featured.

A Guide to Tipping Street Performers

Although you know to tip waiters and waitresses at least 15 percent at the end of a meal if the service was good, the most frustrating thing for street performers and onlookers alike is that there are no rules for what to do when one comes across the busker in his or her natural habitat. Should the average citizen turn around and run the other way or hold out money and hope the performer won't attack? And should the performer put up a sign in their instrument case with a sign showing a suggested donation? And what can a performer do at a place like the Pike Place Market where asking for donations is strictly prohibited?

This is where being a cheap bastard who knows a street musician or two comes in handy.

As veteran market busker Jonny Hahn says, "If you stop and listen for any length of time, [a performer] would like to have that type of appreciation in the form of a tip. Tip size doesn't matter." Better still, if you really like the performer, consider buying a CD. That's how my kids became fans of the group Slim Pickins.

Summer Concerts at the Ballard Locks

Hiram Chittenden Memorial Locks
3015 Northwest 54th St.
(206) 783-7059
www.nws.usace.army.mil/publicmenu/menu.cfm?sitename=lwsc&pagename=mainpage

After 20 years, there's a reason people haven't heard of this music series at one of Seattle's top tourist spots: there's no advertising budget. Zero. Nada. Zilch. And that's too bad because it makes for a great family outing on a sunny Sunday afternoon. Concerts in the ongoing summer series are held on weekends from early June through Labor Day, start at 2 p.m., and run at least an hour. The park sets up 100 chairs on the main lawn in the Carl S. English Jr. Botanical Gardens—you know, the place that you rush through to take visitors to see the ships passing through the locks and the

Here are a few other handy pointers that will help keep both sides of the equation happy and on good terms:

- Make sure to tip more if you've taken a picture of the performer or posed with them.

  "They should pay more, especially if they have an expensive camera," Hahn jokes.
- Remember good camera etiquette. It's okay to take pictures, but it's not okay to be intrusive. These are working artists, after all, not your personal models.
- If you've filmed the performer or used your video camera, you should also consider giving more. After all, if you value the performance enough to want to capture it on video, your tip should reflect that value.
- Whatever you do, never take money from a performer's case. It's more than just theft, it's also bad karma.

Other than that, let your conscience be your guide.

As Hahn says, "In general it's nice to get tips for the ego thing and because we are there trying to make a living."

migrating fish making their way up the salmon ladder—but you can bring your own lawn chairs and blankets and even a picnic. Since the concerts have attracted a slightly older crowd, the music tends to fit their tastes, but organizers work hard to include music that appeals to kids and even find a way to work in a children's theater group along the way. In past years the schedule has been jazz heavy, but has also included groups like the Sound Swing Band, the Puget Sound Symphony Players, the Ballard Sedentary Sousa Band, and the Microsoft Orchestra. As the name suggests, the Sousa band plays march music while sitting. And there's absolutely no truth to the rumor that the Microsoft band started late because it had to reboot.

University Village Concert Series
University Village
25th Avenue Northeast and Northeast 45th Street
(206) 523-0622
www.uvillage.com

Now a summer tradition, University Village Concert Series includes six free family concerts on successive Wednesday nights. The short concert season usually starts two weeks after July fourth. The performances themselves go from 6 to 8:30 p.m. and feature local celebrity bands playing tunes everybody knows. The event also features gourmet bites from many Village restaurants, a beer garden on one side of the stage, and a kids' area on the other with sprinklers, face painting, and other fun stuff for the younger set to do.

FILM:
CHEAP SHOTS

*"You know what your problem is,
it's that you haven't seen enough movies—
all of life's riddles are answered in the movies."*

—STEVE MARTIN

When it comes to movies in Seattle, free is a relative term. There are a few free screenings to be had, but they come at a price. If you love the full on, indoor, theatrical experience, you may want to opt for the cheap theaters, but if you are okay with less than sterile conditions, sitting outdoors, or a little bit of unpredictability, then the free options will likely work for you. Here's a mix of all of the options.

FREE **YEAR**-ROUND

Seattle Film Directors Guild Movie Night
Amore Restaurant
2301 Fifth Ave.
(206) 770-0606
www.tasteofamore.com

The Catch: Two drink minimum.

The Seattle Film Directors Guild screens movies in the restaurant's Theater Lounge from 8 to 10 p.m. on Tuesday nights. There's no cover, but there is a two-drink minimum. It's also worth noting that movie nights at Amore have come and gone, so it's best to check the Web site calendar or call before you go.

Bizarro Movie Night
Aster Coffee Lounge
5615 24th Ave. Northwest
(206) 784-0615
www.astercoffeelounge.com

There may be plenty of bad B movies out there, but there's never been anyone to explain them to you . . . until now. Every second or third Saturday of the month at 8 p.m. Aster screens a cinematic oddity hosted by self-titled Shockologist Tony Kay. The shock-master himself gives a witty introduction providing a bit of context and then lets the oddity roll before your very eyes. Just a warning, there will be weirdness . . . and there may be prizes. There's also free popcorn . . . until the movie starts. Check the Web site or call before you go.

Friday Night at the Meaningful Movies

Keystone Congregational United Church of Christ
5019 Keystone Place North
www.meaningfulmovies.org

Yes, I know it's at a church, but the films aren't church-related and there are no religious messages. If you're an old lefty or you just love movies with a cause, this is the place for you. Every Friday night at 7 p.m. the Wallingford Neighbors for Peace and Justice screen documentaries about social justice issues followed by open discussion. The gatherings are designed to help foster conversation, build community, allow justice groups to publicize their issues, help people do meaningful social justice work, and allow filmmakers to promote their work. But it's okay to show up just because you want to get out of the house and watch a good movie.

JW Film Club

Times and locations vary
www.janetwainwright.com/filmclub.htm

Yes, Virginia, you can see first run movies for free . . . on occasion . . . if you know the right people and happen to have the time. Film fans who sign up for Janet Wainwright's Film Club via an e-mail to jwmovieclub@gmail .com receive free passes to advance movie screenings via e-mail about twice a month, give or take. There's no telling what film will be next, but one thing's certain: you'll need to show up early to make sure you get a seat.

Wayward Coffeehouse

8570 Greenwood Ave. North
(206) 706-3240
www.waywardcoffee.com

Science fiction geeks have a place to call their own on the first Friday of the month when this sci-fi/fantasy themed coffeehouse shows a sci-fi or fantasy movie. Films start at 9 p.m. In addition to being the home of the Seattle Browncoats (fans of *Serenity* and *Firefly*), many of the specialty drinks are named with sci-fi/fantasy references. The Iocane latte is the perfect example. Fans of *The Princess Bride* may remember that Iocane was a highly toxic substance that played an important part in one of the scenes. According to the menu, the latte contains "iocane and vanilla."

The Best Bargain in Town:
The Seattle International Film Festival

Why volunteer to usher at a play and only see that show for free when you could usher at a movie, stay and see the show, and still get a voucher to see another movie free?

Yes, I know there's nothing like free live theater, but getting two things free is even better.

The Seattle International Film Festival (SIFF) has long offered its ushers and other volunteers many ways to go to the movies for free. Depending on their responsibilities during a shift, most volunteer ushers will not only get to see the movie they volunteer at for free, but they'll also get a voucher for a free ticket for every movie they work. Given that most shifts require coverage of three movies, that could mean a total of six free movies.

What makes the vouchers an even better deal is that they don't lose their value once the festival ends. Instead, they are good for a year and can be used at other movie festivals, series, and screenings hosted by SIFF at its year-round theater, SIFF Cinema, or can be converted into an Enthusiast membership level of SIFF. If you have five vouchers to spare, the Enthusiast-level membership makes a good deal even better because members are invited to free previews throughout the year.

ALMOST **FREE**

The Warren Report
www.thewarrenreport.com

The Catch: It costs $20 a year.

For years, the Warren Report has been a kind of smorgasbord for film fans. The truly serious can attend classes and sit in on discussions with movie-

The best news of all is that you don't have to wait until the festival starts to begin racking up vouchers. SIFF needs so many volunteers in the weeks and months before the event that it's easy to spend the better part of the festival sitting in a darkened theater without a care in the world . . . other than wondering how you're going to spend the rest of your vouchers.

Volunteer jobs before the start of the festival include proofreading publications, distributing movie guides around town, answering phones, selling tickets, and stuffing gift bags. If your schedule won't permit ushering, but you want to work during the festival, you can work will-call tables, pick up guests at the airport and drive them back, transport films to venues, or do any of hundreds of other tasks that keep the event going.

Of course, if you're hardcore enough, you could become one of 10 members of the front desk volunteer team who agree to work at least four hours a week for six months. The job involves answering calls, giving top notch customer service to people who visit the office, doing data entry, and helping out with special projects. The reward for all your hard work is a free Festival Pass (which is worth $850).

To volunteer at SIFF Cinema or the festival, sign up at www.siff .net/about/jobs/volunteers.aspx.

makers and actors of all sorts. The real attraction for the dilettantes has been the chance to see advance screenings of new releases. If you were to watch every preview, the per movie cost would easily drop to $1 or less. You have to be fast, though. Warren Etheredge lists them on his Web site and subscribers make reservations. If you snooze, you lose. The former curator of Bumershoot's One Reel Film Festival and all around Northwest film industry maven also offers workshops and hosts other events that aren't free.

See Free Without Standing in Line (sort of)

If you're a parent of young kids, like I am, you don't get much of a chance to see the latest first run blockbusters because you don't have the time or you can't find a babysitter when you want to go. Even renting a movie is iffy because most rentals only last a few days and there are always late fees to contend with. Fortunately, there's an alternative that not only costs nothing, but also is easily accessible and is something that everyone's heard of: the local library.

Both the King County Library and Seattle Public Library systems lend movies on DVD to their card-carrying patrons for longer than your average rental with far lower late fees (overdue fines) than even the most liberal video stores. The disadvantage is that you might not get to see that hot new flick as soon as it's released on DVD, but at least you can get on a waiting list . . . and you do move up pretty quickly.

At the King County Library you can check out a DVD for seven days and renew it up to two times, if needed, and fines are only 10 cents a day (topping out at $3). Don't get the wrong idea, though. The system won't play Mr. Nice Guy forever. Materials out over 29 days past the due date are considered lost and you will be billed. If you accrue fines of over $10, you won't be allowed to check out books. And if your fines reach $25, they'll sic a collection agency on you.

Seattle Public Library loans DVDs for two weeks and allows up to two renewals unless there is a hold on the film. Fines are 15 cents per day with a maximum of $6. Lending privileges are suspended at $15. Once an account reaches $25 or an item has been out more than 50 days, the account is turned over to Unique Management Service. Go ahead, laugh at the name if you will, but whatever it is, it can report you to credit agencies and charge you a $12 processing fee.

Hey, they may be librarians, but they're not pushovers.

CHEAP

In my early days as a poor, starving freelancer, second run movie theaters like the Crest Cinema Center were a staple of my entertainment budget. Of course, in those days, they only charged a dollar or two. As I made more money, the Crest remained the heart of my movie priority rating system. Instead of relying on numbers, I based it on cost. The continuum went this way: Long-awaited, hot new release that I absolutely must see—opening night at full price. New release that I really want to see—matinee. Movies that interested me, but were not top priority—Crest. Shows that I'm so-so on—wait for the video. Films that have captured my curiosity, but I'm not terribly optimistic about—watch after it comes off the new-release wall at my local video store. Over the years, I've been surprised by how few movies have merited opening night rating. How picky am I? Even *Avatar* didn't make the opening night movie cut.

So, if you're patient like me, you may want to consider making these theaters part of your own rating system.

The Crest Cinema Center
16505 5th Ave. Northeast
Shoreline
(206) 781-5755
www.landmarktheatres.com/market/seattle/crestcinemacenter.htm

The Catch: Watch where you park. Neighbors living to the west of the theater are quick to tow illegally parked vehicles.

One of the best ways to judge the popularity of a first-run movie is the length of time it takes to make it to this second-run cinema on the edge of town. If it made the jump in just a few weeks, you may want to rethink your desire to see it. The seats can be hard, but at $3 for all shows at all times for any of the four movies, it's hard to go wrong, especially if you bring your own seat cushion Of course, you could take the view that even if the movie's bad, at least it's cheap. I felt that way until I saw *Basic Instinct*. That's two hours of my life I'll never get back.

East Valley 13
3751 East Valley Rd.
Renton
(425) 873-2077

If you can't find what you like at the Crest, you might consider checking out this multi-multiplex with 13 screens. It, too, is $3 all seats, all times, but you may have to travel the dreaded Interstate 405 to get here.

Gateway Movies 8
2501 South Gateway Center
Federal Way
(253) 946-9224
www.starplexcinemas.com

If this weren't so far from Seattle (and if it began with the letter A or B), it would top the list. It's 22 miles from downtown Seattle, but depending on gas prices and where you are, it could well be worth the drive to spend $2. Better still, wait until Tuesday when tickets are $1. Hot dogs are $1.

The Death of the Matinee

Long, long ago in an Emerald City not so far away, there were theaters that offered matinee showings up until 6 p.m. on weekdays, weekends, and holidays. And there was much rejoicing, especially among those who came home to spend Thanksgiving with the family and realized why they moved away in the first place when they needed a place to escape for a few hours. Some theaters were more persnickety and only had matinees for the first showing of the day, but there was still some rejoicing. All that changed recently when most local cinemas decided to roll back matinee times to 10:30 a.m. and there was much sadness. Now, not only do prodigal sons and daughters have to guess whether or not their relatives will irritate them and take pre-emptive action, they also lose the joy of dramatically storming out of the house when someone inevitably says something that really ticks them off.

The Historic Admiral Theatre

2343 California Ave. Southwest
(206) 938-3456
www.farawayentertainment.com/admiral.html

If you live in the south end of town, rely on buses, or just can't be bothered to drive all the way to the Crest, you can always hit this nautical-themed second run theater in West Seattle. It'll cost you a bit more, though. Movies at this two-screener are $5.50.

SUMMER SCREENINGS

Bellevue Summer Outdoor Movies in the Park

Bellevue Downtown Park
10201 Northeast 4th St.
Bellevue

Family-friendly Tuesday night movies run from early July to late August are presented by Bellevue Parks and Community Services, sponsored by Intelius. The films are free, but each has a themed charity benefit. When the city showed *Hotels for Dogs*, for example, the movie helped raise funds for the Hopelink Food Drive.

Carillon Point Outdoor Movies

Carillon Point Plaza
4100 Carillon Point Rd.
Kirkland

These Saturday night movies running mid-July through August come with a beautiful view as the screen overlooks lovely Lake Washington. Suggested donation is $5 with proceeds going to Hopelink. All movies are family friendly. No showings in the rain.

Fremont Almost Free Outdoor Cinema
Phinney Avenue North and North 35th Street

The granddaddy of them all, this is the gathering that launched the outdoor movie movement in Seattle. It originally started as a wacky, weekly community gathering with bad B films ("The Mysterions want our women!") shown on the wall of a neighborhood parking lot preceded by a variety of goofy contests and competitions including prizes for best urban camp site. The parking lot is gone and the focus is on more recent releases and cult films, but the goofiness remains with pre-show competitions and slightly more spectacular events including a recent zombie walk. Admission free. Suggested donation $5. Saturday from late June through mid-August.

Kent Summer Nights and the Silver Screen
Town Square Plaza
Second Avenue and Harrison Street
Kent
www.kentarts.com

All Friday night movies are family friendly with some screenings especially for kids. Activities start 45 minutes before the start of the show and usually have a theme based on the movie being screened. Admission free, but donations requested.

Marymoor Outdoor Movies
Marymoor Park
6046 West Lake Sammamish Parkway Northeast
Redmond

The Catch: Suggested donation of $5 per person or $15 per family and a mandatory $1 parking fee.

One of the largest and most popular parks in the King County system, Marymoor hosts family-friendly movies at McNair Field in the park on Wednesday nights. There are a few catches, though. It's free, but there's a suggested donation of $5 per person or $15 per family. There's also a $1 charge for parking. Unfortunately, this isn't one of those neighborhood parks where you can go outside the boundaries, find an empty spot on a side street and park there free. No, you're stuck, but on the plus side, how many other places can you park for two hours for only $1?

Mercer Island Outdoor Movies
Mercerdale Park
Mercer Island

Pre-movie entertainment features activities for kids based on the theme of the film. Shows start at dusk. Mid-August.

Moonlight Movies at Liberty Park
Liberty Park
Bronson Way North and Houser Way North
Renton

Free Friday night movies under the stars. Seating starts at 7 p.m. and the movie rolls at dusk.

Movies at the Mural
Seattle Center

One of the best parts of watching a movie while sitting in the shadow of the Space Needle is, if the movie's a stinker, at least you can look up in the sky and marvel over a Seattle landmark. The Saturday night shows are in August and feature a mix of childrens' films and movies that are more popular with adults. All movies are rated PG-13 or under. The soft-sloped lawn makes for a more comfortable experience than the asphalt surface found at most outdoor shows and the 45-foot-wide screen means there's not a bad seat in the bunch. Shows start at dusk.

Redhook Moonlight Cinema
Redhook Brewery
14300 Northeast 145th St.
Woodinville

Is there any way to beat watching *National Lampoon's Vacation* while drinking a beer? Some movies just shouldn't be seen sober. Films are shown Thursday nights from mid-July to mid-August in an amphitheater near Redhook's brewpub, the Forecaster's Pub. There's a beer garden and food is available from the pub. No beer service after the start of the movie. Admission $5 per person.

Summer Outdoor Cinema Series

Tukwila Community Center
12324 42nd Ave. South
Tukwila

Movies run Fridays in late July through mid-August. Admission is free, but there is a suggested donation of a can of food for a local food bank.

Three Dollar Bill Outdoor Cinema

Cal Anderson Park
1635 11th Ave.

Movies run on four successive Fridays in this popular Capitol Hill Park just a block off Broadway.

West Seattle Movies on the Wall

California Ave.

Films are shown on a wall in a courtyard between Dr. Wolff (4400 California Ave.) and Hotwire Coffee (4410 California Ave. Southwest). Free. Family movies shown on Saturday nights from mid-July to mid-August.

COMEDY:
FREE-FOR-ALL

"Dying is easy. Comedy is difficult."

—EDMUND GWENN

Despite its reputation for political correctness, Seattle has long been a great town for comedy. Like any city, we have our share of dreadfully earnest people who wouldn't recognize humor if it hit them with a pie in the face, and irony is not spoken here, but there's still plenty to laugh at: Ballard residents who insist on driving at a snail's pace with their turn signals on long after turning, uptight liberals, cranky conservatives, and a professional baseball team that was once so bad one local comedian said the main reason to go to a game was that "sometimes, they let you pitch." There are venues where it's possible to see top name comics, but you'll have to pay a pretty penny to get in. Or, you could always save your money, take your chances, and see young comedians and old pros alike get their acts together at some of these places.

Amore Restaurant
2301 Fifth Ave.
(206) 770-0606
www.tasteofamore.com

The Catch: Two drink minimum.

As the old song says, "When the moon hits your eye like a big pizza pie, that's . . . pretty damn funny." Okay, it doesn't really say that. Instead, it says, "That's *amore*." And this Amore just happens to have a comedy night one Saturday each month in its Theater Lounge. The show is free. So, don't forget to tip your waitresses and order the veal; I'll be here all week. I've always wanted to say that.

Bamboo Bar & Grill
2806 Alki Ave. Southwest
(206) 937-3023
www.bamboobarandgrill.com

The Catch: $5 cover charge.

Attending open mic nights is always a risky proposition. Sometimes the jokesters are funny, sometimes they aren't. Paying $5 to see an unknown quantity might seem to make it even riskier, but who knows? Maybe all the tacky tiki makes people funnier. Or maybe it's the Mai Tais. Wednesday nights at 9:30 p.m.

The Capitol Club

Cracked Up!
414 Pine St.
(206) 325-2149
www.thecapitolclub.net

The same people who bring you the edgy, alternative comedy sketch show, The Laff Hole, on the first and third Wednesday of the month at Chop Suey ($7 cover, show starts at 10 p.m.) host a more traditional stand-up show in a more intimate setting. The show starts at 8 p.m. on the second and fourth Sunday of the month.

Comedy Underground

109 South Washington St.
(206) 628-0303
www.comedyunderground.com

The Catch: $5 cover.

Shhh. Can you hear that? The sound of an open mic comedian bombing is so quiet, you can almost hear a pun drop. It can be especially deafening at one of Seattle's oldest comedy clubs complete with the obligatory brick wall backdrop featuring a painting of a local landmark. Still, if you had to spend $5 on an open mic night this might be your best bet because it's long been home to some of the area's best comedians. The Sunday night Comedy Showcase and Monday Open Mic Night start at 8 p.m.

Hooters Casino

9635 Des Moines Memorial Dr.
(206) 762-4000
www.washingtonhooters.com

The comedians at this weekly Wednesday night show at Hooters—yes, that Hooters—might be funny, but you might not notice at a place where comedians may fall flat, but the waitresses won't. The show runs from 8 to 10 p.m. and there's no cover.

Jazzbones

2802 6th Ave.
Tacoma
(253) 396-9169
www.jazzbones.com

This music venue features stand-up comedy on Tuesday nights. Just to make sure you know that it's comedy, the club calls it Ha Ha Tuesday. Admission is $5, but the club distributes free comedy passes. Mention the *Cheap Bastard's Guide* for a free comedy pass.

Kona Kitchen
8501 Fifth Ave. Northeast
(206) 517-KONA
www.konakitchen.com

A mix of professionals and amateurs show up for stand up comedy on the second Thursday night of the month for this open mic format show. The fun starts around 8 p.m., comedian standard time, and usually goes until around 10ish.

Laughing Ladies Cafe
17551 15th Ave. Northeast
Shoreline
(206) 362-2026
www.laughingladiescafe.com

A funny thing happened to this café on the way to becoming a comedy-themed coffeehouse. Although the laughing ladies tried to do three comedy nights a month, they had difficulty getting enough people to do that many shows. So, they cut back to having free open mic nights one Thursday night each month. The thing is, it's not always the same Thursday night. Now that's funny. Check the site's calendar for details.

Laughs Comedy Club
12099 124th Ave. Northeast
Kirkland
(425) 823-6306
www.laughscomedy.com

This suburban comedy club has two things Pioneer Square's Comedy Underground doesn't: parking and a less scary neighborhood. Oh, and there's no admission charge for open mic night, which starts at 8:30 p.m. on Tuesday nights. It's enough to make you wonder if suburban comedy is different from the urban version.

Entertainment's Redheaded Stepchild

Go ahead, laugh all you want . . . for now. Just know that things could change on short notice and that tonight's open mic night could easily become tomorrow's poetry reading. Or jazz show. Or karaoke night. Or anything else you can think of. When it comes to adding entertainment to a club's mix of offerings, comedy tends to be the redheaded stepchild. Many club and restaurant owners turn to comedians in hopes of filling seats on quiet nights only to discover it's not as big a crowd pleaser as they first thought. Sometimes it's hard to attract audiences, while other times comedians are in short supply. Occasionally, it just isn't a good fit. For whatever reason, comedy nights seem to come and go rather quickly, so it's best to call before you head out looking for an evening of yuks only to discover it's been replaced by a goth poetry slam or a men's drumming circle.

Owl and Thistle

Seattle Best Comedians Showcase
808 Post Ave.
(206) 621-7777
www.owlnthistle.com

"Best" is such a subjective phrase. And is the club saying the show is the best showcase of comedians or the best comedians in a showcase? And why are they in a showcase? Wouldn't they be funnier on stage? One thing's for sure: the club was quick to point out that this is not, repeat, not an open mic night. The funny begins at 8 p.m on the third Thursday of the month.

Pagliacci Pizza

426 Broadway Ave. E
(206) 726-1717
www.pagliacci.com

Imagine family friendly stand-up comedy. Now that you've finished laughing at the preposterousness of the idea, check out Pagliacci's free comedy night the first Monday of the month. Far from being an open mic night, it features six comics, a professional headliner, audience participation, and not a single genital joke. At least, not usually anyway. The fun starts at 8 and goes until 9:30 p.m. Pizza slices, beer, and wine are available during the show.

Pegasus Pizza
12669 Northeast 85th St.
Kirkland
(425) 822-7400
www.pegasuspizzakirkland.com

It's hard to tell whether the owners are brave or foolhardy, but whatever it is, they have chosen to offer the two most deadly forms of entertainment to their customers: open mic comedy and karaoke. When both diversions are good, they're very, very good, but when they're bad, well, speaking as someone who once bombed during an open mic night, I'd rather not talk about it. The jokes start to fly at 9:30 on Wednesday and continue until about 11 p.m, which usually gives up to 10 comedians enough time to strut their stuff.

People's Republic of Koffee
People's Republic of Komedy
1718 12th Ave.
(206) 755-5727

Now that the Capitol Hill–based Koffee stand has gone from being a window to a full-fledged coffee shop with actual walls and tables, the company plans to add live entertainment including a free open mic show on Friday nights. The comedy troupe named after the café will still do outside engagements including Laff Hole at Chop Suey ($7 cover) and Cracked Up! at the Capitol Club (see above), however.

Tost
The Big Bully Show
13 North 36th St.
(206) 547-0240
www.tostlounge.com

Where are Jamie Farr and J. P. Morgan when you really need them? The regulars on TV's old *Gong Show* would be right at home at this open mic comedy night where performers who amuse more than half the audience get to stay on stage while those who don't get the gong. The show starts at 8 p.m. on the first and third Sunday of the month.

DANCE:
FREE EXPRESSION

"If I can't dance, I don't want to be part of your revolution."

—EMMA GOLDMAN

Contra. Square. Swing. Lindy hop. Seattle has always been a dancing kind of town. In fact, back in the 1950s it was so popular here that it seemed like you couldn't swing a cat without hitting a dance hall. Those glory days are gone, of course, and it's a good thing because cats don't really make good swing partners. As it turns out, they're moody and they prefer to waltz. Who knew? That doesn't mean dance is dead in the Emerald City. There are still places to learn the art or sit back and enjoy watching those who dance, and some of them can be surprisingly inexpensive, if not free.

PERFORMANCE

acornDance
Bellevue
www.acorndance.org

The head of the company works hard to make acornDance's performances available to as many people as possible. As a result, she allows people to volunteer for usher spots, presents occasional pay-what-you-can performances, and even offers discounts for seniors, students, and working artists. The catch is that those opportunities are only available when acornDance produces the show. If the performance is part of a festival or not at acorn's regular venue, the company has no control over whether volunteers will get free tickets or not. For more information about volunteer opportunities, contact the company via its Web page.

Coriolis Dance Collective
Westlake Dance Center
10701 8th Ave. Northeast
(206) 854-1462
www.coriolisdance.com

Coriolis focuses on experimental dance that involves a collaboration among artists from many disciplines. Volunteer slots are available during some performances and often involve jobs including venue setup, ushering, and performance teardown. Volunteers get comp tickets. While it doesn't offer a free class, the company does have one of the cheapest ballet classes around. It's only $5 per session for a drop-in class that allows professionals to strive for the next level and challenge themselves artistically and technically. Classes are Tuesday and Thursday from 10 to 11:30 p.m. at the Westlake Dance Center.

On the Boards
100 West Roy St.
(206) 217-9886
www.ontheboards.org
Ushers per performance: 6 to 8

Many of On The Board's shows feature dance, but not all of them. Some are drama, some are a mix of both, but all rely on volunteer ushers to keep things going smoothly before the curtain goes up. To sign up, e-mail hm@ontheboards.org. Opening night rush tickets sell for $12. There are also a limited number of $12 tickets for dance lovers and a senior discount as well.

Pacific Northwest Ballet
Seattle Center
Marion Oliver McCaw Hall
(206) 441-2424
www.pnb.org

First, the bad news: There is no volunteer ushering at PNB because ushering is a paid position. The company does use volunteers and tickets are earned based on the number of hours of work performed. There are a number of ways to see a show without having to pay the standard $25 to $160 full fare, however. Patrons 25 and under can see the first Thursday and Friday performances of a run for $15 per person or $25 for two. Dress rehearsals are $25 the day before a show opens and include a pre-show lecture. If you just want to attend the lecture, though, it's only $12. Teen Tix tickets are $5, depending on availability. Student and senior rush tickets are also available 90 minutes before each performance. And there are also a few opportunities to get just a taste of a show before it starts. PNB offers an hour-long Friday preview in its studios for $10, but you have to act fast. Once word of the date hits the Web site, it sells out quickly. There are also free lunchtime previews at the Seattle Public Library's Central Library the Tuesday before opening night and a free conversation with the dancers at the Elliott Bay Book Company at 2 p.m. on the Sunday before a show opens.

The Pat Graney Company

925 East Thomas
(206) 329-3705
www.patgraney.org

This dance company's focus is on staging new works. Graney also works with incarcerated women.

Seattle Dance Project

3029 31st Ave. West
(206) 321-0407
www.seattledanceproject.org

This modern dance company was created in 2007 and features top-notch dancers from the likes of the New York City Ballet and the Pacific Northwest Ballet. Volunteer ushers can stay to see the show. In addition, people who volunteer to help out with events after a performance can see the show before the event. SDP also has a Pay What You Will dress rehearsal as well as discounts for students and seniors. It also participates in the Teen Tix program.

Spectrum Dance Theatre

800 Lake Washington Blvd.
(206) 325-4161
www.spectrumdance.org

Since it stages most of its main stage shows at the Moore Theater, which provides its own ushers, Spectrum doesn't need ushers for its larger productions. It can use volunteer meeters-and-greeters during its studio performances at its Lake Washington Boulevard home in late fall. The job typically involves helping set up the studio and taking tickets. Spectrum also offers classes including African dance, childrens' movement, and creative dance and will trade an hour's worth of volunteer work for an hour of dance class. To volunteer, e-mail shirley@spectrumdance.org.

Stone Dance Collective

The Theater at Meydenbauer Center
Bellevue
(206) 799-6004
www.chopshopdance.org

So far, the company only performs at the annual Chop Shop: Bodies of Work, which it also produces, every February. The event is a festival focused on contemporary dance. Prospective dancers can take a free dance class in connection with the event (usually in early January) through the Bellevue Parks Department or take in a free lecture on modern dance and then score a free ticket to a show.

PARTICIPATORY

Balorico
Kenyon Hall
7904 35th Ave. Southwest
(206) 679-7229
www.balorico.blogspot.com

This dance instruction company offers two opportunities to save. The quick and dirty way to do so is to attend its free Latin and ballroom dance lessons from 6 to 7 p.m. on the first Monday of every month at Kenyon Hall. Who knows? If you like it, you can always stick round for the $15 dop-in ballroom/Latin class at 7:30 (or take 7 classes for $80). If Latin and ballroom aren't your thing and you have spare time on your hands, you can become an intern and do administrative and marketing work four hours a week and finally take those Afro-Peruvian classes you've been saving up for. Or opt for something more conventional like tango, quickstep, mambo, or salsa.

The Century Ballroom
915 East Pine St.
(206) 324-7263
www.centuryballroom.com

The Catch: The lesson is free, but you have to pay $5 to attend the dance.

You may not be able to wangle your way into Century's regular weekly dance classes by volunteering or doing light clerical work in the front office, but you can at least get a free half hour lesson before its regular DJ dances. Of course, you still have to pay the $5 admission to the dance. The half hour lessons are usually available before dances on Wednesday, Thursday, Friday, and Sunday. The dances themselves cover a wide variety of styles and typically start at 9:30 (with lessons at 9), but times are subject to change. For more information, check the Century's Web site.

Little Red Hen

7115 Woodlawn Ave. Northeast
(206) 522-1168
www.littleredhen.com

The Catch: The live music isn't free, but the dance lessons are.

You don't have to skedaddle out to a roadhouse on the far end of town to learn how to dance the Bootscoot Boogie, line dances, and other country music dances. Instead, giddy up over to the Greenlake neighborhood. The Hen offers lessons Sunday through Tuesday before the music starts. On Monday, the focus is on line dancing. While the lessons themselves are free all three days, there's a cover charge for the Sunday night dance. Fortunately, the cover charges are usually quite small, ranging from $3 to $5 Thursday through Sunday.

SECTION 2:

Living
in Seattle

FOOD:
ON THE HOUSE

"I went to a restaurant that serves 'breakfast at any time.' So I ordered French toast during the Renaissance."

—STEVEN WRIGHT

If you ask me, Costco has the right idea. Hire a bunch of demonstrators to hand out food samples at peak shopping hours. The goal is to either get you to consider trying something you wouldn't otherwise or at least guilt you into it. Fortunately, the crowds are large enough to provide plausible deniability. You can feign interest in the item, ask where it is on the shelf, walk there, and ignore it as you pass. Some call it product demonstration; I call it lunch. You can do something similar at many shops in Seattle and the Pike Place Market, but you might not want to skulk away because if you stick around, you might just learn a little about something you really want to eat. The same is true of happy hours in Seattle. You can eat it and beat it, but if you stick around you just might order something you've never tried before, just because it's free . . . or cheap.

HAPPY **HOURS**

If you've ever heard the adage, "there's no such thing as a free lunch," you can identify with a lot of happy hour patrons in Seattle because there appears to be no such thing as free happy hour food, either. Ridiculously cheap food, yes, but my research turned up only four places that offered apps on the house. There was a fifth that until recently offered free mini filet mignon sandwiches, but it just decided to start selling four for $6. Hmmm. Maybe there is something to this recession thing after all.

Free Happy Hour Food

Il Fornaio
Pacific Place
600 Pine St.
(206) 264-0994
www.ilfornaio.com

Yes, Virginia, there is free happy hour food in Seattle and it's not that hard to find. The Italian restaurant at pricey Pacific Place rolls out a small, frequently restocked buffet featuring a mix of whatever appetizers catch the chef's fancy each day. Typical apps include pizza squares, crostini, and chicken wings. Beers are $3, wine $4 from 4:30 to 6:30 p.m. Monday through Friday. Get there early; seating is limited.

Oliver's at Mayflower Park
405 Olive Way
(206) 623-8700
www.mayflowerpark.com/olivers.asp

While it's best known for serving some of the best martinis in town, the lounge at the boutique Mayflower Park Hotel also serves free appetizers from 4:30 to 6 p.m. Monday through Friday. The offerings vary from day to day, but there are usually two dishes that include food like egg rolls, spring rolls, chicken wings, and hummus.

Osteria La Spiga
1429 12th Ave., Suite A
(206) 323-8881
www.laspiga.com

Late Night Happy Hour

It may not be enough to fill you up, but there is free food served during La Spiga's *aperitivo* hour from 5 to 6:30 p.m Monday through Friday and 11 p.m. to midnight on Friday and Saturday. The restaurant serves four small plates with a $3 beer or $4 glass of wine. The dishes include olives, Italian cheese, roasted nuts, and a pâté. Other happy hour menu items range from $3 to $10.

Cheap Happy Hour Food

Chao Bistro Bar
1200 East Pike St.
(206) 324-1010
Downtown
www.chaobistro.com

Late Night Happy Hour

Residents of Capitol Hill are divided over whether or not Chao is a good fit for the neighborhood, but one thing is undeniable. It's hard to beat a happy hour where all the food is $3 including spicy tuna roll and California roll. Happy hour runs from 3 to 7 p.m. and 11 p.m. to 1 a.m. daily.

Happy Hours: Not Just for Dinner (or Breakfast) Anymore

Leave it to the city that brought you the Wave, the espresso cart, and the first toothbrush for dogs to come up with a new wrinkle on the happy hour: the late night happy hour. If you were at home, you'd call it a midnight snack, but since you're still out, you're hungry and the restaurant you just passed is still open, those cheap late night specials are a way for eateries to grab a last bit of business and keep you from launching an early morning raid on your fridge. The special menus have worked so well that more and more restaurants are adopting them. And that doesn't even include the places that now offer all-day happy hours, weekend ones, brunch ones, and even a few breakfast versions.

Rather than debate the issue of how any hour can last all day, much less a happy one, we'll just go with the spirit of the thing and say, "Isn't that as it should be? After all, why are we only allowed to get happy right after work when there's so much of the day left?"

Club Contour
807 First Ave.
(206) 447-7704
www.clubcontour.com

This night spot has a specials menu that is as extensive as the happy hour is long. It has 18 items starting with Tomato Honey Basil Soup with cream and grilled baguette for $1.95 all the way to sautéed scallops for $4.95. My favorite deals are the provolone cheeseburger for $2.95 and the croque monsieur for the same price. Beers $3, well drinks $3.75. Menu subject to change. The specials go from 3 to 8 p.m. Monday to Thursday, 3 to 9 p.m. Friday and 2 to 8 p.m. on weekends.

Dragonfish Asian Café
722 Pine St.
(206) 467-7777
www.dragonfishcafe.com

Late Night Happy Hour

Yuppies and the pre-show crowd from the Paramount brush elbows at this pan-Asian style hotel restaurant with one of the best special hours in town. It's hard to go wrong with $1.95 sushi when it's this good. Half rolls range from $1.95 to $2.95, small plates from $1.95 to $4.95. Draft beer, special cocktails, and sake for $2.95 from 3 to 6 p.m. and late night happy hour from 9 p.m. to 1 a.m. Tuesday through Sunday. Happy hour also runs from 3 p.m. to 1 a.m. on Monday.

Elliott's Oyster House
1201 Alaskan Way, Pier 56
(206) 623-4340
www.elliottsoysterhouse.com

If you love oysters, this waterfront eatery is the place to be at 3 p.m. for the start of the Progressive Oyster Happy Hour when the chef's choice of whatever is being freshly shucked is available for 50 cents apiece. Prices jump 25 cents every half hour until they're $1.75 per at 5:30. The fun goes from 3 to 6 p.m., Monday through Friday.

Endolyne Joes
9261 45th Ave. Southwest
(206) 937-5637
www.chowfoods.com/endolyne

The timing of its happy hour may seem odd unless you commute on the Vashon Island Ferry. Joes not only recently added a happy hour after years of requests from patrons who catch the ferry nearby, but also built the schedule around them. It's easy to remember how much everything on the happy hour and late night menus costs because everything has the same price tag. It's all $3 including food specials, draft beers, house wines, and well drinks. It also has a Not So Early Bird Specials menu for late breakfasts where everything is $5 including Caramel Apple French Toast, a breakfast burrito, and a Goat Cheese and Fresh Herb Scramble. Not So Early Bird menu 8:30 to 11 a.m. Monday through Friday. Regular happy hour from 4:40 to 6:55 p.m. Monday through Friday. Late night menu from 10 p.m. to close daily.

5 Spot
1502 Queen Anne Ave. North
(206) 285-7768
www.chowfoods.com/five

This favorite neighborhood eatery at the top of Queen Anne Hill is owned by the same group behind Endolyne Joes and the Hi-Life, Chow Foods. It doesn't have a happy hour or Not So Early Bird menu, but it does have a late night menu where dishes are all $5 including such items as chili and cornbread, red beans and rice, and a hot turkey sandwich with mashed potatoes and gravy. Pints of Pabst Blue Ribbon are $1. Late night menu on offer from 10 p.m. to midnight.

Fonte Cafe and Wine Bar
1321 1st Ave.
(206) 777-6193
www.fontecafe.com

Cheap food and a color coded menu to boot. All drinks and appetizers on the happy hour menu are $3 each including butternut squash soup, mini pork sandwiches, and spiced lamb burger sliders. The best part is that colored squares next to each dish indicate which wines pair well. Happy hour from 5 to 7 p.m.

Hattie's Hat
5231 Ballard Ave. Northwest
(206) 784-0175
www.hattieshat.com

Late Night Happy Hour

I'm not sure who Hattie is, but she has a great old dive bar that appeals to old school Ballard fishermen and blue-collar workers as well as the hipsters. It doesn't have a happy hour menu as such, but it does have discounts on some apps. During its first happy hour of the day from 3 to 7 p.m. selected apps are $1 off. The stakes are raised during the late night happy hour on Monday through Thursday when the apps are $2 off. That means $1.50 fish tacos, $3.25 salmon quesadillas, and around $2 for a pound of fries with tartar sauce. The $2 nightly specials are also good deals—Tuesday is $2 nacho night, Wednesday it's hot wings, and Thursday fish tacos are featured. On Monday all burgers are $5.

The Hi-Life

5425 Russell Ave. Northwest
(206) 784-7272
www.chowfoods.com/hilife

This Ballard favorite is owned by the same company as Endolyne Joes and the 5 Spot, so the concepts are the same. Everything on the happy hour and late night menu is $3 including onion rings, small wood fired pizzas, and sliders as well as draft beers, house wines, and well drinks. Not So Early Bird Specials are $5 and feature such dishes as corned beef hash with eggs, breakfast burrito, or buttermilk flapjacks with bacon. Not So Early Bird Specials run from 8:30 to 11 a.m. Monday through Friday. Regular happy hour 5 to 6:30 p.m. Monday through Friday. Late night menu offered 10 p.m. to close daily.

Kate's Pub

309 Northeast 45th St.
(206) 547-6832

Instead of having a special menu, this eatery does it right by serving all regular menu items at half price, even dessert. Microbrews are $3. Happy hour from 4 to 7 p.m.

Maximilien Restaurant

81A Pike St.
(206) 682-7270
www.maximilienrestaurant.com

Who says French food has to be expensive? The bar in this romantic French eatery in the Pike Place Market not only has a beautiful view of sunset over Puget Sound, it also has beautiful food for next to nothing. All eight of the apps on its happy hour menu go for $2.95 each or you can collect the entire set for $20. If the thought of such an unbelievably low price makes you crazy, you'll probably want to avoid the $5 absinthe. Happy hour from 5 to 7 p.m. Monday through Friday and 8 to 10 p.m. Saturday.

McCormick & Schmick's

McCormick & Schmick's Seafood Restaurant
1103 First Ave.
(206) 623-5500
Happy hour 3 to 6 p.m. Monday through Friday, 4 to 6 p.m. on weekends

Late night 9 to 11:30 p.m. Sunday through Thursday, 10 p.m. to 12:30 a.m. Friday and Saturday

McCormick's Fish House and Bar
722 Fourth Ave.
(206) 682-3900
Happy hour 3:30 to 6 p.m. Monday through Friday
Late night 9:30 to 11 p.m. Monday through Thursday, 10 p.m. to midnight Friday

McCormick & Schmick's Harborside on Lake Union
1200 Westlake Ave. North
(206) 270-9052
Happy hour 4 to 6 pm. daily
Late night 9 to 11 p.m. Sunday through Thursday, 10 p.m. to midnight Friday and Saturday

McCormick & Schmick's Seafood Restaurant
700 Bellevue Way, Suite 115
Bellevue
(425) 454-2606
www.mccormickandschmicks.com
Happy hour 4 to 6 p.m. daily
Late night 9:30 to 11:30 p.m., Monday through Saturday, Sunday from 9 to 10 p.m.

The Catch: $3.50 minimum beverage purchase per diner.

Although McCormick & Schmick's is a chain, its four local restaurants have long had one of the best happy hours around. What's on offer varies from location to location, but prices start at $1.95 and go up to $4.95 at all locations and each menu is anchored by the generous $2.95 half pound cheeseburger with French fries. Combine that with another side and it's more than enough for a meal.

Moshi Moshi Sushi
5324 Ballard Ave.
(206) 971-7424
www.moshiseattle.com

Late Night Happy Hour

It's not every day you can get cheap sushi, Pabst Blue Ribbon, and inexpensive sake all at the same place. But that's only because there's no happy hour on Sunday. There are two happy hours a day to make up for it, though. The selection includes tiger rolls for $2.95, California rolls for $3.95, PBR in cans for $2, and small sake for $1.95. Happy hour is daily from 4:30 to 6 p.m. and a late night happy hour goes from 10 to 11 p.m. Monday through Thursday and 11 p.m. to 1 a.m. on Friday and Saturday.

Norm's Eatery and Ale House
460 North 36th St.
(206) 547-1417

Finally, a happy hour where you can take your best friend. Dog lovers and their pets are welcome as long as they're well behaved and on a leash (the dogs, not the dog lovers). The food isn't free, but portions are generous and you can't beat the company. Specials run from 4 to 7 p.m. Monday through Friday. There's also a brunch happy hour on weekends with $4 bloody Marys and mimosas.

Peso's Kitchen & Lounge
605 Queen Anne Ave. North
(206) 283-9353
www.pesoskitchen.com

Late Night Happy Hour

There are happy hours and then there are *happy hours*. And the one at Peso's gives diners plenty to smile about with almost 50 items listed and more than half going for $4 or less. The selection includes soups, salads, tapas from land and sea, hot sandwiches, tacos, and desserts. The menu modestly describes it as the city's most visited happy hour. I can't speak to that issue, but folks in the know mention it frequently. Peso's also has a breakfast happy hour menu on which all entrees are $6 including steak and eggs. Some items with crab are excluded from the special pricing, however. Breakfast specials 9 to 11 a.m. Monday through Friday. Happy hour 4 to 6 p.m. daily. Late happy hour 10 p.m. to 1 a.m.

Roxy's Diner
462 North 36th St.
(206) 632-3963

If you ride your bike to happy hour here, you get a free appetizer. How you go about proving that it's your bike, I'm not really sure. It's not like you can keep the registration in your glove compartment. You don't have to register bikes in Seattle . . . and they don't have glove compartments. Maybe all you need to do is show your bike helmet. If you walked or drove, you can still get cheap apps like a Reuben spring roll, sliders, or fried pickles for about $3. There's more pedestrian food as well. Me, I still miss their pastrambow (pastrami and sauerkraut in a hombow bun). Happy hour runs from 4 to 6 p.m. Monday through Friday.

Sazerac

Hotel Monaco
1101 Fourth Ave.
(206) 624-7755
www.sazeracrestaurant.com

A taste of New Orleans, Sazerac has a much-loved happy hour with appetizers like hearts of romaine "Caesar style" for $3, two barbecue pulled pork sliders for $4, and 10-inch wood fired pizzas for $6. Beer, wine, and mixed drinks are $3 to $6 from 4 to 8 p.m. Monday through Saturday.

Serious Pie

316 Virginia St.
(206) 838-7388
www.tomdouglas.com

There comes a time in the life of every great city with a great chef when its citizens must ask, "Don't you think you have enough restaurants already? Don't you think we could do without one or two of them?" We thought Seattle's Tom Douglas might have reached this point until he opened Serious Pie along with its happy hour roasted chanterelle, truffle cheese 6-inch mini pizza for $5. With beers for $3, wines for $5, and other pie options including Yukon gold potato and rosemary olive oil; Penn Cove clams, house pancetta, and lemon thyme; or even guanciale, soft egg, and dandelion greens. (Heck, we don't even know what guanciale is, but we bet it's something good.) Now, we find ourselves realizing we might have been a bit hasty. All we have to do now is convince Douglas to change his happy hour times. It goes from 3 to 5 p.m. There have been times when we've just missed the deadline and it's not pretty. And take it from us, no one likes to see a grown man cry.

Talarico's

4718 California Ave. Southwest
(206) 937-3463
www.talaricoswest.com

Late Night Happy Hour

Ginormous slices of pizza are the draw here. It's $4 for a huge slice of pie, $5 for meatball sliders, and draft beer for $3. What more do you need? Happy hours from 4 to 6 p.m. Monday through Friday, and 3 to 6 p.m. Saturday and Sunday. Late night specials from 11 p.m. to 1 a.m. nightly.

Tin Hat Bar & Grill

512 Northwest 65th
(206) 782-2770

The food isn't quite free at this dive bar, but 69 cent hard shell tacos on Tuesdays and $3.95 for spaghetti and Texas toast on Wednesdays isn't far off. And don't forget pulled pork sandwiches on Monday for $4.95 and sloppy joes on Thursday for $3.95. In addition to the all day specials, happy hour runs from 4 to 7 p.m. with $1 off microbrews and well drinks.

Tost Lounge

513 North 36th St.
(206) 547-0240
www.tostlounge.com

Considering the quality of the $5 happy hour pies, this night spot may want to consider renaming itself Pizza. Beer $2.50, well drinks $3. From 5 to 8 p.m. daily.

Toulouse Petit

601 Queen Anne Ave. North
(206) 432-9069

Late Night Happy Hour

The Catch: Minimum $3 beverage order per person.

If you thought the happy hour menu at Peso's was impressive, you ain't seen nothing yet. That's because Peso's owner has opened this New Orleans–inspired eatery featuring a special-filled menu with more than 50 items for $5 or less including such oddities as fried chicken with tasso-black pepper gravy, fried alligator, and Cajun meatloaf sliders. And that doesn't even include the desserts or drinks. As with Peso's, there's also a breakfast happy hour where most items are $6. Breakfast happy hour 9 to 11 a.m. Happy hour 4 to 5:30 p.m. Late night 10 p.m. to 1:30 a.m.

FREE SAMPLES

Beecher's Handmade Cheese
1600 Pike Place
(206) 956-1964
www.beechershandmadecheese.com

If only Miss Muffett had gone here first, that ugly incident involving the spider probably wouldn't have happened. Instead, she could have just stopped in, watched the cheesemakers at work, and sampled its many varieties of curd before looking for a place to sit and eat. Although cheddared curds and the flagship cheese are the only samples readily available, everything in the cheese case is available for sampling. There are even more samples during the annual Seattle Cheese Festival in May.

Borrachini's Bakery
2307 Rainier Ave. South
(206) 325-1550
www.nowcake.com

The historic Italian bakery has been known for its cakes for generations, which have been a part of many family celebrations for four generations of Seattleites. There's more to the South-end institution than just baked goods, though. It's also a deli, an Italian market, and an importer of Mediterranean foods. Despite its diversity, the store's best samples are from the bakery. There's even a shelf where you can sample the cake of the day. Kids and adults are mesmerized by the bakery window where you can watch cakes being decorated.

Sample-palooza

The names for the place are as numerous as its visitors. Some tourists call it Pike Street Market, Pike's Peak Market, or simply Pike's Market. Locals call it the Pike Place Market. Me, I call it a ticket to a free lunch. When I first worked downtown, I used to love going from one inexpensive food stand to another assembling an impossibly inexpensive meal. A cheap humbow here, a day-old pastry there, all topped off by a beautiful piece of whatever fruit happened to be in season.

All that changed, however, when I discovered how many places in the market offered samples all day, every day. Heck, considering the sheer variety of foods there for the asking, it's easy to see that Costco's got nothing on this place. In fact, there are times when going to the mega-retailer on a Saturday in search of free bites almost feels like cheating on Rachel the Pig, the farmers, and all the other characters at the market. Oh, Pike Place, we may not always have Paris, but with merchants like these, we'll always have lunch:

Beecher's Handmade Cheese: Offers cheddared cheese curd and the store's Flagship cheese.

Chukar Cherry Company: Serves preserves and chocolate.

The Confectional: Columbian drinking chocolate and, if you're really lucky, cheesecake, but that's only if a highly skilled cake maker makes a mistake.

Central Market

15505 Westminster Way North
Shoreline
(206) 363-9226
http://central-market.com/

As great as this supermarket is, there's not much central about it. It's so far north from downtown Seattle that it's actually on the southern edge of Shoreline, the next town up. Despite being the size of a small Home Depot, it's still somehow seen as a neighborhood grocery. Friday night summer dinners with live music and other celebrations help. Numerous cooking demonstrations and food sampling events don't hurt, either.

DeLaurenti Specialty Food and Wine: Cheese, olive oils, and balsamic vinegars. Also has a weekly wine tasting.

La Buona Tavola Truffle Café and Specialty Foods: Serves potato leek soup with white truffle oil and provides samples of its gourmet oils, pestos, and pasta sauces.

Market Spice: Serves its signature orange-cinnamon black tea, Market Spice Tea.

Pappardelle's Pasta: Samples its uncooked flavored pastas.

Perennial Tea Room: Has one flavor in a pot ready for sampling and will brew one of four other flavors of the day on demand.

Pure Food Fish: Serves three of the five varieties of its smoked salmon—teriyaki, pepper, and garlic.

Simply the Best: Offers five varieties of apple chips from sweet to sour.

Snoqualmie Valley Honey Farm: Every flavor of honey in the store's line is available for sampling.

Sosio's Fruit and Produce: What fresh fruit is on offer varies based on seasonality.

Sotto Voce: Olive oils and vinegars.

Stackhouse Brothers Orchards: Samples a variety of nuts.

Stewart's Meat Market: Offers pepperoni and jerky.

Woodring Orchards: Fruit spreads, pepper jellies, apple butters, and pumpkin butters.

Chukar Cherry Company

1529-B Pike Place
Pike Place Market (in the center of the Main Arcade)
(206) 623-8043
www.chukar.com

If you can make it with cherries, chances are this company either sells it or has at least considered marketing it. The booth samples a wide range of its products including its dried cherries, curried cherry chutney, and cherry chipotle barbecue sauce. Are you beginning to see a theme here?

Claudio Corallo

2122 Westlake Ave.
(206) 859-3534
www.claudiocorallochocolate.com

At Claudio Corallo, sampling isn't just a good idea, it's almost required if you want to understand what you're buying. The bars are made from heirloom cacao beans picked from plants dating back to the late 1800s and there is such minimal processing that not even vanilla is added. Consequently, visitors get a quick lesson in chocolate making going from tasting cacao beans and nibs with different percentages of pure chocolate all the way to trying all six of the bars the store sells. At $7.50 per 50-gram bar, it isn't cheap, but Carollo's chocolate is gaining in popularity and now's your chance to try it before it becomes the next Fran's Chocolates.

The Confectional

Pike Place Market
1530 Pike Place
(206) 282-4422
www.theconfectional.com

The store always offers samples of its Columbian drinking chocolate, but only puts out cheesecakes for sampling when they top one wrong or make some other mistake that turns it into a factory second. There's no truth to the rumor that there are people circling outside just hoping for a rare sample or even folks who actively try to make them screw up.

DeLaurenti Specialty Food and Wine

Pike Place Market
Southwest corner of First Avenue and Pike Street
(206) 622-0141
www.delaurenti.com

A great stop if you want good food, but don't want to wade all the way into the crowds of the Pike Place Market. At this little Italian market you can get a quick slice of pizza, a sandwich for lunch, sip espresso, and shop for dinner. While you're there, you can also sample antipasti, cheeses, and meats from the deli case—there are nine types of prosciutto, after all, and who knows which one you'll like best? There's also a table where you can try olive oils and vinegars.

Great Harvest Bread

5408 Sand Point Way Northeast; (206) 524-4873; www.greatharvestsand
point.com

2218 Northwest Market St.; (206) 706-3434; www.greatharvestsea.com

4709 California Ave. Southwest; (206) 935-6882; www.greatharvestwest
seattle.com

Lake Forest Park Town Center; 17171 Bothell Way Northeast; Lake Forest Park;
(206) 365-4778; www.greatharvestbreadlakeforestpark.com

Bear Creek Village; 17220 Redmond Way, Redmond; (425) 883-6909

3610 Factoria Blvd. Southeast, Bellevue, (425) 643-8420; www.greatharvest
bellevue.com

Sometimes the places that give free samples are so obvious that we tend to forget them. Great Harvest is a good example. At most locations, a slice of wheat bread or whatever happens to be on offer that day, is yours for the asking usually along with some butter for you to slather on it. Some locations also give out breadsticks for kids. In my neighborhood you can have an additional slice for a dollar. For that matter, my local Great Harvest also has free doggie biscuits.

La Buona Tavola Truffle Café and Specialty Foods
Pike Place Market (in the Triangle Building between Mr. D's Greek Deli and
Mee Sum Pastries)
1524 Pike Place
(206) 292-5555
www.trufflecafe.com

It's easy to get overwhelmed at La Buona Tavola considering the many items that are available for sampling. For starters, there's a potato leek soup with white truffle oil, then there's a taster's table featuring all of their oils—rosemary, garlic, white truffle, and black truffle—plus pestos and pasta sauces.

Market Spice
Pike Place Market Economy Arcade
85A Pike St.
(206) 622-6340

The bulk spice store's pungent signature cinnamon- and orange-spiced tea is one of its star attractions and its most frequently sampled item. On occasion it samples the latest new products in stock. It also offers spiced cider in winter.

Metropolitan Market
10611 Northeast 68th St., Kirkland (slated to open)
Queen Anne, 1908 Queen Anne Ave. North, Seattle; (206) 284-2530
Uptown, 100 Mercer St., Seattle; (206) 213-0778
Admiral/West Seattle, 2320 42nd Ave. Southwest, Seattle; (206) 937-0551
Sand Point, 5250 40th Ave. Northeast, Seattle; (206) 938-6600
Proctor, 2420 North Proctor St., Tacoma; (253) 761-3663
www.metropolitan-market.com

Did you ever want a Dijon ketchup or a really expensive blueberry chipotle salsa? If so, this small regional chain of gourmet groceries is for you. It has long had a loyal following and had the insanely expensive comestible market all to itself until Whole Foods began muscling in on its territory. In addition to occasionally sampling cheese and crackers, many of the stores have food demonstrations and other events where samples are available.

Mick's Peppourri
Pike Place Market
Next to the Skybridge in the Main Arcade
1531 Pike Place
(800) 204-5679
www.micks.com

It may just be coincidence or a stroke of luck, but this purveyor of peppery treats just happens to be located across from Woodring Orchards stand. So, you can set your taste buds a-sizzling with samples of Mick's pepper jelly flavors like hot cranberry, lime, and ginger (or any of the other 25 flavors available for tasting), then douse the flames with a taste of Woodring's cider(when it's in season). The booth also samples its wine jellies, but you have to request a taste; the jellies aren't on the table because they don't want kids getting into them.

PCC Natural Markets

Edmonds PCC, 9803 Edmonds Way, Edmonds; (425) 275-9036
Fremont PCC, 600 North 34th, Seattle; (206) 632-6811
Greenlake PCC, 7504 Aurora Ave. North, Seattle; (206) 525-3586
Issaquah PCC at Pickering Place, 1810 12th Ave. Northwest, Issaquah; (425) 369-1222
Kirkland PCC, 10718 Northeast 68th, Kirkland; (425) 828-4622
Redmond PCC, 11435 Avondale Rd. Northeast, Redmond; (425) 285-1400
Seward Park PCC, 5041 Wilson Ave. South, Seattle; (206) 723-2720
View Ridge PCC, 6514 40th Ave. Northeast, Seattle; (206) 526-7661
West Seattle PCC, 2749 California Ave. Southwest, Seattle; (206) 937-8481
www.pccnaturalmarkets.com

This co-op chain isn't as glamorous as Whole Foods and can occasionally be more expensive than the privately owned Austin, Texas–based behemoth, but PCC still has one key advantage over its competitor. It's local. PCC gives children a free piece of fruit each visit. It also does some sampling for adults including soups, gelato, and other items, depending on location.

Pappardelle's Pasta

Pike Place Market
1501 #8 Pike St.
(206) 340-4114

It might not go so well with tomato sauce, but just the thought of dark chocolate linguine was enough to make me curious. It really does taste like chocolate. I had to stop sampling there, though. Otherwise, I would have been there all day trying such oddities as Curry Angel Hair, Orange Szechuan Linguine, and Basil Garlic Penne. So what if they're not cooked?

Perennial Tea Room

Pike Place Market
1910 Post Alley
www.perennialtearoom.com
(206) 448-4054

Relax, the street is just called an alley, it isn't one really. Need proof? If tea is the height of civility, why would any tea room set up shop in a dangerous neighborhood? In addition to selling everything you need to brew a cup,

Son of Sample-palooza:
Markets for Those Who Can't Be Bothered

Locals love the Pike Place Market, but not the traffic, the crowds, or the hassle of looking for parking Downtown. Fortunately, there's an option for people who love to try and buy from local producers and those who just can't be bothered to run the gauntlet down to Pike Place: They are weekly neighborhood markets and it seems like new ones are opening every year. Here's a list of some of the top neighborhood markets in the region:

Ballard Sunday Farmers Market, Ballard Avenue and 22nd Avenue Northwest, (206) 851-5100, www.fremontmarket.com/ballard. Sundays 10 a.m. to 3 p.m., year-round.

Broadway Farmers Market, 10th Avenue East and East Thomas behind the Capitol Hill Bank of America, www.seattlefarmersmarkets.org/markets/broadway. Sundays 11 a.m. to 3 p.m., May through December.

Columbia City, 4801 Rainier Ave. South, www.seattlefarmersmarkets.org/markets/columbia_city, Wednesdays 3 to 7 p.m., May though October.

Crossroads Farmers Market, Northeast 8th Street and 156th Avenue Northeast, Bellevue, www.crossroadsbellevue.com/farmers-market. Tuesday, noon to 5 p.m. May to October.

Fremont Market, Phinney Avenue and North 34th St., (206) 781-6776, www.fremontmarket.com/fremont. Sundays, 10 a.m. to 4 p.m. in winter, 10 a.m. to 5 p.m. in summer.

Kirkland Wednesday Market, Kirkland Avenue and Lakeshore Plaza Drive, www.kirklandwednesdaymarket.org. Wednesdays, 2 to 7 p.m.

Perennial always has one tea in a pot that visitors can sample freely plus four more they will brew on request. Check the board over the counter to find out which ones are available for taste testing when you stop by.

Lake City Farmers Market, Northeast 125th and 28th Northeast, in front of the Lake City Library, www.seattlefarmersmarkets.org/markets /lake_city. Thursdays, 3 to 7 p.m., June through October.

Lake Forest Park Commons Farmers Market, Lake Forest Park Town Centre, intersection of State Road 522 and Highway 104, www.third placecommons.org/farmersmarket. Sundays, 11 a.m. to 4 p.m., May through October.

Magnolia, next to the Magnolia Community Center, 2550 34th Ave. West, Saturdays 10 a.m. to 2 p.m., www.seattlefarmersmarkets .org/markets/magnolia. June through September.

Mercer Island Farmers Market, 7701 Southeast 32nd St., Mercer Island, (206) 235-1185, www.mifarmersmarket.org. Sundays, 11 a.m. to 3 p.m., June to October.

Phinney, 67th and Phinney Avenue North, in the Phinney Neighborhood Center's lower parking lot, www.seattlefarmersmarkets.org/markets /phinney. Fridays 3 to 7 p.m. May through October.

University District Farmers Market, University Heights Center for the Community, corner of University Way and Northeast 50th Street, (206) 632-5234, Neighborhood Farmers Market Alliance, www.seattle farmersmarkets.org/markets/u_district. Saturdays 9 a.m. to 2 p.m., year-round.

Wallingford Wednesday Farmers Market, Wallingford Center, 1815 North 45th St., (206) 781-6776, www.fremontmarket.com/walling ford. Wednesdays, 3 to 7 p.m., May through September.

West Seattle Farmers Market, California Avenue Southwest and South-west Alaska, www.seattlefarmersmarkets.org/markets/west_seattle. Sunday 10 a.m. to 2 p.m. year-round.

Pure Food Fish
Pike Place Market
1511 Pike Place
(206) 622-5765
www.freshseafood.com

When you're just down the arcade from the guys who are known for throwing fish, you have to try a little harder to catch the public's attention. Offering free samples of smoked fish definitely helps. Smoked salmon samples come in garlic, pepper, and teriyaki flavors.

QFC

www.qfc.com
Queen Anne, 500 Mercer St., Seattle; (206) 352-4020
University Village, 2746 Northeast 45th St., Seattle; (206) 523-5160
Ballard, 5700 24th Ave. Northwest, Seattle; (206) 297-2150
Consult the Web site for additional locations.

What's available for sampling at this Kroger-owned regional chain depends on what departments are at a given location. At a smaller location like the Wedgwood store, for example, baked goods, fruit, crackers, and spread are often offered. At a larger store like the University Village location, the nibbles may also include fish, sushi, shellfish, and the occasional beverage. Some claim you could turn a visit to some QFCs into a meal. I've yet to see it.

Resident Cheesemonger

405 Main St.
Edmonds
(425) 640-8949
www.residentcheesemonger.com

There are plenty of wine and cheese tastings around, but what about a cheese and wine tasting? If you stop in at this little cheese shop on Saturday from 1 to 4 p.m. for a free tasting, then amble down the street to Arista Wine Cellars, you could do just that. And the best part is, Arista is likely to have even more cheese from the Resident Cheesemonger, so it would be like a cheese and wine and cheese tasting. This shop also does a tasting from 5 to 8 p.m. on the third Thursday of the month as part of the city's art walk.

Simply the Best

Pike Place Market (under the clock)
(206) 624-8863
esimplythebest.net

Considering that it's right under the Pike Place Market sign, the stall selling organic dried Washington-grown fruit (and vegetables) should be hard to miss, but it often gets overlooked because of its internationally known neighbors across the hall, those fun-loving, seafood-throwing fish mongers at Pike Place Fish. Fortunately, there's nothing like a taste of a raz-nana to focus the concentration. Although apple chips from sweet to sour are its main samples, you can ask to try any of the stand's products.

Snoqualmie Valley Honey Farm
Pike Place Market (in the Main Arcade)
85 Pike St.
(800) 643-1995
www.honeyexpress.com

This honey stand located among the day stalls offers so many flavors that it would be impossible to decide what to buy if it weren't for its liberal sampling policy and variety packs. After all, how do you choose between ginger lemon, lime, vanilla velvet, or chocolate velvet flavored cream honey without trying it first? I wonder where they found the chocolate velvet bees.

Sosio's Fruit and Produce
Pike Place Market
1527 Pike Place
(206) 622-1370

It probably isn't the cheapest place in the market, but it has the best fresh fruit and the most courteous employees who are more than willing to offer free samples, even if what you're interested in isn't one of the items they are sampling.

Sotto Voce
Pike Place Market
1532 Pike Place
Corner of Pine Street and Pike Place
(206) 624-9998
www.sottovoce.com

It seems like everything's going artisanal these days. Coffee. Chocolate. Vinaigrette? Sotto Voce is known for its hand-crafted, spiced flavored virgin olive oils, vinegars, and its own spicy vinaigrette. All of the oils and vinegars are made and hand bottled in Spanaway not far from Tacoma. All of the oils are on a table for sampling along with pieces of bread for dipping.

Stackhouse Brothers Orchards

Pike Place Market
1531 Western Ave.
(800) 382-7654

Sample nuts including flavored almonds, natural almonds, and a small selection of dried fruits.

Stewart's Meat Market

Pike Place Market
85 Pike Place
(206) 682-7453
www.stewartsmeatmarket.com

Stewart's is an institution at the market and is known for its jerky and pepperoni samples.

Theo Chocolate

3400 Phinney Ave. North
(206) 632-5100
www.theochocolate.com

The country's first organic chocolate factory gives $6 tours every day complete with plenty of samples, but you don't have to shell out the cash to try such treats as the Bread and Chocolate Dark Chocolate or the Coconut Curry Milk Chocolate bars. Instead, you can hit the lobby where tables are filled with chopped up bits of bars there for the taking.

Trader Joe's

www.traderjoes.com
112 West Galer St.; (206) 378-5536
4555 Roosevelt Way Northeast; (206) 547-6299
Consult the Web site for additional locations.

Okay, I know it's wrong, but the samples here are just so good there are times when I try to change the way I look by removing my glasses or taking off my jacket just so I can get seconds. There are only one or two food samples offered at a time, but they're always good. And you can wash them down with the free coffee.

Whole Foods

Interbay, 2001 West 15th Ave., Seattle; (206) 325-5440
Roosevelt, Roosevelt Square, Seattle, 1026 Northeast 64th St.;
(206) 985-1500
Westlake, 2210 Westlake Ave., Seattle; (206) 621-9700
Bellevue, 888 116th Ave. Northeast, Bellevue; (425) 462-1400
Redmond, 17991 Northeast Redmond Way, Redmond; (425) 881-2600

It's nicknamed "Whole Paycheck" for a reason. The produce is beautiful, but pricey. The organic items are exquisite, but expensive. And don't even get me started on the baked goods. Still, all locations offer a variety of samples including cheese, produce, and tofu-based products. Each offers occasional theme-based freebies as well. At the Bellevue store, for example, there's a free coffee tasting every Sunday and a $1 singles happy hour with wine and gourmet bites every first Tuesday of the month. Interbay offers a variety of familiarization tours of departments with free tastes. At the same time, the Roosevelt store has Fondue Friday with wine and fondue pairings for $3. Check each store's calendar for more free food opportunities.

Woodring Orchards

Pike Place Market
1529 Pike Place
(206) 340-2705
www.woodringnorthwest.com

Stop for the jams and pumpkin butter samples, but linger longer for a taste of cider. The stand has 40 fruit spreads open and ready to try including pepper jellies, apple butters, and pumpkin butters. Other items you can try include chutneys, dessert toppings, and pickled vegetables.

NOT **FREE,** BUT **PRETTY** DOGGONE CHEAP

Bakeman's Restaurant

122 Cherry St.
(206) 622-3375

Bakeman's decor may be interesting, but most people don't come to this subterranean restaurant for atmosphere. The lunch crowd lines up around the block for the inexpensive sandwiches served with a side of good-natured abuse from a counterman who keeps things moving along whenever a diner's indecision threatens to slow the pace. Comparisons to the Soup Nazi on the TV show *Seinfeld* are only natural, but not quite accurate. He's more like a sandwich martinet.

Gorditos
www.gorditoshealthymexicanfood.com
213 North 85th St., Seattle; (206) 706-9352
1909 Hewitt Ave., Everett; (425) 252-4641

I admit that the prices on Gorditos' menu seem to violate my goal of keeping listings close to $5, but not when you average it out. Considering that most of the burritos are less than $10 and big enough to feed two people, the price is right. And even when the line is out the door, the service is fast and the food is excellent.

Pho Than Brothers
www.thanbrothers.com
1299 156th Ave. Northeast, #133, Bellevue; (425) 818-4905
7844 Leary Way Northeast, Redmond; (425) 881-3299
22618 Highway 99, #101, Edmonds; (425) 744-0212
7714 Aurora Ave. North; (206) 527-5973
Consult the Web site for more locations.

This place makes me feel like Keye Luke issuing a warning in the movie *Gremlins*. Whatever you do, don't order the large. Not before midnight, not after. Like Luke, I know you won't listen, but don't say I didn't warn you. The small pho is so big, you might consider skipping the medium as well. This ever-expanding chain of Vietnamese soup restaurants has it down to a science. They seat you, give you a menu and a cream puff—you've got to love a place that serves dessert first—take your order in less than five minutes, and have your soup and all its accoutrements at your table before you know it. Sure, it's high volume, but it's good, it's filling enough to keep you going the whole day, and a "small" bowl of soup is about $5.

Seattle Deli
225 12th Ave. South
(206) 328-0106

The International District is filled with inexpensive places to grab a bite, but this could be one of the cheapest. The specialty is bahn mi, a Vietnamese sandwich on a baguette with pickled veggies, mayo, maybe some cilantro, and thinly sliced meat. On the streets of Saigon, it's a treat filled with mystery meat. Here, you'll know what you're getting and at around $2, you can be sure it's a really great bargain.

WINE AND BEER TASTINGS:
CHEAP DRUNK

*"What I like to drink most
is wine that belongs to others."*

—DIOGENES

For wine lovers, one of the advantages of living in Seattle is that they're so close to many of the state's wineries that they face a difficult choice: Take in a tasting at a local wine shop or drive 45 minutes to Woodinville and eliminate the middleman. On the plus side, it's a lovely drive and you can be sure you'll be talking to people who really know their wines. On the flip side, many Woodinville wineries charge for tastings while most of these wine shops don't.

All Things Wine
4605 Northeast 4th St.
Renton
(425) 254-8400
www.allthingswineonline.com
Wednesday and Friday 5 to 7:30 p.m., Saturday noon to 6ish

The result of a hobby grown out of control, this family-owned wine shop was founded by a couple so passionate about wine that they opened their doors without leaving their day jobs. So, they got their mother to run it. And, no, you aren't seeing things after trying one too many. One of their employees is a toy poodle. The store specializes in Northwest and boutique style wines.

Arista Wine Cellars
320 5th Ave. South
Edmonds
(425) 771-7009
www.aristawines.com

This wine shop in a northern suburb with a small town feel offers tastings from 1 to 4:30 p.m. on Saturday and also from 5 to 8 p.m. on the third Thursday of the month in conjunction with the city's Third Thursday Art-walk. Check the store's Web site for the theme of upcoming tastings. Tastings are free and the shop usually pours four to six wines each time. The staff prides itself on being knowledgeable, but not snobbish.

Bottleworks
1710 North 45th St.
(206) 633-2437
www.bottleworksbeerstore.blogspot.com
Check the store's Web site for schedule

There's no set schedule of tastings at this bottle-shop-turned-tavern, but most of the tastings tend to be on Monday from 5 to 7 p.m. to capture the after work crowd. The sessions usually cost about $1 and typically include the full lineup from a specific brewery. There's usually a brewer or a rep on hand to answer questions. Half the crowd at most tastings are regulars, while the other half come to find out more about beer. For a schedule, check the store's Web site.

Champion Wine Cellars
108 Denny Way
(206) 284-8306
www.championwinecellars.com
Saturday 11 a.m. to 5 p.m.

There are so many wines in this cramped little shop that there's hardly any place to walk, but there's still plenty of room to house the owner's expertise. Not too surprisingly, his events aren't designed for big crowds. Instead, the drop-in tastings are informal with Emile Nanaud explaining the wines as he pours.

City Cellars Fine Wines
1710 North 45th St.
(206) 632-7238
www.citycellar.com
Friday 5 to 7 p.m.

The Catch: Tastings cost $3, but there's no charge if you buy a bottle during the tasting.

This neighborhood wine shop is known for two things: its focus on European wines and its selection of high value, low price wines. Seventy percent of the themed tastings are European based with the rest focusing on Northwest wines or comparing similar wines from different places. Most wines in the store are under $40 and there's a wall near the door featuring 100 wines that are $10 or less.

Corky Cellars
22511 Marine View Dr.
Des Moines
(206) 824-9462
www.corkycellars.com
Friday 4 to 6:30 p.m., Saturday 11 a.m. to 6 p.m.

Instead of opting for a theme-based tasting, Corky's goes for the unexpected during its Friday night tastings, opting to introduce tasters to varieties that they've likely never heard of and would otherwise never try, like the casseta wines made from a grape that's only grown on 40 hectares in Italy, or selections from Uruguay. Saturday tastings focus on a single Northwest winery. The store also happens to be located near a meat shop and a flower shop, so it's the ideal place to shop for a guy who's planning a romantic evening or one who's trying to get out of the doghouse.

DeLaurenti Specialty Food and Wine

1435 1st Ave.
(206) 622-0141
www.delaurenti.com
Saturday 2 to 4 p.m.

Italian wines may be the specialty at this Italian market on the edge of the Pike Place Market, but it sells wines from all over. DeLaurenti samples three to five wines each week, pairs them with cheese, and usually has a producer or a representative from a winery on hand to answer questions.

Esquin Wine Merchants

2700 Fourth Ave. South
(206) 682-7374
www.esquin.com
Thursday 5 to 6:30 p.m., Saturday 2 to 5 p.m.

Located in an industrial district not far from Safeco and Qwest fields, Esquin is as down to earth as its surroundings. The staff is helpful, knowledgeable, and always willing to help even the least wine literate among us. We're not saying we fit that description, mind you, but they pointed us in the direction of a good replacement when we couldn't find our favorite bottle of Mogen David. We're just saying . . . The first weekend of every month the store does a sampling with wines featured in its regular mailer.

Fine Wines and Cigars

Redmond Town Center
16535 Northeast 76th St., Suite D-105
Redmond
(425) 869-0869
www.finewinesltd.com

Friday 4 to 7 p.m., Saturday 2 to 5 p.m. During the summer Friday tastings go until 8 and Saturday tastings to 6 p.m.

The combination of tobacco and alcohol used to make perfect sense, until an indoor smoking ban made it impossible to enjoy a good cigar with a nice vintage within the store's confines. The company has managed to skirt the law occasionally by having an outdoor event far enough away to comply with indoor clean air requirements. Generally, though, most tastings are smoke free.

Fremont Wine Warehouse
3601 Fremont Ave. North
(206) 632-1110
www.fremontwines.com
Friday 4 to 7 p.m., Saturday noon to 7 p.m., Sunday noon to 4 p.m.

Has this ever happened to you? Your favorite wine shop is having a free tasting of a wine you've been curious about, but it's on a day or at a time when you just can't make it? That almost never happens at Fremont Wine Warehouse because the store only does tastings on weekends and it pours the same wines all three days (Friday, Saturday, and Sunday). All tastings are free. One last bit of good news for cheap bastards: Although the store focuses on small production wines, all of the wines in stock are under $25.

Grand Cru Wine Shop and Bar
1020 108th Ave. Northeast
Bellevue
(425) 455-4363
www.grandcru-wineshop.com
Saturday noon to 4 p.m.

The combination wine shop and wine bar's Saturday tastings focus on a single winery or importer. The wine bar also offers tastings on Thursday for $5 to $15.

Jack Cellars
8016 15th Ave. Northeast
(206) 729-5988
www.jackcellars.com
Wednesday 5 to 7 p.m., Saturday 4 to 6:30 p.m.

Ask a silly question, get a silly answer. When the owner of this wine shop was asked what his tastings were like, he replied, "For starters, they're clothing optional." His response may be outlandish, but it's in keeping with the informal atmosphere and the emphasis on having fun with wine at the tastings. The place has a neighborhood feel. Because it's located at the intersection of four north-end neighborhoods with completely different characters, however, the events attract an interesting cross-section ranging from young professionals with a budget for wine to people looking for a free buzz. Weekday tastings revolve around four wines, weekends five or six. All are either built around a common theme or showcase a single winery. It was given City Search's award for best local wine store in 2009.

McCarthy & Schiering, Wine Merchants
www.mccarthyandschiering.com
Queen Anne Store; 2401B Queen Anne Ave. North; (206) 282-8500
Ravenna Store; 6500 Ravenna Ave. Northeast; (206) 524-9500
Saturday 11 a.m. to 5 p.m.

Although the two stores sample the same wines at the same time, their characters are decidedly different. The Ravenna shop is known for older specialty bottles while Queen Anne's proximity to a meat shop and a number of restaurants prompts it to focus on rotating stocks of interesting selections for tonight's meal. The sampling includes one-ounce tastes of three to five wines along with maps or information about where the wines are made.

Northwest Wine Academy
South Seattle Community College
6000 16th Ave. Southwest
(206) 764-7942
www.nwwineacademy.southseattle.edu

No matter what their level of expertise, things are always less expensive when students do them. That includes massages, salon services, and even wine. South Seattle Community College's Wine Technology Program is a case in point. Students in the program produce around 1,000 cases a year (which vary depending on what grapes Eastern Washington producers donate to the program) and hold four tastings a year for the general public. The event is open to the public and even children can attend. Oddly enough, the event is held on campus in a place called the Wine and Welding Building. It kind of makes you wonder.

Pete's Wines Eastside
134 105th Ave. Northeast
Bellevue
(425) 454-1100
www.peteswineshop.com
Saturday 3 to 6 p.m.

Pete's is the Eastside sister store to a much loved Eastlake neighborhood grocery known for its wine selection. Unlike its Seattle relative, this Pete's doesn't sell groceries and it does do wine tastings. The store can only serve wine in plastic cups, but you can bring your own glass instead. They also do occasional beer tastings on Saturdays. Check Web site for details.

Pike and Western Wine Shop
Pike Place Market
1934 Pike Place
(206) 441-1307
www.pikeandwestern.com
Friday 3 to 6 p.m.

For 35 years, Pike and Western has catered to an interesting crowd including folks who live in the neighborhood as well as a growing tourist trade attracted by the ever-increasing popularity of the Pike Place Market. And that's exactly who shows up for the store's tastings: locals, pedestrians who happen to be passing by, and tourists roaming the local landmark. Consequently, the focus is on inexpensive wines that are also good values. The shop also does a higher end tasting focusing on more expensive bottles on Wednesday from 4 to 6 p.m. for $5.

Pike Street Beer and Wine
516 East Pike St.
(206) 778-1086
www.pikestreetbeer.com
Friday 5:30 to 7:30 p.m.

Tastings typically focus on a single brewery each week unless it's a sampling where the focus is on a particular theme like Christmas brews. How many beers are poured depends on how many types of beer the brewery makes, up to five.

Portalis Wine Shop and Wine Bar

5205 Ballard Ave. Northwest
(206) 783-2007
www.portaliswines.com
Saturday 3 to 5 p.m., Sunday 11 a.m. to 4 p.m.

Portalis does two markedly different wine tastings on weekends because it sees two markedly different crowds. On Saturdays, part of the focus is on food-wine pairing as it pours two wines based around a theme along with a light appetizer that's been made in-house for shoppers who see the store/wine bar as their main destination. Sundays bring different shoppers because it's smack dab in the heart of the action that is the Ballard Farmer's Market when people come from all over to buy local produce and crafts. On market days, the store pours four reasonably priced wines centered on a theme, usually a regional winemaker. Then, many stay on at the informal 50-seat bar/restaurant and order a bite to eat. Portalis also occasionally offers a pricier presentation when winemakers from outside the U.S. visit. The backroom tastings feature up to six higher-end wines, cheese, and pâté (made in-house). The events are publicized on the Web site and the store's mail list. An RSVP is essential because the room where the events are held is small and fills quickly. Although they cost $15 to $20, $10 of it can be used as store credit.

Seattle Cellars

2505 2nd Ave.
(206) 256-0580
www.seattlecellars.com
Thursday 5 to 7 p.m.

The Catch: You have to purchase a $10 Riedel tasting glass on your first visit.

This Belltown shop sells wine from all over the world, but emphasizes bottles from the Northwest and small boutique producers. There's no food at a tasting, just wine. The tastings are free unless you count the $10 you have to spend during your first visit to buy a Riedel stem. After that, there's no charge for future samplings—as long as you remember to bring the glass with you.

The Shop Agora

6417-A Phinney Ave. North
(206) 782-5551
www.theshopagora.com
Saturday 1 to 5 p.m.

Given its informality, it's hard to tell whether Agora's Saturday afternoon tastings are actually a neighborhood open house where wine just happens to be available for sampling or whether it's a tasting that happens to be an excuse for neighbors to gather. In either case, the shop specializes in Greek wine and has the largest selection of it in Seattle. Depending on the week, Agora may sample up to five wines with appetizers.

Twelfth & Olive Wine Company

1125 East Olive St.
(206) 329-2399
www.12thandolive.com
Friday 5 to 8 p.m., Saturday and Sunday 1 to 5 p.m.

Considering that all of the staffers have degrees in wine-related fields, it's a bit of an understatement to say that the people who run the place are knowledgeable. They aren't snobs, though. Tastings draw a neighborhood crowd, have a casual feel, and are built around some sort of theme.

Vino Verite

208 Boylston Ave. East
(206) 324-0324
www.vinoverite.com
Thursday 6 to 8 p.m., Saturday 4 to 7 pm. No Saturday tastings during the summer.

Imagine that house on your block that always seems to have large potluck dinners going on and you get the atmosphere the shop is trying to cultivate. It's like a living room during the Thursday night tastings when samples of four or five wines are offered, and there's usually an importer or distributor on hand to answer questions. The shop's focus is on good, inexpensive wine and the owner loves to find bargains for his customers.

West Seattle Cellars
6026 California Ave. Southwest
(206) 937-2868
www.wscellars.com
Thursday 5:30 to 8 p.m. (or 9 p.m. during Art Walk on the second Thursday of the month).

If Cheers had been set in a wine shop, it could have been filmed here. It's a friendly place where the owners seem to know everyone's name. It gets a little crowded during tastings as people chat with friends and compare notes. The shop also hosts a monthly Saturday tasting when it samples the most popular wines from its wine club.

WOODINVILLE WINERIES

Tastings at wine shops aren't the only option for people who enjoy trying Northwest wines. Less than an hour away from Downtown Seattle all the way out in Woodinville, there are more than 50 wineries, some with tasting rooms, others with regular tastings. Almost all charge for the chance to sample some of their most popular bottles. The catch is you can get the fee waived, but only if you end up buying something. To be free or not to be free, that is the question.

Here's a partial list of the wineries that offer such tastings:

- **Anton Ville Winery,** 19501 144th Ave. Northeast, Suite D-300, Woodinville, (206) 683-3393. www.antonvillewinery.com. Tasting room open Saturday through Sunday from 1 to 5 p.m. There's a $5 charge for tastings featuring wine paired with either cheese or chocolate. The fee is refundable if wine is purchased.
- **Baer Winery,** 19501 144th Ave. Northeast, Suite #F-100, Woodinville, (425) 483-7060, www.baerwinery.com. Open for tastings Saturday from 1 to 5 p.m. No tasting fee.
- **J. Bookwalter Tasting Studio,** 14810 Northeast 145th St., Building B, (425) 488-1983, www.bookwalterwines.com. Friday and Saturday 11 a.m. to 6 p.m., Sunday through Thursday noon to 5 p.m. $10 fee is refundable with purchase.

- **Brian Carter Cellars,** 14419 Woodinville-Redmond Rd. Northeast (425) 806-9463, www.briancartercellars.com. Open noon to 5 p.m. daily. $8 fee waived with purchase.
- **Columbia Winery,** 4030 Northeast 145th St., (425) 482-7490, www .columbiawinery.com. Open Sunday through Tuesday 11 a.m. to 6 p.m., Wednesday through Saturday 11 a.m. to 7 p.m. The $5 tasting fee is not refundable with purchase, but is refunded if you join the Wine Club. While there's no cost to join the club, you will have to buy two bottles of wine every other month. Sure, there will be a 20 percent discount on the retail price, but that price still ends up being around $72.
- **Efeste Wine,** 19730 144th Ave. Northeast, (425) 398-7200, www.efeste .com. Open Friday to Sunday noon to 5 p.m. $10 fee waived with purchase.
- **Facelli Winery,** 16120 Woodinville-Redmond Rd. Northeast, Suite 1, (425) 488-1020, www.facelliwinery.com. Saturday and Sunday noon to 4 p.m. $5 charge allows visitors to sample 4 of the winery's 18 wines. The tasting fee is applied to purchase.
- **Gordon Brothers Tasting Room,** 19501 144th Ave. Northeast, Suite 800, (425) 398-9323, www.gordonwines.com. Open Friday and Saturday noon to 7 p.m., Sunday from noon to 5 p.m. The $5 tasting fee is refundable with purchase.
- **Guardian Cellars,** 19501 144th Ave. Northeast #E600, (206) 661-6733, www.guardiancellars.com. Saturday and Sunday, 12:30 to 5 p.m. $5 fee applied to wine purchase.
- **Hollywood Hills,** 14366 Woodinville-Redmond Road, (206) 790-4223, www.hollywoodhillvineyards.com. Friday and Saturday noon to 5 p.m. $5 refundable tasting fee.
- **JM Cellars,** 14404 137th Place Northeast, (206) 321-0052, www.jmcellars .com. Friday 2 to 6 p.m., Saturday and Sunday 12 to 5 p.m. $10 refunded with purchase.
- **Matthews Estate,** 16116 140th Pl. Northeast, (425) 487-9810, www .matthewsestate.com. There's a tasting room at the winery as well as a smaller tasting room with a smaller selection at 19495 144th Ave. Northeast, Suite A120. The winery tasting room is open daily from noon to 5 p.m. and the $10 fee is refundable with a wine purchase. The off-site room is open Saturday through Sunday from 12 to 5 p.m. Tastings are $5, refundable with purchase.

- **Northwest Totem Cellars,** 15810 Northeast 136th Place, Redmond, (425) 877-7111, www.nwtotemcellars.com. Tastings on Saturday from 12 to 4 p.m. The tastings are free.
- **Page Cellars,** 19495 144th Ave. Northeast, Suite B, (253) 232-9463, www.pagecellars.com. Open Saturday from noon to 4 p.m., Sunday 1 to 5 p.m. $5 tasting fee waived with purchase of red wine.
- **Patterson Cellars/Washington Wine Co.,** 19501 144th Ave. Northeast, Suite D-600, (425) 483-8600, www.pattersoncellars.com. Friday through Sunday, noon to 5 p.m. $5 tasting fee waived with wine purchase.
- **Red Sky Winery,** 19495 144th Ave. Northeast B220, (425) 481-9864. www.redskywinery.com. Open Saturday, noon to 5 p.m. $5 tasting fee applied to purchase.
- **Sparkman Cellars,** 19501 144th Ave. Northeast, Suite D-700, (425) 398-1045, www.sparkmancellars.com. Open Saturday and Sunday from 1 to 5 p.m. There's a $10 charge for five one-ounce tastings, but the fee is waived with any purchase.
- **Stevens Winery,** 18520 142nd Ave. Northeast, (425) 424-9463, www .stevenswinery.com. Saturday noon to 4:30 p.m. $5 fee refunded with purchase.
- **Tefft Cellars,** 16110 Woodinville Redmond Rd. Northeast, Suite 5, Woodinville, www.tefftcellars.com. Given that the room has barstools and comfortable chairs, it feels more like a wine bar than a tasting room. It also has live music. The room is open from 11 a.m. to 7 p.m. and the owner described the tastings themselves as "extensive and free."
- **Woodhouse Family Cellars,** 15500 Suite C600 Woodinville-Redmond Rd., (425) 527-0608, www.woodhousefamilycellars.com. The winery pours four wines during tastings. $5 fee refunded with purchase.
- **Woodinville Wine Cellars,** 17721 132nd Ave. Northeast, (425) 481-8860, www.woodinvillewinecellars.com. $5 tasting fee.

HAIR AND SPA SERVICES:
FREESTYLE

*"If truth is beauty, how come no one has their
hair done in a library?"*

—LILY TOMLIN

I admit it. I don't know hair because there's baldness on both sides of my family. Yes, that's right, even my mother was bald. Okay, I may be exaggerating there, but my grandfather was as bald as a cue ball, so I never expected to have hair going into my 40s. Consequently, I've always been a Great Clips kind of guy. Now that I'm on the downhill slide to 50 I'm slapping myself for not realizing Seattle had so many places where I could get a great cut and save a little money. So what if I might not get to choose the style or that it could take longer than a typical cut? Most of the people who cut my hair do what they want anyway. Even if you're more particular, the area has quite a few options for people who want to save money on salon services. And if you really want to splurge, you could take the money you saved and spend it on an inexpensive massage or even spa services at clinics run by some local massage schools.

HAIR **SALONS**

Some of the best-known salons in town have training programs where you can go to get cuts and a variety of services from students. These aren't your typical trainees, though. When most people think trainee, they think of the young kid running the register at a burger place or a department store who takes three times as long to ring up your purchase. The trainees in these salons are fully licensed beauticians who know their stuff, but want to take their skills to the next level, so you won't risk falling asleep and waking up with a mullet or a crew cut. There are occasional drawbacks, though. If you agree to be a hair model, for example, you'll save money, but you might not have a say in the style you get and the cut may take a little longer. The training programs are still a good deal even if you aren't a model. You'll pay for the services you get, but it will be far less than the salon's regular prices.

Craigslist
www.seattle.craigslist.org/bts/

Is there any item or service you can't get through this ubiquitous list? If the beauty section is any indication, apparently not. While it never would have occurred to me to look there, an acquaintance who owns the Essence Salon suggested it and lo and behold, there were numerous students looking for hair models for free cuts at a variety of salons including Seven, The Loft, and Gary

Manuel Aveda Institute. The student listings are usually quite specific about the type of model they need, the type of hair they need to work with, and the hairstyle they need to perform. The ads are also sporadic and it's not unusual to see a posting requesting less than a day's notice. As is the case with responding to any Craigslist ad, the usual caveats apply. Be safe. Don't go if it doesn't feel right. And make sure the individual and the organization are legit.

Crux Academy at Habitude Fremont
513 North 36th St.
(206) 633-1339
www.habitude.com

No matter how promising a newly minted graduate with a cosmetology license is, the folks at Habitude believe new stylists need a bit more polish and training before they're ready for the salon floor. That's why it takes new fresh-out-of-school hires and puts them through eight months of advanced training at Crux Academy. Cruxers perform many of the same services as Habitude's more senior stylists, but they do it for less. While a haircut at Habitude's regular salon starts at $35, Crux charges $20. Coloring is $60 at Habitude, $40 at Crux. Academy students also need live models to practice on as they learn new styles. Although they find most of their models via word-of-mouth, the company is open to considering new participants. The good news about being a Crux hair model is that your cut is free. The flip side is that you won't have a say in the cut you get and it will likely take longer than a typical cut.

Gene Juarez Advanced Training Salon
1901 4th Ave.
(206) 622-6611
www.genejuarez.com/education/advanced-training-salon.aspx

There are beauty school dropouts and there are these guys. The advanced training salon is for people who already have their haircutting license and want to go on to the next level . . . whatever that means. Consequently, there are some savings to be had, it's just not as great as it would be if you went to a beauty school where people are just starting to learn their craft. While a cut at a regular Gene Juarez salon would set you back $60, for example, it's $30 here. Although coloring starts around $50 at other salons, it goes for $40 here. Full foils are $80 rather than $110 and bleach and tones start at $60, not $95. They also offer a Perfect Blowdry, which is a wash and blowdry for $20. Me, I'd rather save the money and have an imperfect one.

Phase 3 by Gary Manuel Salon

2123A First Ave. (between Blanchard and Lenora streets, next to Buffalo Deli)
(206) 728-9933
http://garymanuel.com/promises/phase3new.html

This small salon just a few doors down from Gary Manuel's main salon acts as a finishing school for the company. It allows interns to attain the proficiency Gary Manuel requires and more experienced employees to hone their skills. As a result, you can get a cut by a well-trained stylist for around $33 to $37 when a similar cut at GM's main salon would go for $50 to $170. Appointments are available, but the salon also takes walk-ins. Open Tuesday through Saturday 10 a.m. to 6 p.m.

Seven Academy

Westlake Center
400 Pine St.
(206) 903-1299
Open by appointment only

Super models get paid and occasionally get free clothes, hand models also get a decent amount of cash, but in Seattle, apparently, the highly skilled and rewarding job of being a hair model isn't quite what it used to be. Student cuts are no longer free, but at least they're cheap. To become eligible to be a Seven hair model (you must have more than seven hairs to do this) call the model hotline at (206) 903-1299 and an apprentice will get back to you. The cut takes longer, but it is cheaper. Cuts are $10, color service $20, and a combo is $25. We assume that a combo is a mix of the two services and not a pizza with everything on it.

BEAUTY **AND** AESTHETICS **SCHOOLS**

Clover Park Technical College

4500 Steilacoom Blvd. Southwest
Lakewood
(253) 589-5800
www.cptc.edu

Heading south of Tacoma just to save on aesthetic treatments may seem to be taking this whole frugality thing to extremes, but then again, people travel across some states just to get mediocre deals at outlet malls. Given the programs that Clover Park offers it's theoretically possible to get a day of beauty on the cheap. How cheap? Facials in the cosmetology clinic start at $28 and salt scrubs at $32. Not only does the school have a student cosmetology clinic, it also has student clinics for its barber and massage programs. Clover Park's facilities may not be as glamorous as a spa, but knowing how much money you're saving has a funny way of helping most folks to relax. Cosmetology appointments are available, but walk-ins are welcome.

PERSONAL **CARE**

Euro Institute of Skin Care
10904 Southeast Petrovitsky Road
Renton
(425) 255-8100 ext. 6
www.euroinstitute.com

Unlike most aesthetics programs involving students, the Euro Institute operates its spa seven days a week all year long. Clients receive the same services they would at a spa only at much lower rates. Facials start at $43. Other treatments include microdermabrasion (starting at $60), waxing, salt scrubs, and peels. By appointment only.

Gary Manuel Aveda Institute
1514 10th Ave.
(206) 302-1044
www.gmaveda.com

This isn't your grandmother's beauty school. In fact, many people stumble on this salon without an appointment and get a cut without ever realizing that relative students are doing their hair. It provides all the services of its sister salon, Gary Manuel, but at much lower prices. Of course, what you save in money you may end up spending in time because the cuts can take longer. Cuts range from $16 to $22 and include a scalp massage, shampoo, and style.

Greenwood Academy of Hair

8501 Greenwood Ave. North
(206) 782-0220
www.gahseattle.com

It's not the prettiest looking building on its block in Seattle's Greenwood neighborhood, but it's been around long enough that you can be sure it's no fly-by-night operation. Besides, it's outlasted most of its competition. Its Web site features a list of services and their cost. The salon runs on a two-tier system, charging more for services offered by students with more seniority. Cuts range from $10.95 to $13.95, color $42.95 to $48.95, and customized facials are $42.95. There's also a foot facial for $26.95. Who knew feet had a face?

Lake Washington Technical College

Kirkland Beauty School
17311 140th Ave. Northeast
Woodinville
(425) 487-0437
www.kirklandbeautyschool.com

Unlike most programs involving students, this salon isn't on the campus of the school where they're taking classes. Heck, it isn't even in Kirkland. Instead, it's miles away in Woodinville, but it moved and we all know how expensive it can be to change your name, even if it does cause the occasional customer to drive around lost in the wrong town, cursing under her breath. Haircuts are $8.50, color $30, and foils $50. Perms are $35.

Seattle Vocational Institute

1500 Harvard Ave.
(206) 587-5477
http://sviweb.sccd.ctc.edu/p_cosmet.htm

Students in SVI's Cosmetology program offer chemical services, hair cuts, manicures, facials, and waxing Tuesday through Friday at deeply discounted rates. A facial is $15, waxing starts at $5, coloring is $30, and a simple shampoo and hair cut is $9.50. In addition, a 90-minute facial costs $50. Walk-ins are encouraged for most services, but if you want a chemical-based treatment it's best to make an appointment to make sure a student with that area of expertise will be on hand. A 90-minute facial costs $50. Walk-ins welcome. All services supervised by a licensed instructor.

MASSAGE **SCHOOLS**

Bellevue Massage School
15921 Northeast 8th St., Suite C-106
Bellevue
(425) 641-3409
www.bellevuemassageschool.com

The availability of massage at this student clinic varies depending on where the school is in the curriculum and how many people are in a given class. The best times to try are in January through March, May through July, and August through October. Students are observed as they give massages, but you'll never notice, and most of the assessment and instruction occurs after you leave. It's $33 for an hour massage ($28 for those over 55), but you'll need to allow 90 minutes for filling out paperwork and doing student feedback. At these prices, it's worth it. Check the Web site to find out when clinics are scheduled. Sadly, it's not prominently displayed. It's the second bullet under the heading "Schedule an Appointment with Admissions" even though it has absolutely nothing to do with admissions.

Cortiva Institute
425 Pontius Ave. North, Suite #100
(206) 204-3170
www.cortiva.com/locations/seattle/clinic

It's hard to go wrong with an hour massage for $35, but then again, the massages are being offered by students who need to gain experience. So, you're either paying to have a great experience or to be a guinea pig. Considering one of the last massages I had, that's not necessarily a bad thing. Allow an hour and 15 minutes for your appointment so you'll have time for intake and a post-massage assessment of the student. You can also book online at mtc.cortiva.com.

Everest Student Clinic
2111 North Northgate Way, Third Floor
(206) 526-7668
www.everest.edu

There are bargains and then there are *bargains*. Everest's rates definitely fit the latter category with one-hour massages at $30 and two-hour massages at $60. The school also offers a selection of spa massages, such as hot stone massages for $45. There are also scrubs and wraps. To find out what spa treatments are available, call the clinic.

Northwest Academy Health Center
2707 California Ave. Southwest #201
(206) 932-5950
www.nw-academy.com

This school's clinic offers a standard massage that's a combination of a deep tissue and Swedish massage. Appointments are usually available on Monday, but only during certain times of the year. There are also occasional Fridays and Saturdays as well. The best way to find out when appointments are available is to go to the school's Web site. One-hour massages are $35.

Northwest School of Massage
13033 Northeast 70th Place
Kirkland
(866) 713-1212
www.nwschool.com

Massage students here set up and schedule their own appointments. So, all you have to do is call in, leave a message, and wait for someone to get back to you. People typically hear back the same day. Massages cost $25 an hour, but you should budget an extra half-hour to fill out forms.

CHILDREN'S EVENTS AND ACTIVITIES:
FREE TO BE YOU AND ME

*"I take my children everywhere,
but they always find their way back home."*

—ROBERT ORBEN

For many years, there have been stories in the local press talking about how Seattle's population is so skewed towards singles and couples without children that the city just isn't child friendly. Don't you believe it. There may be more childless families than those with kids, but Puget Sound abounds with stuff for the younger set. There are children's theater companies, children's museums, and even playgrounds that are amazing enough to make many adults envious. And that doesn't even include the coffeehouses with play areas, gyms with childcare, or the pervasiveness of baby changing tables in men's bathrooms. Now, if we only had enough preschools to go around.

DESTINATION **PLAYGROUNDS**

Crossroads Water Spray Play Area
Crossroads International Park
999 164th Ave. Northeast
Bellevue
(425) 452-4874

Although it's more watery playground than swimming area, you'll still hear kids shriek with delight as they play among a variety of animals that squirt, spout, or spit, but only in a good way. It's open year-round, but the water is turned on Memorial Day through Labor Day. For more information, call the community center at (425) 452-4874.

Gas Works Park
2101 North Northlake Way
(206) 684-4075
www.seattle.gov/parks/park_detail.asp?id=293

This isn't your grandfather's playfield because . . . well . . . quite frankly, it used to be your grandfather's gas works where coal was converted to gas until cheaper, imported natural gas made it too expensive to run. The land has since been converted into a park and the exhauster-compressor building has become a covered play area. There aren't a lot of traditional play structures on hand, but there are lots of cool machines to play around on.

Gene Coulon Memorial Beach Park
1201 Lake Washington Blvd. North
Renton
(425) 430-6700

Play structures, a waterslide, a beach, and free summer concerts are just a few of the things that keep this park and playground crowded throughout the summer months and it's a good thing. Otherwise, most people wouldn't be willing to make the trip down Interstate 405 to get there.

Green Lake Park
7201 East Green Lake Dr. North
(206) 684-4075
www.seattle.gov/parks/park_detail.asp?id=307

This is a destination playground for everyone in the city, not just kids. Powerwalkers who want to talk about their relationships, rollerbladers, bikers, joggers, and people who want to see and be seen. There are plenty of green areas for kids to run, a swimming pool, and activity rooms in the Greenlake Community Center as well as a playground that always seems to be full of children on the slides, swings, in the sandbox, and playing in the boat in the middle of the sandbox. During the summer, the wading pool here is one of the city's most popular spots for kids to cool off. Rather than waste time looking for a space in the small parking lot, it's best to look for street parking along Greenlake Drive.

The Junior League of Seattle Playground Magnuson Park
7400 Sand Point Way Northeast
(206) 684-4946
www.seattle.gov/parks/magnuson/default.htm

This playground is built on the site of a former naval air station's air control tower and features three climbing structures (including one for toddlers), a big sandbox, and a small track around the play area that's wide enough for kids to ride their bikes on. Another feature that makes it a favorite of small kids: its proximity to an off-leash dog park means that they get to see all types of dogs (on leashes) walking nearby on the way to a playground of their own. Perhaps the best part is that it's next to a huge parking lot where there's almost always parking. The key exception is a weekend in April and another in September when the Seattle Public Library's Friends of the Library holds its semi-annual book sale. Then, you might want to steer clear.

Meridian Park
4649 Sunnyside Ave. North
(206) 684-4075
www.seattle.gov/parks/park_detail.asp?id=1104

It may be a destination playground, but that doesn't mean it's easy to find. Although it's next to a major thoroughfare, the rock wall and shrubbery surrounding it make it blend in with the scenery. Behind the walls, however, is the campus of a former Catholic school for wayward girls-turned-park that's a destination for kids and adults. The playground in what was once an orchard isn't huge, but the play structures are perfectly toddler-sized, including the monkey bars and wide slides surrounded by boulders. One of two sand areas in the park has a button kids can push to open a stream of water, creating a river on a wall next to the sand. When they tire of the play equipment, they can run along the open space, go through the children's garden, or have a picnic without ever realizing there's a busy road on the other side of the shrubs. Adults also like the park because it's home to Seattle Tilth, a non-profit organization that teaches people how to garden organically. None of its classes are free, but it does hold a free harvest festival in September.

Powell Barnett Park
352 Martin Luther King Jr. Way
(206) 684-4075
www.seattle.gov/parks/park_detail.asp?id=345

This is the thinking child's playground. Yes, there are slides and swings, but the play structures are more challenging than those found at typical playgrounds. The structures leading up to slides offer a variety of diversions for children to stop off and play along the way. There are no monkey bars in sight, but plenty of other climbing structures that allow kids to create their own adventures.

Saint Edward State Park
14445 Juanita Dr. Northeast
Kenmore
(425) 823-2992
www.parks.wa.gov/parks/?selectedpark=saint%20edward

This is the type of park that makes you wonder why they didn't have these kinds of playgrounds when you were a kid. Surely, it can't be because playground technology has advanced so much in the last 20 years. The playground is divided into two distinct areas. The Owl Forest is an enclosed play area where toddlers can run free along a boardwalk, play house (or fort), swing, or hop into a wooden airplane. The area for school children features a multi-level play structure with lots of nooks and crannies, slides for sliding, and multiple ways to get from here to there. The park itself can grow with you. Once kids feel they've outgrown playgrounds, there are plenty of hiking trails of varying lengths for the entire family to explore.

STORY **TIMES**

It used to be that the main time to read stories to kids was right before bed. And maybe right before nap. Possibly after school. And maybe on the toilet. But now, everybody's doing it at all times throughout the day. It's no wonder kids are confused. What with all this reading going on for no particular reason other than to keep them entertained, they might get to thinking they were the center of our world or something. And that would be wr—hold on, I'll be right back. I think I hear my kids calling.

Common Folk Kids
Crossroads Mall
15600 Northeast 8th St.
Bellevue
(425) 653-5555
www.cfkidsonline.com

Sunday story time runs from noon until around 12:30 p.m., depending on the attention span of its audience each week. The toy store aims for three stories, but understands that it's playing to a tough crowd and won't take it personally if children begin flitting about after hearing just one.

Crossroads Mall

Northeast 8th and 156th Avenue Northeast
Bellevue
(425) 644-1111
www.crossroadsbellevue.com

Talk about story time central! This community shopping center has several story hours a day almost every day of the week. The options include preschool story time at a children's store; Russian, Mandarin, preschool, and terrific tots readings at the Crossroads branch of the King County Library; and a story time at Barnes & Noble. No story times on Monday, Tuesday, or Saturday.

Izilla Toys

www.izillatoys.com
Capitol Hill Store, 1429 12th Ave. Suite D, Seattle; (206) 322-8697
Wallingford Store, Wallingford Center, 1815 North 45th St., Suite 218, Seattle; (206) 547-5204

Both locations alternate story time with free music classes. Every other Monday in Wallingford and every other Tuesday on Capitol Hill, the toy store offers free story time from 10:30 to 11:30 along with free snacks and juice. On off weeks, local children's musician Doug Fleming Jr. hosts a music class that's part lecture, part hands-on performance, and all fun. Fleming performs, then passes shakers, drums, and other instruments and has a 20-minute jam session with the kids. Note to parents: a pair of ear stoppers might be a worthwhile investment.

The Land of Nod

2660 Northeast 49th St.
(206) 527-9900
www.landofnod.com

As the folks at this high-end kids' furniture store see it, there's more to story time than just reading stories. It's an opportunity for adults to get together and chat while kids listen to stories. Of course, it's also an opportunity to sell stuff. All kids who attend can join the World Readers Program and get a map and a stamp card. Once their card has five stamps on it, they get a small trinket like a book or T-shirt and their parents get 10 percent off any purchase they make during the same visit. Readings are every Thursday at 11 a.m. and generally last about 30 minutes.

What All the Noise is About: Story Time

Libraries are supposed to be quiet places where one can go to do research, gather one's thoughts, write, read peacefully, and maybe even take a nice nap amidst the hush. All those thoughts go out the door during story times, however, when the decibel level rises and the effectiveness of a well-timed "Shhhh!" is practically nil. If you're a parent with a child that needs to get your kid out of the house, it's the perfect time to go, but if you're just someone seeking solitude, you may want to delay your arrival or step out for coffee.

It's important to remember that reading times vary, so it makes the most sense to list the types of story times available at each branch, but not the specific times for each. The information was correct at press time, but it's best to call before you go.

Seattle Public Library System—www.spl.org

Ballard Library: Baby, preschool, toddler
Beacon Hill: Preschool, toddler
Broadview: Preschool
Capitol Hill: Family
Central Library: Toddler
Columbia City: Family
Delridge: Pajama
Douglass-Truth: Family
Greenlake: Family
Greenwood: Toddler, preschool, baby, bilingual
High Point: Toddler
International District: Family
Lake City: Mandarin Chinese, family, hora de cuentos (Spanish)
Madrona: Family
Montlake: Toddler, preschool
Magnolia: Family
Montlake: Family
New Holly: Family
Northeast: Preschool, family, toddler, baby
Northgate: Family

Queen Anne: Family
Rainier Beach: Preschool, Mandarin Chinese
South Park: Bilingual preschool
Southwest: Preschool, toddler, baby
University: Baby
West Seattle: Toddler

King County Library System—www.kcls.org
If you need to go to a library and you're not inside Seattle city limits, then you're probably going to hit a library in the King County system.

Algona-Pacific: Baby, pajama
Auburn: Toddler ABC, preschool ABC, Baby Bounces, Wacky Wednesday family, sleepy
Bellevue: Mother Goose, young toddler, toddler, baby, preschool, family, Mandarin Chinese, Korean
Black Diamond: Discover stories family
Bothell: Korean, toddler, preschool, Once Upon a Wednesday, Russian, Spanish
Boulevard Park: Spanish, family
Burien Library: Alphabet, Mistress Moon's Evening, Cinnamon Bear's Toddler, Bear Hugs: early toddler, Spanish, Baby and Me: lap sit
Covington: Toddler Tales, Preschool Pizzazz, Spanish English, family
Crossroads: Russian, preschool, Spanish, Terrific Tots, Chinese
Des Moines: Raising Readers pajama, Raising Readers preschool, Raising Readers baby and young toddler, Spanish
Issaquah: Preschool, Spanish, toddler, young toddler
Kent: Sleepy, preschool, baby and toddler, family
Kirkland: Toddler, preschool, family, evening
Lake Forest Park: Toddler, preschool, pajama
Mercer Island: Preschool, wonderful ones, terrific twos, Italian
Redmond: Chinese, family, Hindi, preschool, young toddler, toddler, Japanese, baby
Skyway: Baby and toddler, preschool
Southcenter: Cozy Cove
White Center: Alphabet Soup family, Vietnamese

Mockingbird Books

7220 Woodlawn Ave. Northeast
(206) 518-5886
www.mockingbirdbooksgl.com

This children's bookstore has the most ambitious story schedule in the area with a story hour from 11 to 11:30 a.m. every day except Sunday. Because of its schedule, it doesn't set an age range on the readings and is open to whoever shows up even if it means that the audience is made up of nursing moms. If your kids get a little antsy in the middle of a reading, they can always visit the train table, play with a puzzle, or spend time at the chalk table.

Pottery Barn Kids Book Club

www.potterybarnkids.com/customer-service/book-club.html
Bellevue Square, 1050 Bellevue Square, Bellevue; (425) 451-2966
University Village, 4633 26th Ave. Northeast, Seattle; (206) 527-5560

This story hour could well be a gateway to create a whole new generation of young Pottery Barn shoppers . . . or just a chance to keep your kids entertained. Every Tuesday at 11 a.m. both stores read kids' books aloud for a half hour. If you get there early enough, your special someone can pick one of the books, as long as it's not too long. Even if you don't get there early, they can still get a stampable passport. After attending five readings and getting five stamps, they (read: you) will get $10 off any purchase. Most Pottery Barn Kids also offer free decorating classes on some Saturdays, but times vary. Call your local store to find out more.

Queen Anne Books

1811 Queen Anne Ave. North #103
(206) 283-5624
www.queenannebooks.com

This independent bookseller at the top of Queen Anne has a free story hour the third Sunday of the month at 2 p.m. Your kids can sit on a blanket, listen to a story, and finish off with a cookie. Get there early and calm your jangled nerves with a café con leche or other coffee drink at El Diablo Coffee in the same building.

Seattle Mobile Espresso

13000 Linden Ave. North, Suite 106
(206) 420-4719
www.seattlemobileespresso.com

This place really knows how to make its assets work for it. The coffeehouse is located on the bottom floor of a mixed-use building that also happens to house condos for seniors, so the owner has wisely recruited one of the residents to lead a story hour from 9 to 11 a.m. on Tuesdays. When kids get fidgety, the birthday-cake-hat-wearing former librarian whips out a variety of mini craft projects to keep the children distracted. When story time is done, take your kids across the street to the playground at Bitter Lake Park and you have the makings of a perfect morning. Then you can either have a snack in the park or come back for lunch.

Secret Garden Bookshop

2214 Northwest Market St.
(206) 789-5006
www.secretgardenbooks.com

Although it sells books for all ages, it's also one of Seattle's best-loved children's book stores and for good reason. Secret Garden takes story time to a whole new level with its Ultimate Tuesday readings. The gatherings are held at 7 p.m. on the last Tuesday of the month (hence, the Ultimate Tuesday moniker) and the stories are read by either the author of the book or the person who illustrated it.

Third Place Books

Lake Forest Park Town Center, 17171 Bothell Way Northeast, Lake Forest Park;
(206) 366-3333; www.thirdplacebooks.com
Ravenna Third Place, 6504 20th Ave. Northeast, Seattle; (206) 525-2347;
www.ravennathirdplace.com

The big store does story time on Fridays at 10 a.m., while its smaller sister in Ravenna does books for kids on Saturdays at 11 a.m. The Ravenna reading is easy to find, but the Lake Forest Park gathering can be difficult to locate because it's tucked away in a small corner of a large (children's) section. Arrive a few minutes early to find your way.

Tugboat Story Hour

Center for Wooden Boats
1002 Valley St.
(206) 447-9800
www.nwseaport.org

The appropriately named Tugboat Story Hour takes the prize for the coolest location for a reading: on board the historic tugboat, Arthur Foss. In keeping with the theme, all of the stories are maritime-centric, focusing on some of its audience's favorite things. Namely, boats, sea-bound adventure, and people their own age. Second and fourth Thursday of the month at 11 a.m.

University Book Store

www.bookstore.washington.edu
4326 University Way Northeast, Seattle; (206) 634-3400
990 102nd Ave. Northeast, Bellevue; (425) 462-4500
Mill Creek Town Center, 15311 Main St., Mill Creek; (425) 385-3530

Maybe they're trying to cultivate an audience or just get kids familiar with the places they'll be buying books when they go to the school at one of the local branches of the University of Washington, but all three stores have story hours for kids. The main branch store in Seattle has readings at 11 a.m. on Tuesday and Saturday. The Bellevue and Mill Creek stores have readings at 11 a.m. on Thursday. Children at the Mill Creek store color before the reading and have cookies or donuts after. Mill Creek also has a teen book club that meets the first Monday of every month at 6:30 p.m. to discuss a young adult novel.

Village Play Days

University Village
2660 Northeast 49th St. (25th Avenue Northeast and Northeast 45th Street)
(206) 523-0622
www.uvillage.com

It's hard to know where to put this weekly Tuesday morning activity because there's so much overlap. One week there may be story time with a celebrity reader at Barnes & Noble, the next it could be craft making at Kids Club, and the week after that it could be yoga for children at Lululemon Athletica. The one thing U Village is sure of is that the classes and events will go from 10 to 11 a.m. For more details about what's coming up each week, check the Web site. Many participating merchants also offer discounts each play day.

CHEAP, **BUT** NOT **FREE**

Toddler Tales and Trails
Seward Park
5902 Lake Washington Blvd. South
(206) 652-2444

As with story time at the Miller Library, there's more to this story time than just reading. Once the reading is finished, participants head outside for a themed walk. As a rule, the walks are stroller friendly and easy. Unlike the Miller Library, there is a small charge. While it's free for its intended audience of toddlers up to age 4, it costs $2 for kids 5 to 14 and $4 for adults. The readings are from 10 to 11 a.m. on the second and fourth Wednesday of the month and at 11 a.m. every other Saturday.

ARTS, **CRAFTS**, AND **PERFORMANCE**

Bellevue Arts Museum
510 Bellevue Way Northeast
Bellevue
(425) 519-0770
www.bellevuearts.org

The Catch: $2 materials fee

Kids can get crafty with a variety of media every Saturday during a weekly event appropriately called Get Crafty Saturday, which runs from 1 to 3 p.m. Every two weeks there's a new activity relating to a current exhibit at BAM. Events in early 2010 included making shoes, applying gold paints to objects, and making homemade window stickers. Participation costs $2 for materials or is free with a museum admission. There are also specific teen activities during Student Wednesday, on the second Wednesday of the month from 1 to 5 p.m.

Common Folk Kids

Crossroads Mall
15600 Northeast 8th St., Suite F-5
(425) 653-5555
Bellevue
www.cfkidsonline.com

Craft projects at CF Kids are created with preschool-aged children in mind and are designed to create practical things the makers can use at home: puppets, noodle necklaces, and holiday related items such as St. Valentine's Day cards. Most projects take 15 to 20 minutes to complete. Thursday from 11 a.m. to noon.

Home Depot

11616 Aurora Ave. North
(206) 361-9600
www.homedepot.com
Consult the Web Site for additional information.

Maybe the workshops offered on the first Saturday of every month will allow children to succeed where we have failed. I have no doubt that the classes that teach them how to build things like rain gauges and race cars will make them feel more comfortable around tools at an earlier age. What I want to know is, will it help them learn the secret to finding where all the employees are hiding whenever you have a question? Classes go from 9 a.m. to noon, there are no materials fees, and kids get to keep what they build and they even get a child-sized orange apron, which should come in handy when they play hide-and-seek.

Izilla Toys

www.izillatoys.com
Capitol Hill Store, 1429 12th Ave., Suite D; (206) 322-8697
Wallingford Center, 1815 North 45th St.; (206) 547-5204
This crazy toy store like no other offers one drop-in craft class each month at each of its locations. There's no charge and no reservations for what it calls Crafternoons, just a table filled with stuff kids can use to make something to take home with them. It could be something as seasonal as Valentine print making or as wild as Google Eye Puffball critters, whatever those are. The event runs from 4 to 6 p.m. Check the Web site for dates and details. The monthly event always happens on a Thursday, but which Thursday varies from month to month. Izilla is also planning to introduce a monthly game

night from 5 to 8 p.m., but the date has not yet been determined. One thing is for sure, though. There will be free pizza and beverages.

Lowe's Build and Grow Clinic
12525 Aurora Ave. North, Seattle
(206) 366-0365
www.lowes.com
Consult the Web Site for additional information.

Even if you aren't terribly handy, you can inspire your little ones to be by taking them to a Lowe's class with a building project. Provided that they don't hate you forever and need counseling for the rest of their lives because you made them get up so early on a Saturday. Each class tackles a different project like a table-top basketball game or a toy that's a car on one side and a robot on the other. Attendees not only get to keep their finished projects, they also get a free apron, safety glasses, and a patch. The classes are free and typically run at 10 a.m. every other Saturday at all Seattle locations.

Miller Library
Center for Urban Horticulture
3501 Northeast 41st St.
(206) 543-0415
www.millerlibrary.org

Not just your average story time, the Saturday morning gatherings at the Miller Library in the Center for Urban Horticulture also include a craft activity that celebrates gardens, plants, and nature. Children generally color or tackle a small craft project based around a theme like "growing kindness" or "hooray for mud." The events are free and held at 10:30 a.m. on the first Saturday of the month except July and August when the library is closed and the event moves to Monday nights.

Pratt Fine Arts Center
1902 South Main St.
(206) 328-2200
www.pratt.org

Instead of offering drop-in art or craft classes, the Pratt prefers to work with children on a longer time frame, producing more ambitious projects including painting, collage, and silk screening. Classes are divided by age group—kindergarten; second grade; third through fifth grade; and sixth

Big, Watery Fun

No matter how old you are, it seems like you're never too old to enjoy watery fun. Think about it. Every child's love of water goes back to happy times in the tub, then to wading pools and family trips to the beach. And if you think you outgrow it, you may not have been paying attention. As you get older, you graduate to other types of activities including swimming, snorkeling, scuba diving, kayaking, canoeing, water skiing, and jet skiing. Heck, it could even be said that snow skiing involves water. It's hard, flaky, and frozen water, but it's water no less. Here are some places where that love affair begins.

On those rare summer days when the weather gets really hot, it seems like there's no more popular place for toddlers than one of the many wading pools found in parks throughout the city. Seattle Parks and Recreation operates 25 in all (see appendix for locations) and most are open seven days a week from late June to early September. For more details on when the nearest wading pool will open and its operating hours, call the wading pool hotline (206) 684-7796.

While the area's best water spray park could well be Bellevue's Water Spray Play Area (see Destination Playgrounds in this chapter), Seattle is no slouch, either. Ballard Commons Park (5701 22nd Ave. Northwest) has a variety of water squirters including fixed sprayers and ones that pop up. At the same time, the Dr. Blanche Lavizzo Water Play Area at Pratt Park (1800 South Main St.) has water cannons and animal sculptures that squirt.

And if you've ever needed proof that you're never too old to enjoy the water, you need look no further than the International Fountain at the Seattle Center. Located in the middle of a vast expanse of lawn at the center, the water feature is a draw for kids and adults alike. The sides of the fountain gently slope toward a silver dome that shoots water high into the air often in time to music piped in from speakers on the fountain's sides. If the delighted screams of children are any indication, the seeming random order of sprays from a combination of micro shooters and super shooters are a big hit. The same is true with adults who are too old for wading pools but need relief from the heat just the same.

through eighth grade—and last for eight weeks each quarter. There is a suggested $15 donation, but it's not a requirement. You do have to move quickly if you want to get your budding artist into a class, though. There's only space for 25 students and registration is open as soon as the quarterly course catalog is published.

Seattle Asian Art Museum
Volunteer Park
1400 East Prospect St.
(206) 654-3100
www.seattleartmuseum.org

As part of its Free First Saturday event, SAAM offers art projects for children usually based around the theme of a current exhibition on display. Parents and singles can belly up to the art table, too, and create their own art from 11 a.m. to 2 p.m. The museum also shows a family friendly movie at 1:30 p.m.

Wing Luke Asian Museum
719 King St.
(206) 623-5124
www.wingluke.org

The third Saturday of the month is Family Fun Day when admission is free and kids are invited to take on a craft project that allows them to interact with the artists who created the activity. The projects are things that kids can do quickly and spend of the rest of their time adding details.

FUN **WITH** SCIENCE

Discovery Park
3801 West Government Way
(206) 386-4236

At 534 acres, this is one of the city's largest parks and there's plenty for kids to do. There's a small children's play area, but what may interest them more is the Environmental Learning Center. The center uses interactive exhibits and a play room where they can do all the things kids love doing including playing and coloring while learning more about the nature surrounding them. If they're old enough, there are also a number of books covering bird watching, botany, and roaming trails. Families with children seven or under can get a pass that allows them to drive down and park near the beach. There are only eight passes available, however. Because the park is located on Magnolia Bluff, it has amazing views of area mountains and Puget Sound.

Seattle Audubon Birdwatch Bird Banding
Seward Park Environmental and Audubon Center
5902 Lake Washington Blvd. South
(206) 652-2444
www.sewardparkaudobon.org

Kids and adults can watch and learn as the Puget Sound Bird Observatory and the Audobon BirdWatch Service Corps do a regular bird banding near the Seward Park Environmental and Audubon Center. Attendees will see captured birds tagged and released and will also have a chance to get their questions about the process answered as it occurs. Fourth Saturday of the month from 9 a.m. to noon.

THE **GAMES** PEOPLE **PLAY**

Blue Highway Games
2203 Queen Anne Ave. North
(206) 282-0540
www.bluehighwaygames.com

There are worse ways to spend a Saturday night than whiling away the hours playing board games with close friends, but I'm hard pressed to think of any that are quite as fun. Does that make me a nerd? If it doesn't, I'm sure something else does. I am a writer after all. Game night runs from 7 to 11 p.m. every Saturday. Although the store focuses on and teaches a few games each month, you can try anything in the store for free. Also worth mentioning are Puzzle Sundays from 11 a.m. to 5 p.m. when the store puts out a puzzle and invites customers to stop by and add a few pieces.

Common Folk Kids

Crossroads Mall
15600 Northeast 8th St.
(425) 653-5555
Bellevue
www.cfkidsonline.com

There's nothing like getting kids all wound up playing with toys and games before a concert, but there's also no requirement that you and your family attend the Friday night performance at Crossroads Mall, either. Heck, you can begin playing at 6 p.m. when Toy Demo Night starts and keep on until right before closing at 9 p.m. CF provides free popcorn and shows movies on TVs inside the store.

Uncle's Games

Crossroads Mall
15600 Northeast 8th Ave.
Bellevue
(425) 746-1539
www.unclesgames.com

He's not really a relative, but his store wants to bring your family together for Family Game Night every Thursday from 5 to 9 p.m. Don't feel like you have to buy one of the demo games, but if you do, you'll get 15 percent off. C'mon, would it kill you to visit your uncle once in a while? There's also a General Games Night every Saturday from 7 p.m. to midnight.

FAMILY FILM

Regal Family Film Festival

www.regmovies.com (select "now showing")
Thornton Place Stadium 14 & IMAX; 316 Northeast Thornton Place, Seattle; (206) 517-9943
Crossroads Stadium 8; 1200 156th Ave. Northeast, Bellevue; (425) 562-6596
Alderwood Stadium 7; 3501 184th St. Southwest, Lynnwood; (425) 672-2077

Remember those movies our parents used to drop us off at when we were kids so they could get a few hours of peace and we could run wild through the aisles? Well, Regal has brought them back. Participating theaters show one G-rated and one PG-rated movie starting at 10 a.m. on Tuesday and Wednesday from June through August and there are no restrictions on age. Seats are limited and available on a first come, first serve basis. I wonder if a corporate owned theater chain has any better luck controlling the little devils than the ushers at the mom-and-pop theaters we used to go to.

Afternoon at the Movies
Delridge Community Center
4501 Delridge Way South
(206) 684-7423

Catch a free family film from 1 to 3:30 p.m. on the third Saturday of the month at this community center.

Family Movie Night
Jefferson Community Center
3801 Beacon Ave. South
(206) 684-7481
www.seattle.gov/parks/centers/jeffercc.htm

Jefferson hosts a family movie night on a Friday night once a quarter featuring a film that will please kids and adults alike. There's also popcorn and refreshments. The fun starts at 6 p.m.

Family Movie Night
Carnation Library
4804 Tolt Ave.
Carnation
(425) 333-4398

A laid back early evening at the library where kids can wear pajamas and parents can hang out with their kids while watching family appropriate entertainment. From 6:30 to 8 p.m. on Thursday.

Friday Family Flicks and Food

Ravenna Eckstein Community Center
6535 Ravenna Ave. Northeast
(206) 684-7534

The Catch: $3 activity fee

Spend the first Friday night of the month watching a movie and hanging out with the kids without being stuck at home. There is a $3 activity fee or $10 for families of four or more, but the snacks are free. Movies run from 6 to 8 p.m.

Magnuson Cinema Festival

Magnuson Community Center
7110 62nd Ave. Northeast
(206) 684-7026
www.seattle.gov

There's no activity fee for this weekly afternoon showing of family films on a big screen television, but there aren't any free snacks, either. Movies show at 1:30 p.m. on Saturday.

ODDS **AND** ENDS

Outdoor Opportunities

Camp Long, (206) 684-0797
Discovery Park, (206) 390-1018

Today's playgrounds aren't the only things that make me wish I were still a kid. So do programs like this one. Nicknamed O2, its goal is to introduce multi-ethnic teenagers to such issues as environmental awareness and urban conservation. As part of the program, kids aged 15 to 19 are able to go on two overnight trips as well as service projects and weekly workshops. The trips include a variety of activities ranging from snowboarding and snow-shoeing to sailing and kayaking. And the best part is, it's all free.

KIDS **EAT** FREE

As a parent of two toddlers, I know that some restaurants offer free meals for kids, but I wonder if anyone has asked, "Is this a good thing?" I understand that it helps bring more people into restaurants while allowing beleaguered parents a chance to save a little money on a night out, but I have to ask if we really want to inflict our kids on others, no matter how well-mannered our offspring may be. Still, there are times when we have no choice in the matter and really must clean them up and take them out. So, it's nice to know there are places like these that help improve the bottom line. Just remember to read all the fine print before ordering. Some places only allow one kid's dish per adult entrée purchased and most require the free meal to come from the kids' menu, which can often be a junk food junkie's delight.

Ballard Brothers Seafood and Burgers
5303 15th Ave. Northwest
(206) 784-4440
www.ballardbrothers.com

Most fast food joints have menus filled with burgers and just one fish sandwich. The Ballard Brothers menu is lousy with fish sandwiches and seafood baskets. And kids eat free on Monday and Wednesday.

Beach House Bar & Grill
6023 Lake Washington Blvd.
Kirkland
(425) 968-5587
www.beachhousekirkland.com

Kids 10 and under eat free on Sunday at this casual waterfront restaurant.

Celtic Bayou Irish Pub & Cajun Cafe
7281 West Lake Sammamish Parkway Northeast
Redmond
(425) 869-5933
www.celticbayou.com

The combination of Irish and Cajun may sound like a train wreck in the making, but they must be doing something right because this place has been open for years. Kids 10 and under eat free on Saturday and Sunday.

Charlestown Street Cafe
3800 California Ave. Southwest
(206) 937-3800
www.charlestownchowder.com

This West Seattle restaurant known for its breakfasts and its chowder has plenty of fine print on its offer. It's available after 5 p.m. daily for kids 10 and under. If parents order two regular items from the menu, up to three children can get a free dinner from the children's menu. Offer limited to three free meals per family per day. Kind of makes you wonder . . .

Desert Fire
Redmond Town Center
7211 166th Ave. Northeast
(425) 895-1500
www.desertfiremex.com

Kids 12 and under eat free all day Monday. Dine in only.

Eat's Market Café
2600 Southwest Barton St.
(206) 933-1200
www.eatsmarket.com

Children eat free from 4 to 9 p.m. on Wednesday. One free kids meal with each adult meal purchased. Dine in only.

International House of Pancakes
1002 Aurora Ave. North, Seattle; (206) 517-4467
17250 Southcenter Parkway #104, Tukwila; (206) 575-0330

On Thursday, children 12 and under eat free with one child's meal free per every paying adult at IHOP's Seattle location; children 12 and under eat free from 4 to 10 p.m. in Tukwila.

Marie Callender's
www.mariecallenders.com
9538 1st Ave. Northeast, Seattle; (206) 526-5785
31920 Gateway Center Blvd., Federal Way; (253) 839-8322

Children 12 and under get a free kid's meal with purchase of adult entree on Tuesday and Saturday. The meals include a choice of ice cream sundae or slice of apple or chocolate cream pie. Beverages not included. Not available on holidays.

Pallino Pastaria
www.pallino.com
University Village, 2626 Northeast 46th St., Seattle; (206) 522-8617
Columbia Center Tower, Third Floor Mezzanine, 701 5th Ave., Seattle; (206) 624-2412
East Lake Sammamish Shopping Center, 6150 East Lake Sammamish Parkway Southeast, Issaquah; (425) 394-1090
Seattle Tacoma International Airport, 17801 Pacific Highway South, Seattle; (206) 444-4796
Redmond Town Center, 7545 166th Ave. Northeast, Space D110, Redmond; (425) 861-6900
17848 Garden Way Northeast, Suite 102, Woodinville; (425) 488-7900
Consult the Web site for additional locations.

Children 12 and under eat free all day Sunday and Wednesday when an adult purchases a full price entrée. Kids must order from the children's menu.

Rikki Rikki
442 Parkplace
Kirkland
(425) 828-0707
www.rikkirikki.com

Children 10 and under eat free all day on Tuesday at this Eastside Japanese restaurant.

Romio's Pizza and Pasta
11422 Northeast 124th St., Kirkland; (425) 820-3300
3615 Factoria Blvd. Southeast, Bellevue; (425) 747-3000

Children under 10 eat free from 4 to 9 p.m. on Monday and Tuesday. Dine in only.

Ruby's Diner
www.rubys.com
3000 184th St. Southwest, Lynnwood; (425) 778-8729
16501 Northeast 74th St., Redmond; (425) 861-7829
13706 Northeast 175th St., Woodinville; (425) 489-1173

Children 12 and under get a free meal from the kids' menu from 4 p.m. to close on Tuesday.

Seattle Crab Company
1710 Northeast 104th St.
(206) 366-9225
www.seattlecrabco.net

Kids 13 and under eat free meals from the kids' menu all day every day.

Sunflour Bakery Café
3118 Northeast 65th St.
(206) 525-1034

One of the few places on the list that isn't part of a larger chain, this much-loved neighborhood café offers free kids' meals for children under 10 all day Monday. Kids have to order from the kids' menu and it's valid for one child per adult.

Whistle Stop Ale House
809 South 4th St.
Renton
(425) 277-3039
www.whistlestopalehouse.com

Kids eat free from 4 p.m. to close on Monday with no restrictions on the number of kids per party. Dine in only.

Zoopa
393 Strander Blvd.
Tukwila
(206) 575-0500
www.freshchoice.com/locations_page_wa.html

Kids under two always eat free at this all-you-can-eat mega buffet, but how much do they really eat anyway? On Tuesday all kids nine and under eat free. At other times, 3- to 5-year-olds eat for $1.99 and 6- to 12-year-olds eat for $4.99.

INSURANCE

Washington Apple Health for Kids
(877) 543-7669
http://hrsa.dshs.wa.gov/applehealth/index.shtml

This program could well address the concerns of parents of the state's 75,000 uninsured children . . . if only they knew about it. The needs-based program covers major medical and certain preventive health care visits at an extremely affordable price for kids through age 18. The only catch is that eligibility is based on income. If a family makes less than 200 percent of the Federal Poverty Level, or less than $44,100 for a family of four, for example, the insurance would be free. Up to $55,125, families would pay for $20 a month per child and $30 a month per child for incomes of up to $66,150.

LITERATURE, LIBRARIES, AND OTHER LIFE LESSONS: FREE ASSOCIATION

"We're going to have the best-educated American people in the world."

—FORMER VICE-PRESIDENT DAN QUAYLE

It was a dark and stormy night . . . that lasted all winter. It doesn't snow much in Seattle, but it sure turns grey and rainy in the winter. Not the gullywashers they get in the Midwest, mind you, or the monsoons of Southeast Asia. Instead, it's the slow hanging mist and drizzle that is the stuff of film noir. While lesser folk might be inclined to curl up with a good book and go into hibernation for the season, we Seattleites are made of sterner stuff. Once the weather turns grey, we jauntily pull our seasonal affective disorder treatment lamps until we've recharged ourselves enough to trudge in the rain, go out and try to be social or curl up with a good book at someone else's place like a café, coffeehouse, or bookstore. We know we have to do these things during the dreary months because when the weather turns nice we won't want to be stuck indoors. And who knows? If we find something we like now, we may do it during the summer for a change of pace. Here are some of the free things with which we busy ourselves to prevent the onset of cabin fever during winter.

READINGS **AND** OTHER **LITERARY** EVENTS

Barnes & Noble
www.barnesandnoble.com
Pacific Place, 600 Pine St., Seattle; (206) 264-0156
University Village, 2675 Northeast University Village St., Seattle: (206) 517-4107
Northgate Mall, 401 Northgate Way, Seattle; (206) 417-2967.
South Center, 300 Andover Park West, Tukwila; (206) 575-3965
Westwood Village, 2600 Southwest Barton St., Seattle; (206) 932-0328
626 106th Ave. Northeast, Bellevue; (425) 451-8463
Crossroads, 15600 Northeast 8th St., Bellevue; (425) 644-1650
Pickering Place, 1530 11th Ave. Northwest, Issaquah; (425) 557-8808

In some places, B&N is the only game in town for people who want to attend an author reading. Not so, Seattle, where just two independent booksellers put on a total of 700 author events between them. And that doesn't even include the smaller fish in the market. Still, it never hurts to put in the effort. After all, most B&Ns are at big malls or shopping centers, so people can attend a reading and then do their shopping. The same can't be said for most independent booksellers, however.

Cheap Beer and Prose
Richard Hugo House
1634 11th Ave.
(206) 322-7030
www.hugohouse.org

When you have a name like this, what more do you need to say? A spinoff of the Hugo House's Cheap Wine and Poetry, the program features four writers doing long readings from their own works, and Pabst Blue Ribbon for a buck. After they're done, there's time for about 10 open mic readers to strut their stuff for five minutes each. The event occurs on a semi-regular basis, whenever it suits the curator. It starts at 7 p.m., but if you want a seat you'll need to get there early because it often attracts between 100 and 200 people and it's held in a small cabaret space. Admission is free, the crowd is lively, and the beer is . . . cheap. Check the Web site to find out when the next one will be.

Cheap Wine and Poetry
Richard Hugo House
1634 11th Ave.
(206) 322-7030
www.hugohouse.org

There are those who find the idea of an evening of wine and poetry hopelessly pretentious. This gathering is anything but. For starters, it's $1 for a glass of Charles Shaw's finest (known around these parts as Two Buck Chuck) and the crowd can get rather raucous, responding to readers and even joining them on stage if the situation calls for it. Recent performances have included a lip-synching dog and a chance for audience members to play rock-paper-scissors with someone dressed like Jesus. Admission is free and the turnout is always big. Check the Web site or contact Hugo House for dates and additional details.

Eagle Harbor Book Company
157 Winslow Way East
Bainbridge Island
(206) 842-5332

Eagle Harbor may be small, but it's mighty. The community bookstore in downtown Winslow, a half hour ferry ride from Seattle, has developed a reputation for bringing in top-notch authors you'd typically expect to see at larger venues including such names as Malcolm Gladwell, Barbara Kingsolver, and Christopher Moore. The store also hosts several book groups.

Elliott Bay Book Company
1521 10th Ave.
(206) 624-6600
www.elliottbaybook.com

One of the staples of my entertainment budget when I was a poor, starving freelance writer, author readings occur almost every night at this recently relocated Seattle institution. In fact, there are times when there have been as many as three a day. It does about 400 readings a year and most of them are free. Although it had a children's section at its Pioneer Square store, children's book readings were long forgotten until the move when it planned to start offering story hour at 11 a.m. on Saturday. Most evening readings start at 7 p.m., unless there are two scheduled the same evening. Then, the first usually starts at 5. Sunday readings typically deal with more serious topics like social justice, slow food, or even progressive Christianity. The store also does readings off site in partnership with other organizations. To see who's scheduled to read this month, check out the Web site. And don't be surprised if the mix includes folks like David Sedaris and Walter Moseley.

Island Books
3014 78th Ave. Southeast
Mercer Island
(206) 232-6920
www.mercerislandbooks.com

The only bookshop in a small downtown area on a small island between Seattle and Bellevue serves its clientele well with a mix of book groups and occasional readings. The staff is friendly and knowledgeable and the store stubbornly refuses to put a shopping cart on its Web site because the staff would really rather you come in to buy, spend some time, and maybe even chew the fat with a new friend. What's your rush? It is an island, isn't it? Okay, maybe not that kind of island, but still . . .

Meet the Author
King County Library System
Various branches
www.kcls.org

Most of us think about libraries when we want to read a particular book that we can't find at our local bookstore, aren't sure we want to spend the money on, or just don't want to keep, but have we ever thought of such treasure troves of the written word as a good place to see an author reading? Probably not, considering that most authors do readings in hopes of selling their books, not lending them out. And that's too bad because KCLS does a monthly Northwest Author Spotlight event at the Bellevue Library and also holds a number of author readings each month at branches throughout the system. The author's books are usually on sale at the events. So, you won't have to worry about having the author sign a library book.

Open Books: A Poem Emporium
2414 North 45th St.
(206) 633-0811
www.openpoetrybooks.com

Not only is this Seattle's only all-poetry bookstore, it's also one of only two in the country, making it a destination bookstore. It has several readings a month by poets from near and far. Weeknight readings start at 7:30 p.m., weekend readings usually begin around 3 p.m. The readings last about 40 to 60 minutes and all feature a published poet publicizing a book, not amateurs who are suffering for their art.

Pilot Books
Upstairs in the Alley Building
219 Broadway East
(206) 229-7181

A new entry on Seattle's literary scene, Pilot prides itself on only selling indie lit. It hosts a weekly writing group, does occasional readings, and hosts a small press fest featuring writers from tiny publishers. When it's not doing the fest, Pilot averages four events a month, which include readings, workshops, and even a meeting of a group that writes letters to prisoners.

Queen Anne Avenue Books

1811 Queen Anne Ave. North
www.queenannebooks.com
(206) 283-5624

This relatively small Queen Anne neighborhood bookstore hosts far fewer readings than its other independent bookselling brethren, but the events are a joy to attend. Part of it could be that the store occasionally serves snacks that match the theme of the reading. It could also be attributable to the coziness of the reading space and the friendliness of the staff. Or it could have something to do with the quality of the café con leches and other coffee beverages at El Diablo Coffee, which is attached and is accessible through a door at the front of the store. Queen Anne also hosts book groups and a book mixer where people gather to discuss a book, then adjourn to a nearby bar.

Seattle Public Library

Various locations
www.spl.org

SPL holds a variety of author events and lectures for adults every month ranging from book groups to author readings. All author readings are free and there's a pretty good chance that you'll be able to get an author to autograph a book, but only if you buy it somewhere else and bring it with you because the library prohibits sales of merchandise at any events that occur on site. For more information about lectures and readings, go to the Web site at www.spl.org

Stage Fright

Richard Hugo House
1634 11th Ave.
(206) 322-7030
www.hugohouse.org

Sometimes, it's hard to know where to list an event. Stage Fright is a case in point. Does it go in the children's section because it involves teens or does it go in the literary section, because it involves spoken word performance? I'm putting it here. The oldest youth open mic night in the city is a chance for 8th through 12th graders to gather and share their prose, whether it be fiction, poetry, or even a song they just wrote. There are anywhere from 5 to 15 readers a night, depending on the month. The event is held the second

Going to Your Special Place

When is a bookstore more than just a bookstore? When it's Third Place Books.

Shopping center developer Ron Sher developed the 30,000-square-foot space with a plan to make it as much a gathering space as a retail place. He based his ideas on the work of sociologist Ray Oldenburg who suggested that every person has three important places where they spend most of their lives. Home is the first place, work is the second. The third is a friendly place where members of the community come together in their off hours to be social and exchange ideas. The concept not only proved successful here and at Third Place Books in Ravenna, but also at Crossroads in Bellevue where his ideas helped save a mall that was on the brink of disaster. The city surrounding the bookstore, Lake Forest Park, and much of Seattle has happily embraced Sher's brainchild, attending the more than 1,000 events held here every year, stopping in for a bite to eat, taking in readings by their favorite authors, attending musical performances, holding meetings, hanging out with friends, and, yes, even buying books.

Wednesday of every month from 7:30 to 9 p.m. The best part is that it's free and snacks are provided. The Hugo House also hosts a weekly drop in writing circle every Wednesday night from 6 to 7 p.m. and many of the writers stay for the show.

Third Place Books

17171 Bothell Way Northeast, Lake Forest Park; (206) 366-3333
6504 20th Ave. Northeast, Seattle; (206) 525-2347

Third Place Books' main store in Lake Forest Park is so big it has three possible locations to choose from for its readings—the children's department for the younger set, a small in-store area near travel books and mysteries with room for 50 or so, and Third Place Commons, an indoor area next to the store with the capacity to seat several hundred. All readings here are free and start at 7 p.m., but participation in the signings may require purchase of a book at the store for events involving highly popular authors. The Ravenna store is smaller and has a smaller event space where readings are typically scheduled for Tuesday and Wednesday. There the focus is on local authors. Readings start at 7 p.m.

University Book Store

www.bookstore.washington.edu
4326 University Way Northeast, Seattle; (206) 634-3400
990 102nd Ave. Northeast, Bellevue; (425) 462-4500.
Mill Creek Town Center, 15311 Main St., Mill Creek; (425) 385-3530

Unlike most Seattle booksellers, the University Book Store's main branch never has to worry about running out of space for one of its readings. If turnout is a concern, the store can always schedule in one of the auditoriums at the University of Washington nearby, which it has done numerous times over the years. The company hosts over 500 readings a year split among its stores. Although all three host events covering a wide range of genres, the Seattle store is known for doing science fiction and fantasy readings well while the Bellevue location has built a following for hosting authors of popular thrillers and mysteries such as Stewart Woods and Phillip Margolin. Literary fiction events are also popular at the Eastside store. Most in-store events are free and begin between 7 and 7:30 p.m. on a weeknight. The chain tries to avoid scheduling weekend readings because turnout tends to be lighter than during the week. The store also co-sponsors a series of science lectures held at Town Hall, but those events usually cost around $5.

RIDICULOUSLY **CHEAP** SPOKEN **WORD**

Seattle has always been a quirky kind of place, but that brand of silliness doesn't always come free. Sometimes, you have to shell out a few bucks to get in the door, but if you've got an odd sense of humor, you won't regret the investment.

Ignite Seattle

King Cat Theatre
2130 6th Ave.
www.igniteseattle.com

An event that only a geek or someone with a healthy sense of the absurd could love. Ignite's tagline is "Enlighten us, but make it quick." For good reason. Ignite participants have only 5 minutes and a 20-slide Powerpoint presentation to enlighten, inform, amuse, or downright baffle their audience. And there's one other catch: the slides automatically rotate after 15 seconds. The quarterly event costs just $5. Of course, you could save the money by waiting until the presentations are posted on the Internet, but you won't get to experience the roar of the greasepaint and the smell of the crowd . . . or something like that.

Seattle Spelling Bee
Jillian's Billiard Club
731 Westlake Ave. North
(206) 223-0300

The Catch: Contestants pay $5 entry fee.

Did you ever wish you had been good enough to win the annual Scripps-Howard spell-off for the school-aged set? Do you still have nightmares of that one spelling error that knocked you off the competition in the final round? Do you wake up late at night in a cold sweat yelling, "I should have said 'i-e' not 'e-i'"? If so, this adult spelling bee is your chance for vindication or redemption. And if you don't win this time, there's always next month. The bee takes place the second Monday of the month and starts at 8 p.m. It's free to watch, but $5 to play.

Seattle Poetry Slam
The Re-bar
1114 Powell St.
www.seattlepoetryslam.org

Seattle is hardly the first city to hold poetry slams, nor will it be the last, but if you're a poetry fan who digs watching poets compete, the Re-bar is the place to be on a Tuesday night. Open mic starts at 8:30 p.m., featured poet at 9 p.m., Slam starts at 10 p.m. Cover is $5. It all builds up to a Grand Slam in the spring where poets compete for the right to represent the city at the National Poetry Slam.

Brainy Competitions

When it comes to brainy competitions, the adult spelling bee at Jillian's Billiard Club (see p. 161) isn't the only inexpensive and smart bar competition in town. At many local bars, pub trivia isn't just a cheap way to pass a night; it may also be a way to turn a tidy profit if you and your team are at the top of your game on the right night. Although the set up varies from bar to bar, teams usually pay a nominal amount to play, a quizmaster asks several rounds of questions, and the team with the most correct answers at the end of the evening wins the kitty or some other prize. There are far too many pub trivia quizzes in the area to list them all, but here's a quick sampling of what's available when, how much it costs, maximum team size, and possible prizes.

Admiral Pub, 2306 California Ave. Southwest, Seattle, (206) 933-9500. Wednesday, 7 p.m. $2 per person, up to five players per team. Multimedia trivia night. Winning team gets 70 percent of pot; second place, 20 percent; third, 10 percent.

Ballard Loft, 5105 Ballard Ave. Northwest, Seattle, (206) 420-2737. Offers free trivia at 8 p.m. Tuesday

Celtic Bayou, 7281 West Lake Sammamish Parkway, Redmond, (425) 869-5933. Monday at 8 p.m. $2 per person, up to eight players per

FREE CLASSES WITH CLASS

There are times when a book just isn't good enough. We want to know more, gosh darn it, but we don't want to pay for it. Either that, or we're just looking for an excuse to get out of our houses and hang out with other people so that we won't go stir crazy during those short days when the sun refuses to show its face and daylight lasts from about 9 a.m. to, oh, let's say about 3 p.m.—if we're lucky.

team. Winning team gets half the pot, second place 30 percent, third, 20 percent.

College Inn Pub, 4006 University Way Northeast, Seattle; (206) 634-2307. First Thursday of the month, 8 p.m. Free, up to six players per team. Hosted by the Burke Museum of Natural History; prizes are drink vouchers and museum passes.

Cooper's Alehouse, 8065 Lake City Way Northeast, Seattle; (206) 522-2923. Tuesday, 8:45 p.m. $1 per player, no team size limit. Top placing teams divide pot, other top finishers get prizes.

Finn MacCool's, 4217 University Way Northeast, Seattle, (206) 675-0885, offers free trivia starting at 9 p.m. on Monday with the winning team getting $25 taken off its tab.

Lottie's Lounge, 4900 Rainier Ave. South, Seattle; (206) 725-0519. Sunday, 7:30 p.m. $5 per team, up to four players per team. Cash prizes.

The Monkey Pub, 5305 Roosevelt Way Northeast, Seattle; (206) 523-6457. Friday, 8 p.m. $3 per player, up to six per team. First place team gets entire pot.

There are also a number of free pub trivia nights in the area as well, but most don't offer cash prizes.

In A Class By Itself

Seattle Free School
Locations vary
(253) 642-6365
www.seattlefreeschool.org

The name really says it all. There are no hidden fees or attempts to sell you stuff, just free classes on whatever the mix of unpaid instructors feel passionate enough about to teach. Of course, that also means that there's no regular class schedule. Instead, the sessions are announced on the Web site and the school's blog. Over the last year the offerings have included crafts, instruction on how to make your own cheese, and even a class on how to

Giving the L-I-B-R-A-R-Y some R-E-S-P-E-C-T

If you needed proof that Seattle area residents value the offerings of their local libraries, you need look no further than famed novelty wholesaler and retailer to the masses, Archie McPhee. The same Seattle-based company that brought you the Moses, Jesus, and Freud Action Figure dolls also created a Librarian Action Figure and based it on much-loved local librarian Nancy Pearl. If Pearl's name sounds familiar, it probably should. She's the author of *Book Lust*, *More Book Lust*, *Book Lust Journal*, and, now, *Book Crush* for kids. All of the books list recommended reads based on everything from age and personality to occasion and mood.

Although she's no longer with the Seattle Public Library, there's no question that Pearl is a librarian with class. But she's not the only class at many local libraries. In fact, most offer a wide array of classes for every age and interest.

The Seattle metro area has two main library systems, the Seattle Public Library (www.spl.org) and the Bellevue-based King County Library System (www.kcls.org). Here's a quick look at some of the subject areas their classes cover:

Anime	Health insurance benefits
Arts and crafts	Homework
Art & technology	Internet instruction
Book groups	Job searches
Budgeting	Library catalogues
Business	Music
Citizenship	Mythology
Computer skills	Nutrition
Cooking	Online marketing
Crafts with duct tape	Resume basics
Dance	SAT prep
Disaster preparedness	Science
English/Second Language	Singers
Finance	Taxes
Foreign languages	Theater
Gardening	Writing
Genealogy	

become an Irish citizen. Locations also vary, but many classes have been held at the Seattle Public Library Central Library, the Cascade People's Center, and Street Bean Espresso. It's also worth noting that the blog lists other free classes around town, even if they aren't offered by SFS.

Arts

Teen Art Studios
Gage Academy of Art
1501 10th Ave. East
(206) 526-2787
www.gageacademy.org/youth

Every Friday night this school not only provides a place for 13- to 18-year-olds to express themselves through art, but also the art supplies and snacks to help them do it for free. The popular drop-in event goes from 6:30 to 9:30 p.m. and centers on a different theme or medium every month ranging from figure drawing and printmaking to anything else they can dream up. Gage also has two free art lectures for adults every month. One is called Art Talks and features an interview with a working artist. The other, Artist Tool Kit, covers the practical side of being a professional artist including how to promote your art and make a living being an artist.

Fitness

Lululemon Athletica
www.lululemon.com
Pacific Place, 600 Pine St., Suite 210, Seattle; (206) 682-1286
Bellevue Square, 575 Bellevue Way Northeast, Bellevue; (425) 462-5530

Two of this company's three Seattle locations offer regular weekly fitness classes. In fact, the Pacific Place location offers two chances for its customers to get physical. There's free yoga on Sunday from 9:30 to 10:30 a.m. and a Wednesday afternoon run club that meets at 5:30 p.m. The Bellevue store offers either yoga or a fitness class every Sunday at 9 a.m. For more details on any of the events see each store's community calendar.

Food and *Beverage*

Caffe Vita Public Brewing School
1005 East Pike
(206) 709-4440
www.caffevita.com

Starbucks is great and all, but if you really want to learn how to make a great cup of coffee, Caffe Vita has a class for you. The two-hour gathering covers different brewing methods and discusses the importance of manual brewing versus the automatic coffee machine approach. Although dates vary, the class is typically held from 10 to noon on the third Saturday of the month.

Redmond Whole Foods
7991 Redmond Way
Redmond
(425) 881-2600
www.wholefoodsmarket.com/stores/redmond

As a rule, Whole Foods is so expensive that even the classes it offers are a bit spendy, but two classes offered by the Redmond store cost nothing. Healthy Eating on a Budget is essentially a store tour that teaches Whole Foodies how to score deals and make easy meals. At press time the store also planned to offer a special diet store tour. Times and dates vary from month to month, so it's best to call the store or check its Web site.

Sur La Table
www.surlatable.com
90 Central Way, Kirkland; (425) 827-1311
84 Pine St., Seattle; (206) 448-2244
The Bravern, 11111 Northeast 8th St., Bellevue; (425) 450-4010

The national gourmet kitchen shop offers a variety of product demos in its stores on Saturday at 11 a.m. Recent examples include a knife skills classes, donut making, and Sous Vide cooking. The Kirkland store also holds a variety of cooking classes each month with prices ranging from $39 to $150.

Williams Sonoma
www.williams-sonoma.com
University Village, 2530 Northeast University Village, Seattle; (206) 523-3733
Pacific Place, 600 Pine St., Seattle; (206) 624-1422

Bellevue Square, 212 Bellevue Square, Bellevue; (425) 454-7007
Alderwood Mall, 3000 184th St. Southwest, Lynnwood; (425) 778-8053

What's a cheap bastard like you doing in an expensive place like this? Taking a free class, of course. The purveyor of pricey pots, pans, and other kitchen paraphernalia offers complimentary cooking technique classes several Sundays a month starting at 10 a.m. They may be free, but don't forget to call and sign up in advance. Not too surprisingly, the Bellevue Square store has found a way to cash in on the interest in cooking classes and is now offering additional classes . . . for a price.

Languages

Mango Languages
Seattle Public Library
(206) 386-INFO
www.spl.org

Sometimes you don't even need to leave your house to take a free class. Mango Languages is a good example. Anyone with a valid Seattle Public Library card can login to SPL's Web site, find mangolanguages on its list of databases, sign up, and begin learning French, Portuguese, Russian, Italian, Japanese, or a variety of other languages for free. Before you know it, it really could be Greek to you.

Rick Steves Europe Through the Back Door
Rick Steves Travel Center
130 4th Ave. North
Edmonds
(425) 771-8303
www.ricksteves.com/about/travelcenter.htm

Considering that most of the classes only last an hour to an hour and a half, you're not going to leave any of the language classes here with the fluency of a native speaker. The crash courses should provide you with at least enough knowledge to cover the basics including getting to your hotel, ordering in a restaurant, and asking where the bathroom is. Classes are held Thursday and Saturday and languages include Czech, Italian, and Turkish. Classes are free, but reservations are required.

Travel and Other Adventures

REI

Seattle Flagship Store, 222 Yale Ave. North, Seattle; (206) 223-1944
www.rei.com/stores/11
Redmond Town Center, 7500 166th Ave. Northeast, Redmond; (425) 882-1158
www.rei.com/stores/20
735 Northwest Gilman Blvd., Issaquah; (425) 313-1660
www.rei.com/stores/116
240 Andover Park West, Tukwila; (206) 248-1938
www.rei.com/stores/78
Alderwood Mall, 3000 184th St. Southwest, Lynnwood; (425) 640-6200
www.rei.com/stores/35

Of course, you could just go into an REI store, get outfitted for your next trip, then walk out the door never to return or at least not until you needed more stuff, but wouldn't it be helpful to learn how to use the stuff? Or be inspired to do so much more? Every location in the region offers free classes covering a wide range of topics of interest to people not because they want to adopt the protective colorings of a Northwesterner and just fit in, but because they want to learn more about their favorite active pastimes. Recent offerings have included such topics as how to use your GPS unit, Washington's weather extremes, snowshoeing and preparing for climbing Mt Rainier. Although the classes are free, space is limited so advanced registration is suggested. For more details on classes go to each store's Web site.

Rick Steves Europe Through the Back Door

Rick Steves Travel Center
130 4th Ave. North
Edmonds
(425) 771-8303
www.ricksteves.com/about/travelcenter.htm

Don't let the name fool you. Even though Steves has made his name on his Europe Through the Back Door books and guided trips, it's still okay to enter the shop through the front door. Once you're there you can even sit in on one of the free classes, as long as you pre-registered and you're there on a Thursday or Saturday. The sessions cover some things you might expect, like how to pack light and digital photography, as well as others you might not, such as volunteer travel. Most classes are held at the Travel Center, but others are offered at Edmonds Theater and the Edmonds Center for the Arts.

The Savvy Traveler
112 5th Ave. South
Edmonds
(425) 744-6076
www.savvytraveleredmonds.com

Not far from the headquarters of Rick Steves' off-the-beaten-path travel empire is a smaller, less well known travel store that also offers free seminars and classes. While the schedule tends to be destination-oriented, it also offers classes on packing, volunteer travel, and the like. The only thing it does that Steves' operation doesn't is offer more detailed language classes. Where most of Steves' language courses are one-dayers, a recent Italian class at Savvy Traveler had four two-hour sessions.

Odds And Ends

Babeland
707 East Pike St.
(206) 328-2914
www.babeland.com/events

Under normal circumstances, you might not think of a sex shop as a good place to take a class, but Babeland isn't your typical adult store. The Capitol Hill shop offers a variety of classes ranging from free all the way to $35. Recent freebies included a flirting tips class, a cheap date night lesson on sexual positions, and a lecture on how to talk to kids about the birds and the bees taught by sex educator Amy Lang. Most free classes typically last an hour and serve as introductions to a particular topic while pay classes go two hours or longer and go into greater detail. The store also has a free Sunday morning brunch once a month and a free Kinky Crafts class where you can make a sex toy on the cheap (there may be a small fee for materials). If you would like to attend a pay class, but can't afford it, you may be able to negotiate a rate on a sliding scale.

Sew Up Seattle
Goods for the Planet
525 Dexter Ave. North
(206) 652-2327
www.sewupseattle.blogspot.com

A class about how to sew and turn recycled fabric scraps taught at a store that specializes in eco-friendly products. The classes are held at 11 a.m. on the last Saturday of the month. The classes are free, but signing up in advance is a good idea as space is limited. Recent classes have covered mending and remaking, buttons and buttonholes, and bags for the beach.

UW Graduate School Public Lecture Series
Kane Hall, Room 130
University of Washington Campus
(206) 543-0540
www.grad.washington.edu/lectures

Every year, the graduate school hosts a monthly series of lectures by an eclectic mix of scholars on a wide range of topics. In 2009–10, for example, film maker Girish Karnad talked about the impact British colonialism had on modern day entertainment in India, journalist Hedrick Smith spoke about the new polluters, and paleontologist Louise Leakey gave a lecture titled "Origins and Evolution: How We Became Human." Although the lectures are open to the public, the best way to make sure you'll have a seat is to register in advance by calling the UW Alumni Office at the above number. The series runs from October through April.

Meditation

Free Meditation in Seattle
Thai Exotic Importers
85 Yesler Way
(206) 682-2190

There are worse places to meditate than an art gallery, but there probably aren't any as interesting. The gathering occurs on Wednesday from 7 to 8:30 p.m. Although offerings are appreciated, it's not necessary to donate. After all, its name is "Free Meditation in Seattle."

Sahaja Meditation

Crossroads Mall Community Room
156th Northeast and Northeast 8th
Bellevue
(425) 753-0634

Meditation in a mall. On the Eastside no less. Who'd have thunk it? The method is said to be very easy and the curious are invited in to drop in and experience internal peace. And if that doesn't work, you can always cut out early and contemplate bargains.

Seattle Shambhala Center

3107 East Harrison St.
(206) 860-4060
www.seattle.shambhala.org

The center offers free meditation instruction on Monday and Thursday at 6:30 p.m. and from 9 a.m. to noon on Sunday. The organization suggests that newcomers to meditation attend the Thursday session because it is followed by an open house where you can ask questions about meditation, the center's technique, or whatever else you can think of.

Vidyana Foundation

Talaris Conference Center
4000 Northeast 41st St.
(206) 949-7933
www.thewayofseeing.com

Free beginning meditation classes are held every Monday at 6:30 p.m. It may be nice to achieve the relaxed state meditation can bring you and gain useful tools for helping cope with aspects of our everyday lives, but apparently, the organizers aren't as relaxed about your comings and goings. The organization's Web site suggests arriving a few minutes early because the doors are locked promptly at 6:30. Does that mean you can zone out any time you'd like, but you may never leave?

HEALTH AND MEDICINE:
LIVE FREE OR DIE

"We Americans live in a nation where the medical-care system is second to none in the world, unless you count maybe 25 or 30 little scuzzball countries like Scotland that we could vaporize in seconds if we felt like it."

—DAVE BARRY

Even if you have health insurance, the price of health care seems to keep going higher and higher, especially if you have health insurance. While the best way to save money on medicine and other care is to not get sick or, at least, keep from getting kicked off your insurance company rolls simply because you actually needed to use your insurance, there are times when you just can't avoid spending money. Even if you're a guy and you insist that the huge gash in your chest is "only a flesh wound." That's when some of these organizations come in handy. You might not be able to do anything about the high cost of insurance, but some of the options below might help lighten the impact on your wallet or purse.

Seattle-King County Public Health
(206) 296-0100
www.kingcounty.gov/healthservices/health.aspx

The go-to place for advice on all sorts of medical issues and concerns. The department runs 11 public health centers, a variety of clinics (including dental, family planning, HIV/STD, and Teen Health), smoking cessation, and substance abuse programs to name just a few. In fact, the department is also responsible for restaurant inspections and environmental health. If its medical personnel can't treat you, they will be able to point you in the right direction for affordable options.

TESTING, **TESTING** . . . IS **THIS** THING **WORKING?:** CLINICAL **STUDIES**

The University of Washington Medical Center. Children's Hospital. The Seattle Cancer Care Alliance. Fred Hutchison Cancer Research Center. With so many medical research facilities located here, there's no shortage of opportunities for you to become a human guinea pig. Of course, not everyone who signs up for a particular clinical study is sick. Some do it just because they want to advance medical science and others do it for pay (or the free health care that's involved). If you're one of the people looking for a miracle cure, though, it's important to remember that there's always a control group that's given a placebo, so there's no guarantee the medicine you're trying will help. Of course, the hope is that it won't hurt, either.

Participating in such trials isn't for everyone. They can be time-consuming, call for changes in lifestyle, or even be potentially risky because not all of the side effects of the drug are known at the start, but here's where to look if you're willing to become an explorer on the frontiers of medicine.

AIDS Clinical Trial Information Service: (800) 874-2572, www.aidsinfo .nih.gov
Center Watch: listing by category, www.centerwatch.com
Clinical Trials Search: www.clinicaltrialssearch.org
National Cancer Institute: www.cancer.gov/clinical_trials
National Library of Medicine: www.clinicaltrials.gov

Area medical centers looking for volunteers:
Children's Hospital: www.seattlechildrens.org/research
Evergreen Hospital Medical Center: www.evergreenhospital.org/landing .cfm?id=340
Fred Hutchinson Cancer Research Center: www.fhcrc.org/patient /treatment/trials/index.php
Group Health Cooperative Center for Health Studies: www.group healthresearch.org/participate/joinastudy.html
Seattle Cancer Care Alliance: www.seattlecca.org/clinical-trials-at-scca .cfm
Swedish Medical Center: www.swedish.org/body.cfm?id=371
University of Washington Warren G. Magnuson Health Sciences Center: www.washington.edu/healthresearch
VA Puget Sound Health Care System: www1.va.gov/pugetsound
Valley Medical Center: www.valleymed.org/our_services/clinical_research _program.htm

FREE **CONDOMS**

Gay City Health Project
511 East Pike St.
(206) 860-6969
www.gaycity.org

This health organization for gay men is one of the top HIV and STD testing organizations in the area. It tries to forward the cause of a healthy lifestyle among gay and bisexual men by building self-esteem and creating a supportive community.

Homohealth.org
The Catch: Be warned. The site is not appropriate for children and contains material you may find objectionable.

Instead of just waiting for people to come into their offices and grab free condoms, the program sponsored by the Lifelong Aids Awareness Foundation takes them to where the need is greatest: the places where people hook up. The condoms are part of a free safer sex packet featuring lubricants and education cards that can be found at gay bars throughout town.

Lambert House
1818 15th Ave. (between East Howell and East Denny Way)
(206) 322-2515
www.lamberthouse.org

A drop-in center for gay, lesbian, bisexual, and transgendered youth, Lambert House keeps its supply of free condoms in a basket near a resource center filled with pamphlets on a variety of health topics of concern to its target population. The center is designed to be a safe hang-out for people 22 years old and younger and provides counseling and support groups as well as a variety of activities and events.

Planned Parenthood
www.plannedparenthood.org
5020 Roosevelt Way Northeast, Unit 1, Seattle
4500 9th Ave. Northeast, #324, Seattle
2001 East Madison St., Seattle

9641 28th Ave. Southwest, Seattle
1420 156th Northeast #C, Bellevue
1105 South 348th St., Federal Way
75 Northwest Dogwood St., Suite B, Issaquah
6610 Northeast 181st, #2, Kenmore
10056 Southeast 240th, #A, Kent
19505 76th Ave. West, Lynnwood
(800) 769-0045

Condoms are easy to come by at the nationally known, much-protested reproductive health organization. They're often sitting in a fishbowl or some other container in the reception area of most of its clinics.

ALTERNATIVE CARE

Bastyr Center for Natural Health Care
3670 Stone Way North (38th and Stone)
(206) 834-4100
www.bastyrcenter.org

Bastyr University may be all the way out in Kenmore, but the teaching clinic for its naturopathic medicine, acupuncture, and nutrition programs is more conveniently located in Wallingford. The first visit usually takes 90 minutes with two students taking patient history and doing an exam, then consulting with a supervising, more experienced naturopath to reach a diagnosis and a treatment plan. Follow-up visits for treatment typically take an hour. Remember that this is alternative medicine. On the plus side, that means longer consult times with the people treating you rather than the drive-by gawkings at many Western medical doctor's offices. On the negative side, the ways of alternative medicine can seem strange to people accustomed to another medical model. The good news is that, unlike many Western medical treatments, when naturopathic and acupuncture treatments don't work, they usually don't make things worse. Seniors pay a flat $20 fee for treatments while student fees are on a sliding scale based on income, which usually puts the cost around $20. HIV-positive patient visits to the Immune Wellness Program are free.

Seattle Institute of Oriental Medicine
916 Northeast 65th St.
(206) 517-4541
www.siom.edu

When my friends found out I once went to an acupuncture teaching clinic, they asked if the needles used in treatment hurt. After having reassured them that I barely felt them, I told them the real pain came from the sledge-hammers they used to pound them in. I'M JOKING! The needles are small, there are no sledgehammers, and all of the practitioners here are third year students working under the supervision of a licensed acupuncturist. Community clinics held from 8:30 a.m. to 12:30 p.m. Monday and Friday cost $15 and require an appointment. Community clinic patients sit in lounge chairs in a large room with as many as five other patients while they are treated. More private treatments start at around $35.

FITNESS AND FUN:
FREE KICKS

"You can't leave footprints in the sands of time if you're sitting on your butt. And who wants to leave buttprints in the sands of time?"

—BOB MOAWAD

Seattleites are an interesting lot. Not only are many seemingly not as materialistic as folks in other cities across the country, but a great number of us so value quality of life that stories abound of folks taking pay cuts to move here just so they could live in a place with so many outdoor recreational possibilities. Kayaking. Hiking. Biking. Skiing. Boating. Sailing. Running. Jumping. Sitting here writing this in the middle of winter, it hurts just to think about it. Still, it's not unusual for corporate offices to empty out on the day the ski slopes open in winter and the first nice day of spring. Those days are so eagerly anticipated that some spend top dollar to get the latest, most expensive equipment just to be prepared, no matter what the sport. So much for a lack of materialism. The bad news is that spending so much on equipment doesn't leave a lot to spend on actually leaving town so they have no choice but to look for low priced activities. The good news is that there are plenty of them that aren't far away.

PARK **IT** HERE: **NEARBY** GETAWAYS **THAT** WILL **KEEP** YOU **BUSY** ALL **DAY**

Green Lake/Woodlawn Park Zoo
7201 Green Lake Dr. North
(206) 684-4075
www.cityofseattle.net/parks/park_detail.asp?id=307

These parks are so close together, it's hard to tell where one ends and the other begins. In any case, the opportunities seem endless. There's a 3-mile path around the lake popular with walkers, bikers, skaters, and those who just want to people watch while they walk, a small beach, boat rentals, kayaking, a nine-hole golf course, a community center with an indoor swimming pool and weight room, outdoor tennis courts, baseball fields, a basketball court, a playground, and a wading pool. And that doesn't even include the picnic areas, lawn bowling courts, and the Woodland Park Zoo (the zoo has an admission fee) all located uphill from the lake. It's also a popular venue for theater in the park performances during the summer.

Marymoor Park

6046 West Lake Sammamish Parkway Northeast
Redmond
(206) 205-3661
www.kingcounty.gov/recreation/parks/inventory/marymoor.aspx

At 640 acres, Marymoor isn't just one of King County's largest urban parks, it's also one of its most popular. Located near the end of 520, the park has plenty of ways to while away the day. There are three playgrounds, a velo-drome (bicycle race course), a climbing rock, and playing fields for sports like soccer, lacrosse, rugby, and cricket, as well as an off-leash dog area and a bird loop trail. In the summer you can also catch a free outdoor movie, shell out the big money for a concert, or just keep walking. The park has a connector trail that links the 27-mile Burke Gilman Trail with the 11-mile East Lake Sammamish River Trail. If you have a need for a bit more speed, you can even take advantage of a program funded by a donation from the Dasani Corp. and ride a Trek Classic Cruiser along the route for free. Once you're through with all that walking or riding, you can take your tired feet to the reflexology trail before heading home.

Warren G. Magnuson Park

7400 Sand Point Way Northeast
(206) 684-4946
www.cityofseattle.net/parks/magnuson/

When the federal government created a base closure commission, Magnuson Park is probably the type of result it had in mind. The 350-acre Sand Point Naval Airbase has become Seattle's second largest park and it has plenty to recommend it. Located on the shore of Lake Washington, it is a popular place for boat launching, wind surfing, picnicking, and hanging out on a beach. It's also a popular walking spot with lots of trails throughout the park including the Burke-Gilman, which runs along Magnuson's edge. The park also includes tennis and a number of sports fields. It's also a hit with the younger set because of its large playground, off-leash dog area, kite flying, and motorized airplane flying area. In addition, it's also home to a wide range of community organizations including the Cascade Bicycle Club, EarthCorps, and the outdoor recreation group, the Mountaineers.

RECREATION **CENTERS** AND **POOLS**

One of the joys of living in a large metro area is that there are plenty of recreational options nearby and a little further away. If you like the local mix, you can go to your neighborhood recreation center and partake. If not, you can go to another locality's recreation program and mooch off them. It is getting harder to do it for free, though. While Seattle doesn't ask for proof of residency, Bellevue charges non-residents more to take classes or swim in the community pool, for example. Even so, most parks and recreation department programs are far cheaper than similar offerings you might find at private sector alternatives like fitness clubs. While gyms require memberships, locals can do a drop-in workout at a Seattle Community Center with a fitness room for $2, even less if they get a punch card. Even better, that same $2 could also give a parent a bit of relief when they've got a kid stuck inside on a rainy day. Many community centers operate drop-in indoor play programs or toddler gyms. In fact, most local recreation centers do a great job with programming for kids and seniors.

The Catch: Fitness room fees haven't changed in several years, so an increase is probably due.

Seattle Parks and Recreation
(206) 684-4075
www.cityofseattle.net/parks

The city of Seattle has 26 community centers with 11 pools, 30 wading pools, and six weight rooms (see appendix for locations). Currently, non-residents are subject to the same fee schedule for the use of pools and weight rooms as residents. Youth and seniors pay $2.75 per pool visit while adults 18 to 64 pay $4. You can save a little by buying a multi-use pass, however. A 10-visit swim card is $25 for youth and seniors, $37.50 for adults. A month-long personal fitness fast pass is $35 for seniors, $50 for adults. Drop-in use of weight rooms is $2 per visit but multi-use passes are available. The city also runs four municipal golf courses.

King County Parks and Recreation
(206) 296-0100
www.kingcounty.gov/recreation/parks.aspx

As the department's Web page is quick to point out, the county has "180 parks, 175 miles of trail, 25,000 acres of open space." It operates three community centers, two outdoor pools, and one indoor pool, the Weyerhauser King County Aquatic Center, which was built for the 1990 Goodwill Games. Fees range from $3.25 per person for a family swim in the recreation pool and $5 per adult in the competition pool to $6.25 for an adult to take a water exercise class. A 10-visit card for fitness class is available at a reduced rate.

City of Redmond Parks and Recreation Department
Redmond
(425) 556-2900
www.redmond.gov

The city has one community center and pool, but the community center doesn't offer recreational opportunities and the city doesn't operate the pool. Pool fees range from $3 per person during family swim on late Friday afternoons to $5.25 per adult for lap swimming. Discount punch cards are available. The city also operates a variety of walking trails. All activities at Redmond Parks are offered on a two-tier fee system with residents and non-residents paying different rates. Non-residents even have a different registration date for programs.

Bellevue Parks and Community Services
Bellevue
(425) 452-6885
www.ci.bellevue.wa.us/parks-community-services.htm

Bellevue has five community centers and an indoor aquatics center with two pools. Swim fees range from $4.75 for youth open swim to $5.75 for adults. A membership card offering 12 swims for the price of 10 and discounted three-month passes are also available. The South Bellevue Community Center has a 2,500-square-foot fitness center including free weights, treadmills, weight machines, and elliptical trainers. Fees range from $5 for drop-in ($6 for non-residents) and a three-month pass for $100 ($120 non-residents) to an annual pass for an individual at $315 ($378 non-resident) and a pass for a family with two adults and children for $564 ($684 non-residents).

Kirkland Parks and Community Services

(425) 587-3000
www.ci.kirkland.wa.us/depart/parks.htm

Kirkland operates two community centers and has a range of fitness classes. One offers a variety of fitness activities, while the other specializes in programs for kids and seniors. The city also operates a heated outdoor pool, which is open June through September. Single admission is $3 for all ages, a 10-visit pass is $25, and a season pass for an individual is $70. Household passes are $210.

FREE **CHI:** FREE **YOGA** AND **OTHER** STUFF

Discover Yoga

16615 Redmond Way
Redmond
(425) 861-1318
www.discoveryoga.com

There's plenty of need for grounding and relaxation here in the land of Microsoft what with the long hours and even longer commutes. Fortunately, there's a place where people can try something new for not a lot of money, even if they have plenty of it. Discover holds a free class one Friday each month from 6 to 7:30 p.m.

8 Limbs Yoga

Capitol Hill, 500 East Pike St. Second Floor; (206) 325-1511
West Seattle, 4546 ½ California Ave. Southwest; (206) 933-YOGA (9642)
Wedgwood, 7345 35th Ave. Northeast; (206) 523-9722
www.8limbsyoga.com

Three of 8 Limbs branches offer a free class called Yoga 101 once a month. Although the introductory class is designed to get new people to sign up for pay classes, the company won't resort to high pressure sales tactics if you only show up for this class every month. The class is held at 3:30 p.m. on the first Saturday of the month at the West Seattle location, the first Sunday at Capitol Hill, and the last Sunday at Wedgwood. All Yoga 101 classes begin at 3:30 p.m.

NW Community Yoga
701 Northwest 70th St.
(206) 706-4727
www.nwcommyoga.com

You can work out a one-for-one trade by volunteering for yoga. Although what type of work you tackle will have an impact on the hourly accrual rate, tasks like an hour spent posting flyers for the center will be worth an hour of classes at $15 per class. Other possible tasks include cleaning the studio, gardening, or cleaning the mats. The studio also offers a free monthly yoga class, usually on a Sunday. For more information about the time and date of the class, visit the Web site.

Samadhi Yoga
1205 East Pike St.
(206) 329-4070
www.samadhi-yoga.com

This Capitol Hill yoga studio offers a free yoga class to the community on Saturday from 2:30 to 3:45 p.m. According to Samadhi's Web site, most classes feature "breath work, chanting, seated meditation, and inspirational words and music."

The Samarya Center
1806 East Yesler Way
(206) 568-8335
www.samaryacenter.org

Getting anything free is always a good way to start off a weekend and starting it off with free yoga is even better. The center offers a free community yoga class Saturday at 8 a.m. Its classes remain a bargain through the rest of the week as well because they're all only $8, about half the price of most yoga centers in Seattle. Class size is limited to 25 people.

Tai Chi

Third Place Books
17171 Bothell Way Northeast
Lake Forest Park
(206) 366-3333
www.thirdplacebooks.com

This is yet another one of those times when Third Place proves it really is trying to be all things to all people. The weekly Tai Chi drop-in gathering runs from 8:45 to 9:45 a.m. on Saturday and is open to all, regardless of age, experience, or ability.

Yoga Life

8 Boston St.
(206) 283-9642
www.yogalife.com

Yoga Life's Queen Anne studio offers a free community class from 2:15 to 3:30 p.m. on Saturday. Although it's offered for eight weeks at a time, the studio accepts drop-in participants. The class is good for all levels of experience ranging from beginners to folks with more experience.

SPORTING **EVENTS**

Things aren't the way they were in our grandparents' day. You know, when you could take in an entire major league baseball game by looking through a hole in a wooden fence . . . as long as the local constabulary didn't happen along, catch you in the act, and chase you off. At today's superstadiums there aren't any wooden fences with knotholes in them and it seems like there's nothing free, but there are a few places you can go to see action for nothing or next to nothing. Who knows? A team you knew nothing about could suddenly become your favorite. It worked for curling in the Vancouver Winter Olympics, didn't it?

The Everett Aquasox

3802 Broadway
Everett
(425) 258-3673
www.aquasox.com

If the cost of Seattle Mariners games at Safeco Field are getting too rich for your blood, you can go see some of the team's future stars today just an hour away when you head north and watch the M's Short Season A Classification farm team, the Everett Aquasox, play at Everett Memorial Stadium. At $6, the price of being a bleacher bum is a little higher than it used to be, but there's a family friendly feel here you won't find down in Sodo Center. Kids run around free chasing after foul balls and there are more chances for children to run the bases after a game here than there are at Safeco Field. In 2009, the club also had a lottery ticket promotion where fans who had a non-winning lottery ticket could get a $7 general admission seat for $2.

Seattle Mariners

www.mariners.mlb.com
Safeco Field
1250 First Ave. South
(206) 346-4000

There are plenty of reasons to catch a major league baseball game at Safeco Field and the team is just one of them. There's the beauty of the stadium, the pretty sunsets you can see over Elliott Bay if you get the right seats, and the sounds of the trains as they pass by. I mention all these things on the off chance that you happen to have this book with you when you're at an M's game and they're in the middle of their summer swoon. Just so you can't say I didn't warn you. At $7, the cheapest seats in the house are still less than what you'd pay for a movie and there are also a variety of specials that push down the cost of $20 Reserved View Level seats to prices nearing affordability. On Monday and Tuesday Half Price Family Nights, View Level seats are half off. On Senior Sundays, the seats are $10 off for people over 60. The same is true of Military Nights. The seats can go down to $8 on college nights or when there's a group of 40 or more buying a block of tickets.

Seattle Pacific University

Brougham Pavilion
3414 3rd Ave. West
(206) 281-2000
www.spufalcons.com

The only thing you'll find that's free at any competition involving the SPU Falcons could well be a free throw from courtside in basketball. Otherwise, all games by the school's National Collegiate Athletic Association Division II teams are ridiculously cheap, especially for students, youth, or seniors. They pay $3. Adult general admission to all events is $6. Soccer matches are played at Interbay Stadium on 17th Avenue West and Dravus Street.

Seattle Sounders

www.soundersfc.com
Starfire Sports Complex, 14800 Starfire Way, Tukwila
Occidental Park, Occidental Avenue South and South Main Street, Seattle
Qwest Field, 800 Occidental Ave., Seattle
1-877-MLS-GOAL

The games played by Seattle's Major League Soccer expansion team, the Sounders FC, aren't free, either, but there are two free events that help get people in the right mood for the season and the game. In a throwback to our grandparents' day, you can see training sessions and reserve team games at Starfire Sports Complex as long as you don't mind watching through the perimeter fence. Training typically starts at 10 or 11 a.m. It's also a chance to see some of the players up close and maybe even get an autograph or two. On game day, there's also a March to the Match that starts in Occidental Square 90 minutes before the game with the team's marching band, chanting, singing, and a bit of boisterous walking. There's been no soccer hooliganism, however, because this is Seattle and, well, that just wouldn't be polite.

Seattle Thunderbirds

ShoWare Center
625 West James St.
Kent
(253) 856-6999
www.seattlethunderbirds.com

They're called the Seattle Thunderbirds, but they play down south in Kent. Regular season tickets for the Western Hockey League team's games range from $16 to $40, but it's possible to see training camp practices and scrimmages free at the ShoWare Center. Although practices are usually held on the Thursday or Friday before Labor Day, the best way to make sure you have the right day is to check the Web site or get the latest updates by subscribing to the club's e-news.

Seattle University
Logan Field
14th and Cherry
(206) 296-6000
www.goseattleu.com

The NCAA Division I school's team, the Redhawks, participates in 14 sports including basketball, baseball, cross country, and golf. The only sport that's free to see is softball.

The Storm
North Seattle Community College
9600 College Way North
www.northseattle.edu/storm

No, the women's professional basketball team of the same name hasn't left Key Arena and suddenly moved north. Instead, The Storm is the name for the mens' and womens' basketball teams from North Seattle Community College, which play in the Northwest Athletic Association of Community Colleges league. Also, this Storm team charges nothing for its games.

Tacoma Rainiers
Cheney Stadium
2502 South Tyler St.
Tacoma
(253) 752-7707
www.tacomarainiers.com

If Everett isn't your kind of town or you don't like the name Aquasox, but you've still got a Jones for cheap baseball, head south to the City of Destiny and catch a game by the Mariners Triple-A farm team. At 7 bucks for bleacher seats and reserved seats for $11 ($10 for kids and members of the military), the Rainiers aren't cheaper than the Aquasox, but the caliber of play may be a little lower given the AAA designation. The club does have a free Kids' Night Out late in the season. The catch is that you have to find the tickets. They're typically distributed through charities and local non-profit agencies including the YMCA and the Boys and Girls Club.

University of Washington
Locations vary

There are lots of venues and events where you can yell "Go Huskies," but only a few of them are free. They include mens' and womens' tennis at the Nordstrom Athletic Center, Rowing on the Montlake Cut, and indoor and outdoor track and field meets.

GROUP **BIKE** RIDES **AND** RUNS

Why let a silly thing like rain get in the way of a good time? Although some Seattle motorists seem to forget how to drive in the wet once the first rainfall of the season comes, those of fleeter foot and wheel seem to do just fine, thank you, as is evidenced by the number of groups that ride and run even in the ugly months.

The Balanced Athlete
The Landing
800 North 10th Place, Suite F
Renton
(425) 282-4556

The store has free group runs Tuesday and Thursday evenings at 6 p.m and on Sunday at 8 a.m.

Cascade Bicycle Club
7400 Sandpoint Way Northeast
(206) 522-3222
www.cascade.org

Bike riding doesn't get more organized than this. Cascade has several free bike rides a day every day of the year, all listed on the calendar on its Web site, including some that are only listed on its site. The listings include terrain, pace, ride description, and conditions under which the ride will be cancelled. Some list steady rain, others list ice and snow. Participants need to arrive at the meeting point 15 minutes before scheduled start and be ready to leave at the appointed time. They must also sign a waiver before the ride starts. If you have questions about a day's ride, contact the ride leader of the specific ride listed on the ride description.

Critical Mass
www.seattlecriticalmass.org

Locals either love or hate this controversial group. Considering that many of the members' goals include advocating biking as a healthy and fun alternative to driving, building community, and convincing more people to opt for two wheels rather than four, CM would seem to have its heart in the right place. The problem is in the execution. Its effort to assert bicyclists' right to the road through its Friday afternoon rides in Downtown Seattle has led to confrontations when the group has ended up blocking intersections during rush hour. Most rides have gone off without a hitch, however. The group meets at Westlake Center at 5:30 p.m. on the last Friday of the month.

Evergreen Tandem Club
www.evergreentandemclub.org

If you and your co-pilot have ever felt out of place at a regular group ride, the Evergreen Tandem Club has your back . . . well, both your backs, really, because it offers a ride almost every weekend for people who own bicycles built for two.

Fleet Feet Sports
911 East Pine St.
(206) 329-1466
www.fleetfeetseattle.com

Fleet Feet does three regular runs each week. On Sundays the group meets at an area trailhead at 7:30 a.m. for a moderate trail run. On Tuesdays and Thursdays, the group meets at the store at 6 p.m. for a run with a more urban flavor. The run goes for 5 to 6 miles on Tuesday and up to 6 miles on Thursday.

Niketown Running Club
Sixth and Pike
(206) 447-6453
nikerunning.com/runningclub

Runners and walkers can just do it on Tuesday at 6 p.m. The run starts at the store, is open to all levels and all paces, and goes for anywhere from 2 to 8 miles depending on participants. After the run, the store provides free refreshments including fruit and water.

Roadrunner Sports
Kent Station
444 Ramsay Way
Kent
(253) 850-6200
www.roadrunnersports.com

The Kent branch of this national company offers a run at 6 p.m. every Tuesday and Thursday. The group welcomes people of all running abilities.

Seattle Bicycle Club
www.seattlebicycleclub.org

SBC does a bike ride every week for all levels of bike rider, as long as the weather cooperates. Most of the rides are in and around Seattle. There are monthly rides to destinations further afield, however, that last up to three days and include such places as the Washington Coast, Mount Rainier, and Vancouver Island.

Veloce Velo
98 Front St. South
Issaquah
(425) 427-6383

The shop offers rides each Saturday at 8 a.m. There's a 25.4-mile bike ride along Lake Sammamish and through Marymoor Park every week and a Cyclocross ride up High School Trail from late August through December. If there's interest, the shop also offers a mountain bike ride up Grand Ridge. All rides start at the shop.

West Seattle Runners

(206) 938-2416
www.westseattlerunners.org

Running may be their main reason for getting together, but this organization that one member describes as a running group for everybody also does potlucks, biking, and other activities. The group has three runs a week. On Tuesdays they have a run at Lincoln Park at 5:30 p.m. (meeting point is the large parking lot on Fauntleroy). On Thursdays, they have a 6:30 p.m. run at Alki Beach (meeting point is the Statue of Liberty at 61st Avenue Southwest and Alki Avenue Southwest). WSR also does a weekend run along Alki on Sundays at 8:30 a.m. followed by cinnamon rolls and coffee at the Alki Bakery.

THRIFT STORES:
ONE MAN'S TRASH IS ANOTHER MAN'S FURNITURE

"My heart starts to palpitate when I see an open sign at a thrift store. Especially, an uncharted one I've never seen before."

—ELIZABETH MASON,
OWNER OF THE PAPER BAG PRINCESS

Let's face it, Seattle is a recycling kind of town. Where in some cities you'd have to drive around the night before garbage day looking for a great piece of furniture, here people just leave it out with a "Free" sign on it, hoping it will just go away. More often than not the items are garage sale rejects, but there have been some good values. Not long ago, my wife and I found ourselves actively considering a large dining room cabinet with marble counters that someone had left on the curb in front of the house they had just moved into.

We changed our minds when it started to rain, however.

Over my 22 years in Seattle, I have seen the following items left on the sidewalk by owners who are either looking for good homes for their old stuff or just want to get it out of their houses. Heck, I've even left some of this stuff myself:

Bar stools	Desks/desk chairs	Potted plants
Baskets	Diaper changing table	River rocks
Bookcases (man, they looked great)	End tables	Sofas
	File cabinets	Television
Building materials	Lamps	Tires
Chairs	Microwave oven	Wood
Computer monitors	Movie posters	Vanity (bathroom)

Of course, the better the neighborhood, the better the quality. Sure, curbside stuff is plentiful in the Central District, the University District, and Capitol Hill, but if you want a better class of castoff, you have to go to the same areas to which kids travel across town to go Trick-or-Treating during Halloween and for which garage salers make a beeline early on Saturday mornings.

That's why I like Mercer Island, Kirkland, and Madison Park.

If you can't find it on the street for free, though, I know some really great places to get stuff for free or next to nothing.

Craigslist
http://seattle.craigslist.org/bar/
http://seattle.craigslist.org/zip/

Apparently, there are some things that the ubiquitous list won't sell, but that's only because it's helping people give them away via the free and barter categories under the "for sale" section. The free section is self-explanatory. If you can pick it up and take it with you, these folks are more than happy for you to have it for absolutely nothing. Zero. Zilch. Zippo. Nada. Recent listings on the Seattle list have included a hot tub, a giant ruler used to measure a Mentos/soda geyser, a sofa and chair, as well as what one person called a "tire cover thingy for Jeep Grand Cherokee Loredo [sic]." The barter category features an equally eclectic mix with a catch. Although many of the sellers will take money, they're also just as willing to take something in trade. One seller wanted unopened software for a new camera. Another wanted to trade an SUV for an ATV quad. And, my personal favorite, the owner of high-end classical guitars said he would trade "for things that go bang."

Buffalo Exchange
www.buffaloexchange.com
4530 Northeast University Way, Seattle; (206) 545-0175
2232 Northwest Market St., Seattle; (206) 297-5920

It isn't the cheapest thrift store in town, but the clothing selection is a little more stylish than at other stores. That's especially true at the University District location where many of the clothes are purchased from students.

Cloud 9 Consignment Shop
6518 Roosevelt Way Northeast
(206) 525-4440
www.cloud9consign.org

The great news about this church-run consignment store is that they don't mess around when it comes to moving stuff out the door. If an item has been there for more than 30 days, it will be marked down 25 percent. Two weeks later, the price drops to 50 percent. It's great news for shoppers, not so great news if you're the original owner of the item.

Freecycle
www.freecycle.org

If you have something you want to get rid of and want to get listed on the site, Freecycle can be a real pain in the butt. It's not easy to use and even when you think you've figured it out, you probably haven't. Fortunately, there are people unlike us mere mortals who have the intestinal fortitude and the stick-to-itiveness to list the items they're trying to move out of their houses. Even more fortunately, it takes absolutely no know-how to go to the site and sign up for the Seattle/Mercer Island group (there are also groups for other King County cities). Before you know it, you'll find out about more freebies than you ever wanted, and others that make you scratch your head in wonderment. During a recent weekend on the Seattle group, postings included someone looking to give away slices of soy cheese and soy yogurt as well as another person who wanted to get rid of an opened package of Café Lladro Diablo Blend coffee. Of course, there were also more standard items like an office desk phone, an answering machine, and a television cabinet. And if you're not finding what you're looking for, you can always do a wanted listing.

Goodwill Outlet
1765 6th Ave. South
(206) 957-5516
www.seattlegoodwill.org/shop/stores/seattleoutlet

The bins! The bins! Considering that this is where Seattle Goodwill sends all of the merchandise that hasn't sold in any of its regular thrift stores, it's the type of place where only the serious need apply. If you've got a great eye for values that other people miss, this is the place for you. New bins filled with merchandise are rolled out frequently throughout the day and shoppers are required to stay behind the blue line until all the bins have been secured and store employees have reached a safe distance. Then, shoppers lunge for their shot at the next round of bargains. The place is also good for people on an extremely tight budget as most items are sold by the pound. Clothes and linens sell for $1.49 a pound. If you buy more than 50 pounds, the price drops to $1.09. Over 100 pounds it's 89 cents. Small electronics sell for 49 cents a pound.

Labels
7212 Greenwood Ave. North
(206) 781-1194
labelsseattle.com

Labels has been operating at the same spot for more than 30 years for a good reason: Good value. It's neat and tidy, it's relatively easy to find what you want, and it charges a third of the original price for designer clothing. It also sells maternity clothes and clothes for kids and specializes in purses. A writer friend I know is still bragging about a Kenneth Cole purse she got for under $20 in early 2009. With prices like these, it's no wonder the store has had a loyal following since the early 1980s.

Le Petit Shoppe
3432 Northeast 45th St.
(206) 525-0619

One of the most frustrating things about thrift stores and consignment shops that specialize in kids' clothes is that they look like my kids' playroom after they've been stuck inside on a rainy day. Not so, Le Petit. Everything is just so, the clothing is gently used, and the prices are surprisingly low.

Seattle Goodwill
www.seattlegoodwill.org
Ballard, 6400 8th Ave. Northwest, Seattle; (206) 957-5544
Bellevue, 14515 Northeast 20th St., Bellevue; (425) 649-2080
Burien, 1031 Southwest 128th St., Burien; (206) 957-1020
Seattle, 1400 South Lane St., Seattle; (206) 860-5711
Shoreline, 14500 15th Ave. Northeast, Shoreline; (206) 631-8454
Southcenter, 1174 Andover Park West, Tukwila; (206) 575-4944

Although I've listed most of the area Goodwill shops, a few are worth special mention. Perhaps it may be because of its Eastside location, but the Bellevue Goodwill has a reputation for having a better class of merchandise at unbelievably good prices. The Seattle store is known for its Glitter Gala (an off-site fundraiser) and its Glitter Sale in mid-November when it sells jewelry, formal wear, and high-end accessories. Although I'm not fashion savvy enough to buy clothes at thrift shops, a friend who is assures me that the Ballard Goodwill has a good selection of stylish clothes. "People in Ballard know how to dress," she assured me. Ballard. Who knew?

Value Village
www.valuevillage.com
Capitol Hill, 1525 11th Ave., Seattle; (206) 322-7789
Crown Hill, 8532 15th Ave. Northwest, Seattle; (206) 783-4648
Lake City, 12548 Lake City Way Northeast, Seattle; (206) 365-8232
Burien, 131 Southwest 157th St., Burien; (206) 246-6237
Totem Lake, 12515 116th Ave. Northeast, Kirkland; (425) 821-7186
Redmond, 16771 Redmond Way, Redmond; (425) 883-2049

The idea of a chain of thrift stores doesn't seem right, somehow, but Value Village seems to have just about everything you'd need in its huge stores— you just have to be willing to do a bit of work to find what you want. And isn't that what being a cheap bastard is all about? The best time to get great bargains is on holidays like Labor Day and Memorial Day when the store is open and everything's on sale. If you drop off your castoffs on the day you shop you can save even more because the store gives you a coupon for a percentage off your next purchase.

Not Exactly a Thrift Store, but . . .

Yes, I know the semi-annual Friends of the [Seattle Public] Library Book Sale isn't exactly a thrift store, but the prices are worthy of a thrift shop. CDs, DVDs, and books all sell for $1 each and the selection is large enough to take up an entire airplane hangar at the former Sandpoint Naval Air Station. The mid-April and mid-September sales are so popular that people start lining up outside the building around 5 a.m., at least four hours before the sale starts, sometimes earlier, no matter what the weather. The bargains are so good that even used bookstore owners stake out a place in line. Want to beat the crowds? Members of Friends of the Library can attend the preview sale on Friday night and buy up to 25 books, but only if they've paid their $15 annual dues before the sale (membership the day of the sale goes up to $30). Even then you can't avoid the lines, though, because people start lining up long before the doors open.

There are still two other ways to save even more on books at the sale. Volunteers may not be able to buy books in advance, but they can scope them out and, if they're sneaky enough, hide them away until the time when they're ready to exchange their hours for books. People who don't have the time to volunteer can always save by putting off their shopping until Sunday when everything is half price. The selection will have been fairly well picked over by then but there will still be plenty of hidden treasures.

BUILDING **SUPPLIES**

Habitat for Humanity Home Improvement Outlet
21 South Nevada St.
(206) 957-6914
www.seattlehabitatoutlet.org

Like the ReStore, the Habitat outlet also sells used building materials at a discount, but it also has a great deal of new merchandise. That's because local contractors often donate appliances and other materials purchased for projects that ended up not being used. The store also sells a small selection of furniture and other odds and ends. All of the proceeds go to Habitat for Humanity, which uses the money to build houses for needy families.

The ReStore
1440 Northwest 52nd St.
(206) 297-9119
www.re-store.org

If you can't find the building supplies you need on the street, the ReStore is the next best thing. The store sells salvage building materials, plus a whole lot more. The store accepts drop-offs of old building materials from contractors and everyday do-it-yourselfers and even has a field crew that will go out to a demolition site and collect usable used materials, then turns around and sells it for up to half the original price. That not only means cheap molding and doors, but also inexpensive antique lighting, door pulls, tubs, and a lot of stuff you never even considered. If you bring in a donation you'll get a store credit for 25 percent of the resale value of the item you donated. So, if the ReStore believes it can resell your item for $50, you'll get $12.50 off your next purchase.

Second Use Building Materials
7953 2nd Ave. S
(206) 763-6929
www.seconduse.com

Like the ReStore, Second Use salvages and sells old building materials for substantially less than new, allowing contractors and DIYers to save money while keeping perfectly useable supplies out of the dump. The biggest difference between that other salvage store and Second Use is its location. While ReStore is in easy-to-get-to Ballard, Second Use is in the out-of-the-way South Park neighborhood.

FURNITURE

Goodwill and Value Village, are great places to get ridiculously cheap furnishings, but when you reach a point where you want to go to the next level, you may want to consider this place:

Armadillo Consignment
12421 Greenwood Ave. North
(206) 363-6700
www.armadilloconsignment.com

When I talk to people about inexpensive furniture, Armadillo comes up again and again. On its Web site, its owner takes great pains to explain it's not a thrift store, it's a consignment shop where people bring their goods to be sold hoping to get some money back. What makes the store stand out is its discount pricing policy. Since the store prefers to keep items no longer than 60 days, it cuts prices three times to keep things moving along. At 30 days, the discount is 15 percent. After 45 days it drops 25 percent and at 60 days it's 50 percent off, which can make for a great bargain. Even the price tags in the store show the discount with each tag listing the current price as well as the what the price will be lowered to if the item is still on hand and the date each markdown will occur. While it's a great policy, it's also important for thrift and consignment shoppers to have what my wife calls a "Moscow mentality." If you see it, like it, and can't live without it, don't wait. Otherwise, it could be gone. If it's something you're not sure about and you think is just a little too expensive, you can take the chance, but there's no guarantee it will be there when you come back.

SPORTING **GOODS**

Play it Again Sports
19513 Highway 99, Lynnwood; (425) 670-1184
17622 108th Ave. Southeast, Renton; (425) 227-8777
1304 Stewart St., Seattle; (206) 264-9255
13210 Northeast 175th St., Woodinville; (425) 481-8676

Although there never seems to be any shortage of golf clubs or baseball mitts stacked amongst the stuff people pile curbside, they're mighty hard to come by when you decide you want to take up golf or want to join a softball team on the spur of the moment. Some would call this a used sporting goods store. Me, I call it an equipment thrift shop. While all of the shops carry the standard mix of golf clubs and baseball bats, each store seems to have its own specialty. Seattle's focus has been on skis, bikes, and boards. Renton has weight and fitness equipment. Lynnwood features hockey equipment.

WALKING TOURS:
A CENTS OF PLACE

"Anywhere is walking distance, if you've got the time."

—STEPHEN WRIGHT

The Ballard Locks. The *Seattle Times*. Benaroya Hall. The Washington Park Arboretum. These local institutions have been part of our lives for so long that we feel we know them like the backs of our hands. We take all our out-of-town guests to see the fish ladder and watch boats go from Puget Sound to the Ship Canal and back again. We read the *Times* every day. Whenever we want a dose of high culture, the home of the Seattle Symphony is one of our favorite go-to places. And when we want to go out for a nice walk on a pretty day, the Arboretum is the natural choice. But can you name most of the flowers you see during your walk? Did you know there are organ concerts at Benaroya? Were you aware that the *Seattle Times* isn't printed in Seattle? And do you know how the locks work or why they're even necessary? Many of the free tours available in the Seattle area not only help out-of-towners learn more about the local culture, they also help locals understand many of the things they take for granted.

GOVERNMENT **BUILDINGS** AND **OTHER** FACILITIES

Alki Point Lighthouse
3201 Alki Ave. Southwest
(206) 841-3519

It's now automated and the grounds aren't open to the public, but it's still possible to tour the Alki Point Lighthouse tower from the first weekend in June to the last weekend in August. Tours run every 20 minutes or so from 1 to 4 p.m. on Saturdays and Sundays. The tours meet at the parking lot at the gate. Access is limited because the two homes on the site currently house senior Coast Guard officers.

Hiram M. Chittenden Locks Visitors Center
3015 Northwest 54th St.
(206) 783-7059
www.nws.usace.army.mil/publicmenu/menu.cfm?sitename=lwsc&pagename
=mainpage

While it's always fun to take your children or out-of-town visitors to the Ballard Locks and the fish ladder, it always leaves so many questions. How were the locks built? Why are they necessary? And how do you train a fish to use a ladder, anyway? When those questions finally get the better of you, you can always take this hour-long, ranger-led tour that covers the history of the locks and how they work and answers all the questions you've always had, but only your children were brave enough to ask. Tours start at 1 p.m. and 3 p.m. daily, March to April and in October. An 11 a.m. tour is also available May 1 through September. No tours December through February.

Klondike Goldrush National Park
319 2nd Ave. South
(206) 220-4240
www.nps.gov/klse/index.htm

When most people think about national parks, the gritty urban neighborhood of Pioneer Square probably isn't the first place that comes to mind. Unless you count pigeons squirrels and late-night bar patrons, there's not a lot of wildlife, few trees, and no open space. Yet, somehow, there's still a guided tour given by a national park ranger. The tour leaves at 2 p.m. daily June 15 through Labor Day and not only covers the historic district's role in the rush for gold in the Klondike, but also discusses the area's architecture. If you get stuck in traffic or can't find parking and just miss the tour, you may be able to whip out your cell phone and get a recorded version of the tour. Although it was not available at press time, the park expected to add the service and the ability to download the tour to your MP3 player from its Web site in 2010.

Seattle Public Library
1000 Fourth Ave.
(206) 386-4636
www.spl.org

Just the thought of a tour of a public library is enough to make the eyes roll into your head from boredom, but the Seattle Central Library isn't your average library. Dutch architect Rem Koolhaas designed the now-six year-old building with a variety of cool architectural features including a reference library section called the Mixing Chamber and the Book Spiral, which is essentially a gently sloping spiral ramp that takes people through the book stacks, following the Dewey Decimal System from bottom to top. Don't take my word for it, though. The best way to see all the Koolhaas cool is to take one of the regularly scheduled tours. The times of the tour can vary, so it's best to call or check the Web site before your visit, but the library offers a general tour, which serves as an introduction to how the institution works, and an architectural tour. All tours start at the Welcome Desk on Level 3.

FACTORY **TOURS**

Boehm's Candies
255 Northeast Gilman Blvd.
Issaquah
(425) 392-6652
www.boehmscandies.com

At this candy factory and retail store in a chalet you not only get your choice of a variety of confections including truffles, peanut brittle, and seasonal sweets, you also get to choose your tour experience. You can take a self-guided window walking tour of the factory where you can watch workers produce pounds and pounds of the company's products or you can take a guided tour where you get up close and personal. The windows on the self-guided tour give a glimpse of the kitchen, the hand dipping area, and the factory where clusters are made. The guided walking tour costs $4, but if you want fresh samples, it's worth it. The factory typically runs until 3:30 p.m. You can't stop in and do a guided tour at the last minute, though. You need to have a confirmed reservation before you go.

Seattle Times Printing Plant
North Creek Facility
19200 120th Ave. Northeast
Bothell
(425) 489-7015
www.seattletimes.com

Did you ever wonder how a newspaper comes together, but were afraid to ask? I'm not talking about how the stories get in there. Heck, you can see old episodes of *Lou Grant* to figure that out, but if you've ever wondered how a paper was actually printed and put together, this is the tour for you. You can see the process from the beginning when robots move the rolls of newsprint onto the presses through to the moment when it's loaded on the trucks. The tour is free, but is only available on Thursday afternoons because that's the day the *Times* prints the non-news sections of the Sunday paper. There's room for up to 35 people on a tour. You don't have to be part of a group to take the tour, but you do have to call Kate Palmer to make reservations. Children under the age of eight are not allowed.

BUILDING **TOURS**

Benaroya Hall
200 University
(206) 215-4800
www.seattlesymphony.org

No matter how hard I try, whenever my wife and I go to the Seattle Symphony we get there so late that we barely have time to find our seats much less really get to enjoy the place. Which is why a tour of the hall sounds like such a great idea. Now, all we have to do is find some free time at noon or 1 p.m. on Tuesday or Friday when the tours begin. I have it on good authority that the best time to go on the 45-minute tour is on Tuesday at noon because the symphony holds rehearsals on Tuesday at 12:30 and if your tour group is small enough you'll be able to catch 10 minutes of the practice. The tour meets at Benaroya's Grand Lobby Entrance at the corner of Third Avenue and University Street.

5th Avenue Theatre
1308 5th Ave.
(206) 625-1900
www.5thavenue.org

This grand 1926 movie house, which was saved from a wrecking ball in the 1970s, has a range of impressive Chinoise-style architectural features that you might miss when you're focused on the show on stage. That's why the beautifully restored theater offers a 20-minute tour of the building at noon on Monday. The tour is quite popular with silent movie fans. It's best to register in advance so the 5th Avenue can contact you if a tour is cancelled.

Moore Theatre
1932 2nd Ave.
www.stgpresents.org
(206) 682-6414

Benaroya may be one of the area's newest venues with tours and the 5th Avenue may go back to the days of Vaudeville, but the Moore is one of Seattle's oldest theaters and well worth a behind-the-scenes look. Tours are on the second Saturday of the month, start at 10 a.m. at the theater's main entrance, and last 90 minutes.

Paramount Theatre
911 Pine St.
www.stgpresents.org

Originally called the Seattle, the Paramount was a movie palace built by the movie studio of the same name in 1928. Although it fell on hard times and was eventually reduced to showing second run films, a $20 million restoration in 1995 returned it to its original glory. Theater buffs can take tours of the movie house where Frances Farmer and Bruce Lee once ushered (but not at the same time) on the first Saturday of the month at 10 a.m. Tours meet at the Paramount's main entrance and last about 90 minutes.

NATURE **TOURS**

Mercer Slough Nature Park
1625 118th Ave. Southeast
Bellevue
(425) 452-6885
www.bellevuewa.gov/mseec.htm

Mercer Slough is an oasis within the city of Bellevue. The 320-acre park near downtown is the longest standing preserved open space in the area and is on a major migratory path for birds. As a result, the park is often filled with wildlife, whether it be blue heron, green heron, or beaver and river otters, just to name a few. Every Saturday afternoon at 2 p.m., Mercer Slough offers a guided ranger walk that starts at the environmental education center and continues into the park where visitors learn about the freshwater wetland ecosystem. The park also offers other free programs including a family ranger program that focuses on different nature themes (including camouflage and great migrations) on the first Sunday of the month at 2:30 p.m. It also has a Friday Family Movie Night on the last Friday of the month.

Seward Park Environmental and Audubon Center
5902 Lake Washington Blvd. South
(206) 652-2444
sewardpark.audubon.org

Learn the natural history of the park and all the things that grow there during this 90-minute walk in the park. Along the way, you'll find out stuff you never even considered when it comes to salamanders, salmon, and the area's many other inhabitants. Third Saturday of the month. Toddler to age 4 free, youth to age 14 $2 and adults $4.

Third Saturday Free Walks in Southeast Seattle
Locations vary
(206) 684-7434

As the name suggests, on the third Saturday of every month, Camp Long leads guided tours of area parks and green spaces from 2 to 4 p.m. for people aged one and up. Each walk typically focuses on a particular theme, but all of them are in Seattle parks and are designed to get people up and walking. In early 2010, the areas visited included the old growth forest in Schmitz Park, a greenbelt in Jose Rizal Park, and an unusual park called Deadhorse Canyon. All of the walks are free. (In early 2010, the park planned to have the non-profit walking advocacy organization Feet First conduct the tours with a suggested donation of $5.) Camp Long, which sponsors the walks, also offers a monthly nature walk for two- to three-year-olds with a parent on Tuesday mornings. Carkeek Park has a similar program with themed walks every Thursday from 10 to 11:15 a.m. Discovery Park's themed Tot Treks are on the first and third Wednesday and second and fourth Saturday of the month from 10:30 to 11:45 a.m. The tot nature walks aren't free, however. The cost for all of the walks (except the Third Saturday Walk) is $7 for a parent and child and $3.50 for each additional person.

Third Saturday Walks in Southwest Seattle
Locations vary
(206) 684-7434

Apparently, the same folks who bring you the walks in Southeast Seattle must have to double-time it across town because they offer these walks from 11 a.m. to 1 p.m. In early 2010 tour destinations included Fauntleroy Park, Puget Park, and Me-Kwa-Mooks Park.

Washington Park Arboretum
Graham Visitors Center
2300 Arboretum Dr. East
(206) 543-8800
depts.washington.edu/uwbg/visit/tours.shtml

The arboretum is a great place, but there are times when I feel like I can't tell the players without a program. That's why the free Sunday tours of the park are such a great resource. There are two docent-led tours every week. The first 90-minute weekend walk starts at 11 a.m. and usually focuses on the Pacific Connections Garden, a new 12-acre garden featuring plants from the Northwest and four other Pacific Rim countries. The second goes from 1 to 2:30 p.m. and focuses on whatever strikes the fancy of the garden guide on that day. You can also download park tours to your MP3 player and go whenever you want.

GALLERY WALKS:
FREE-FORM FETES

"Artists ought to walk a mile in someone else's pants. That way you're a mile away and you have their pants."

—JOSEPH P. BLODGETT

In the beginning, there was the first Thursday of the month in Seattle, and it was good because it was the night before Friday. And then an artist or organizer or someone looking to make a buck came up with the idea of turning it into a night to go from art gallery to art gallery in Pioneer Square devouring art with our eyes and maybe having some free wine and cheese along the way. And it was very good. And then it came to pass that some enterprising soul decided to expand it to other parts of downtown and to museums, restaurants, and other non-arts-related businesses and it was even better. Soon one art walk begat another and another and another and before we knew it, it seemed like there was a different gallery walk in a different part of the city almost every night of the month. And it was very, very good.

Here's a quick look at one of the best ways to enjoy high culture at no cost in neighborhoods throughout the city all while going out for a walk to get a little exercise.

GALLERY **WALKS**

Art Up Greenwood-Phinney
Second Friday
From Greenwood Avenue North and 87th Street south to Phinney Avenue and 65th Street

This fledgling effort boasts a mix of art exhibitions, live music, and restaurants and businesses either displaying artists' work or offering special Art Up discounts. About half of the venues are art galleries in their own right. The event runs from 6 to 9 p.m.

Ballard Art Walk
Second Saturday
Corner of Northwest Market Street and Ballard Avenue Northwest
(206) 784-9705
www.ballardchamber.com

The first thing you'll notice about many of the galleries participating in this art walk is that they aren't galleries at all. Instead, the ever-changing cast of characters includes restaurants, boutiques, salons, a wine shop, and, yes, even a couple of galleries. It is possible to walk the entire route between 6 and 9 p.m., but it's a bit of a hike from the heart of the event to the east Ballard participants. Fortunately, there are a few bars and even a grocery store along the way to fortify you for the trip. Print out a map of the month's route at the Ballard Chamber Web site before you go.

Belltown Art Walk and More
Third Thursday
www.belltownartwalk.com

This art event changed dates from Friday to Thursday when the organizers realized that the area known for its nightlife really didn't need any help to attract people on the weekends. In addition to the standard mix of art gallery exhibition openings, the event also features street musicians and two-for-one specials at participating restaurants and bars. The event goes from 6 p.m. until closing.

Capitol Hill Art Walk
Second Thursday
www.blitzcapitolhill.com

Capitol Hill has always been a bit edgy, so there should be no surprise that one of the 50 art venues participating in its monthly art extravaganza is Babeland, an adult sex shop, but you don't have to go there if you don't want to. The rest of the event is similar to most other art walks if not a little bit racier. It runs from 5 to 8 p.m. and also features live music as well as a literary component. For a complete list of venues and a map, go to Blitz's Web site.

Edmonds Third Thursday Art Walk
Edmonds
(425) 776-3778
www.edmondswa.com/events/third-thursday-art-walk.html

With more than 40 businesses participating in this monthly event north of Seattle, Edmonds claims it is one of the biggest art walks in the state. While I can't speak to that issue, there are several reasons to venture north for this art event including live music as well as live artist demonstrations. And did we mention the free food? There's a wine tasting at Arista, a cheese tasting at Resident Cheesemonger, and during the summer one of the banks has been known to bring in some barbecue. The event runs year round from 5 to 8 p.m. Get maps at www.edmondswa.com.

First Thursday

Pioneer Square and throughout Downtown Seattle
www.firstthursdayseattle.com

When it comes to holding a big art event, the organizers of one of the country's first gallery walks don't mess around. It runs from noon to 8 p.m.—which allows plenty of time to cover the distance between Pioneer Square and the Seattle Art Museum—involves 80 venues, includes street musicians and art in the park, and even prompts museums as far away as the Experience Music Project at the Seattle Center to offer free admission. The event itself is in its late 40s, but it's still going strong and doesn't look a day over 39.

Fremont First Friday Art Walk

fremontfirstfriday.blogspot.com

The one-time artsy bohemian area that calls itself the Center of the Universe may have gone so upscale that the artists who made its reputation can no longer afford to live there, but its penchant for the odd lives on. This walk goes on from 6 to 9 p.m. and takes place under the watchful eyes of a Ukrainian statue of Vladimir Lenin and a sculpture of a Volkswagen-Beetle-eating troll. In early 2010, there were 13 participants and the boundaries of the art walk went from 34th Street below Highway 99 north to 36th Street and continued west along 35th and 36th Streets to Leary Way and 1st Avenue.

Georgetown Second Saturday Art Attack

www.georgetownartattack.com

I love industrial art districts because they're filled with surprises. Once the original businesses that inhabit many of the warehouses have moved out, shut down, or gone belly up, artists often move in and change the way we see everything. And then they become victims of their own success by making an area so desirable that they can no longer afford it. Such is the case with Georgetown, the new arts frontier. This monthly event is part art show, part extended public relations effort to make the public aware of the community in order to save it from gentrification. While it has a mix of art, Art Attack could well be the only art walk in the city with a comic shop as a participant. And yes, it does comic art.

Second Thursdays on Park Lane
Downtown Kirkland
(425) 893-8766

Artsy little Park Lane in downtown Kirkland closes to traffic from 6 to 9 p.m. and its three art galleries, a number of boutiques, and restaurants get in on the act, displaying the work of local artists. There will also be live jazz music and a chalk art competition. The event runs May through October.

Wallingford Art Walk
First Wednesday
(206) 547-5177
www.wallingfordartwalk.org

Now in its fourth year, Wallingford's event is the only art walk to address the walkability issue by providing a free shuttle tour. Provided courtesy of the Wallingford Community Senior Center, the bus leaves at 6:45 and provides a 90-minute tour with stops at several participating businesses. The event also features live music, artist demonstrations, a youth art contest, a raffle, restaurant discounts, and . . . rickshaws. The walk goes from 6 to 9 p.m. In early 2010, the event expanded to a year-round schedule.

West Seattle Art Walk
Second Thursday
westseattleartwalk.blogspot.com

In the old days of cartoons, the character who had survived a fall off a cliff would say, "That first step is a doozy." In the case of the West Seattle Art Walk, it's the last stop that's the killer because participating business Gail Ann Photography is nowhere near the junction of California Avenue and Alaskan Way. In fact, it's about 3 miles away. Many of the businesses in this event feature the works of their talented employees. The event goes from 6 to 9 p.m. with many of the venues centered in the Junction, a shopping district with a friendly neighborhood feel. The best time to go is when the event coincides with the area's annual art festival in July because the street is closed to traffic and there's more room to spread out. Participating businesses include a coffeehouse and an insurance office.

GETTING AROUND SEATTLE: FREE RIDES AND FREEWAYS

"Why do they call it rush hour when nothing moves?"

—ROBIN WILLIAMS FROM *MORK AND MINDY*

It seems like traffic in downtown Seattle is always a mess no matter what the reason. If it's not a baseball game at Safeco Field, a football game at Qwest Field, or a concert at the Seattle Center, there seems to be some other inexplicably odd occurrence that messes up the traffic pattern. We've had a truck driver lose control of his vehicle and take out a historic landmark, Critical Mass rides blocking intersections during Friday afternoon rush hours, and even a World Trade Organization meeting-turned-weeklong-riot. And that doesn't even include the random construction projects the city throws up without warning just to keep us on our toes.

And things may be about to get a whole lot worse before they get better. Should city officials ever decide how they're going to replace the earthquake-damaged Alaskan Way Viaduct—tunnel or raised road—the resulting construction project will alter the traffic pattern for years to come.

While this isn't justification for avoiding downtown all together, it is reason enough to start rethinking your options when you have to head into the heart of parkinglessness. Suddenly, transit is starting to look good again. While many of the options aren't necessarily free, most of them are a heck of a lot cheaper than paying the ever-increasing cost of parking. And that doesn't even include the wear and tear on your jangled nerves. Or your car. Thanks to rush hour express buses and Metro transit tunnels that allow Metro vehicles to avoid some of downtown's busiest streets, there are times when busing it really is the fastest option. Either that, or finding a carpool so you can use the High Occupancy Vehicle (HOV) lanes on local highways.

So, sit back, relax, enjoy the ride, and maybe even bring a book while you take advantage of one of these options.

Craigslist
Craigslist.com

Although it's really a more practical option for people who are looking for longer rides, say to San Francisco or Portland, a few intrepid, carless souls do advertise here to carpool from Bellevue to Seattle or wherever their work life happens to take them. The ads are free, but you should offer to kick in a few dollars for gas. Even splitting fuel cost is still cheaper than paying full freight for parking. Remember, you are doing this at your own risk, though, so play it safe. If it doesn't feel right, look for another ride.

Erideshare.com

Where Craigslist's rideshare category seems to lean more toward long distance trips than carpooling and commuting, this site tries to do both by matching those requesting rides with car owners offering same. Potential passengers and drivers alike join the site, then list their neighborhood or city, desired destination, when they need to go, and whether they are offering a ride, seeking one, or want to take turns. The information posts to a table listing what everyone is looking for in hopes that they will find a match. Although the public can see the table, you have to be a member to respond and the only way to contact a member is through the site, so there is some identity protection built in.

King County Water Taxi
Pier 50, Seattle
Seacrest Dock, 1660 Harbor Ave. Southwest, West Seattle
www.kingcounty.gov/watertaxi

The small ferry that runs across Elliott Bay from Downtown Seattle to West Seattle isn't exactly free, but what it can end up saving you in time and money make it as good as free . . . as long as you bus downtown. To begin with, there's only one key route to West Seattle and all it takes is a minor accident to cause a major backup. Then, there's the issue of parking. If you plan on visiting Alki Beach you could easily spend a great deal of time looking for a place to put your car and there isn't much free parking. And besides, given the one-way $3.50 fare (round trip is $7) during the route's April to September run, it's a great cheap way to get out on the water on a sunny day and get to where you're going quickly. The water taxi also operates two free shuttle buses that take people to the area's most popular spots including the Admiral District and the Junction.

There's an interesting reverse catch when it comes to fares for the water taxi. If you have an ORCA card or other regional transit pass, your fare goes down to $3 each way. If the value of your pass exceeds $3 (which it would if you rode Light Link Rail from Downtown for over $4, for example), you won't have to pay to board the water taxi. The water taxi also operates a run from Seattle to Vashon Island, but it's mostly a commuter route and only travels during rush hour.

Metro

(206) 553-3000

metro.kingcounty.gov

The Catch: Light rail and Metro routes 116, 118, and 119 are not part of the Downtown Ride Free Area.

Believe it or not, it is possible to ride King County's transit system for free. Yes, you read that right. Free. As long as you're in the Downtown Seattle Ride Free Area, which stretches from South Jackson Street north to Battery Street and east from the waterfront to 6th Avenue, between 6 a.m. and 7 p.m. All you have to do is hop a bus and ride it as far as you need. Of course, it helps to know if the bus is headed to your destination. If you don't know the route, it's best to ask because some routes zig zag or go in directions that don't make any sense. If you've boarded in the area, but stay on past the boundary, you'll pay as you leave the bus. There are a few exceptions, however. Metro routes 116, 118, and 119 and Sound Transit's Link Light Rail don't participate in the ride free area.

Metro operates on a two-zone system. All destinations within Seattle city limits are one zone while those outside the city are in a second. It further divides fares into peak hours from 6 to 9 a.m. and 3 to 6 p.m. on weekdays and off-peak hours. A one-zone peak hour fare for adults age 19 to 64 is $2.25, a two-zone fare is $2.75. Off-peak is $2 for one or two zones. Students and seniors pay 75 cents regardless of time or zone. (Keep in mind that the rates were current at press time, but are subject to change.)

There are a few ways you can save additional money. A one-month ORCA Pass for peak hours costs $99; off-peak costs $72 while youth and seniors pay only $27. The passes can also be used for Community Transit, Everett Transit, Kitsap Transit, and Sound Transit Service, which would allow you to go all the way from Tacoma in the south to Everett in the North, West to Poulsbo and east to the tiny town of Carnation. That's quite a lot of territory for not a lot of money.

One last way to get a free trip out of Metro is to travel with children 5 and under during the week or kids 18 and under on weekends and holidays. Under those conditions, up to four children can ride free with a paying adult.

More Than Just Buses

When most people think of Metro, they just think about buses. The agency also offers other transportation services as well.

Carpool creator. Using the Web site www.rideshareonline.com, Metro helps people looking for rideshares and carpools to hook up and find a more economical, environmentally friendly way to their destination, whether it be the office, the big game, or the kids' school. Yes, you saw that right, Metro/Rideshare's Schoolpool can even help you find a carpool for your kids. Heck, if there's enough interest and enough people wanting to go your way, you might even be able to start a vanpool. There are even vanshares if you just need to carpool on one leg of your commute—between the ferry dock and train station, for example.

Biking Buddy Finder. What's that you say, Bunky? You'd be more likely to bike to work if you had someone to bike with? Metro can help you find that, too.

Slugging facilitator. No, I'm not talking about a new baseball position or boxing coach. Instead, I'm referring to a practice now popular on the east coast that allows car drivers to find riders at the last minute so they can drive in the HOV lanes. It's like going to the Home Depot to find a day laborer except that it has involved going to a Park-and-Ride lot and picking up additional passengers on an informal basis. Now, Metro has formalized the practice with dynamic ride matching, only you won't have to wait out in the cold. Now you can do it via cell phone.

Airport Shuttle Service. Making the dreaded phone call to a friend to ask for a ride to the airport could become a thing of the past if you travel light enough. Instead of spending $50 on a town car or around $25 on a shuttle, depending on where you live, you could pay as little as $2.75 each way to ride a bus or as little as $2 on a Sounder train.

Sound Transit

(206) 398-5000
www.soundtransit.org

After years of votes, battling, and building, the region finally managed to make light rail service a reality in 2009, making it possible to go from Tacoma in the south all the way up to Everett via the Sounder Train. Fares are based on distance and start at $2.55 but go up 5.5 cents a mile. As a result, an adult trip from Tacoma to Seattle is $4.75, youth pay $3.50, and seniors pay $2.25. It also costs $4.50 to go from Everett to Seattle. The best way to save money is to buy a monthly pass for $171. Again, it may sound expensive, but do the math including wear and tear on your car, gas, and parking, and the savings add up quickly.

Washington State Ferries

Colman Ferry Dock
801 Alaskan Way
(206) 464-6400
www.wsdot.wa.gov/ferries

Why spend $17 on an hour-long cruise around the harbor to see Elliott Bay when you could spend $6.25 for ferry rides back and forth across Puget Sound to Bainbridge Island? You won't get the narration about what you're seeing as you pass by, but you won't have to listen to the jokes that the tour guide thinks are funny, either. On the flip side, you'll get to see the city skyline coming and going and you'll even get a nice day trip to a small, walkable town on the other end for almost nothing. If you just want a cheap, roundtrip ferry ride, you can save even more by hopping the Vashon Ferry in West Seattle. Without a car it's $4.45 per person.

GETTING **OUT** OF **TOWN**

Ridepenguin
www.ridepenguin.com

There may never be such a thing as free taxi service, but Ridepenguin helps take the bite out of getting to the airport by helping you line up additional paying riders to hitch along or by helping you find a cab ride to hook up with. The service is available for trips to and from Seattle-Tacoma International Airport and can be coordinated using a computer or cell phone. Apparently, there is an app for that.

Ridester
www.ridester.com

If you want to put a lot of distance between Seattle and yourself for not a lot of money, this is a good place to start. It's a site where people planning trips longer than 20 miles can look for riders and riders can look for drivers. There's no charge to register with the site and the only fee a rider has to pay is a $2 service charge plus the amount the driver requests for the trip, which usually covers gas costs. Recent listings featured an odd mix of rates. A driver looking for riders from Johnson City, Tennessee, to Mercer Island, for example, was asking only $1 while a driver from Seattle to Brattleboro, Vermont, wanted $200. Riders pay Ridester and the money is forwarded to the driver. Ridester charges drivers a 9.5 percent processing fee based on the asking price for the ride. Maybe that's why Mr. Tennessee only wanted to charge $1. The service is available in cities all over the country.

GARDENS AND GARDENING:
FREE RANGE

"A perfect summer day is when the sun is shining, the breeze is blowing, the birds are singing, and the lawn mower is broken."

—JAMES DENT

One of the main reasons we are so willing to put up with winter's grey, rainy days is that we know what they lead to: beautiful blooms in the spring and summer. Seattle has been named the Emerald City for a reason, and this is it. The area is so green and sunny and the temperatures so pleasant that more than a few visitors have been fooled into moving here because they think it's this beautiful all year. It's not. Summer quickly gives way to fall and fall quickly fades into winter and the dark months. That's why we all rush up north to see the first tulips in bloom in April and scramble to area gardens to see as many flowers as we can as quickly as possible because we know they won't be around long. The displays at many public gardens are so impressive that we just can't help but be inspired to start a garden of our own, even if we don't have the foggiest idea of what we're doing. Fortunately, there's plenty of support for people like us, much of it is free, and none of it requires us to stand in a room and say, "My name is David . . . and I'm a plant-aholic."

GARDENS

Bellevue Botanical Gardens
12001 Main St.
Bellevue
(425) 452-2750
www.bellevuebotanical.org

Just because Eastsiders have a reputation for shopping doesn't mean they don't appreciate a good garden. And this one is a good one. Not only is it known for its annual holiday display, Garden d'lights, when its collection is festooned with lights, but it also includes a Waterwise Garden where water conservation is emphasized, an Alpine Rock Garden, and a 19-acre Botanical Reserve. It also offers free Living Laboratory classes for children from kindergarten to fourth grade level in spring and early summer.

Carl S. English Botanical Garden

3015 Northwest 54th St.

(206) 783-7059

www.nws.usace.army.mil/publicmenu/menu.cfm?sitename=lwsc&pagename
=mainpage

How many times can you possibly go to the Ballard Locks and the fish ladder and not stop and smell the roses? For me, it took 10 visits before I finally succumbed to its charms. Before horticulturist Carl English laid his hands on it, the seven-acre plot was a graveled extension of the construction site left after the completion of the locks. Over 43 years on the job, English remade it into a garden in English landscape style. By the time he finished, the garden featured 500 plant species and 1,500 varieties from all over the world. Despite all the effort, most Seattleites are so focused on taking visiting friends and family to see ladder-scaling salmon and boats rising and falling that they barely notice it.

The Center for Urban Horticulture

3502 Northeast 41st St.

(206) 543-8616

www.uwbotanicgardens.org

The center and the Washington Park Arboretum are the two individual parks that make up the gardens that comprise the University of Washington Botanical Gardens. The center focuses on issues surrounding the use and growth of plants in cities including pollution and unusual natural conditions flora face in an urban environment. It's more than just a dry academic setting, though. The center itself is the first "green" building on the UW campus and includes the Soest Herbacious Display Garden, the Otis Douglas Hyde Herbarium, and the Seattle Garden Club Fragrance Garden, all of which are open to the public. It's also home to the 74-acre Union Bay Natural Area, a public wildlife area that not only has 4 miles of shoreline, but is also believed to be the city's best place for bird watching. Numerous environmental and garden groups meet here as well and it's home to the King County Master Gardener Foundation.

Kubota Garden

9817 55th Ave. South (Rainier Avenue South and 55th Avenue South)

(206) 684-4584

www.kubotagarden.org

It's not exactly accurate to call Kubota a formal Japanese garden because it combines Japanese technique with Northwest plants. And there's also its hands-on policy that allows visitors to touch the plants and structures in this 20-acre city park that was originally the headquarters of a well-loved, family-owned local gardening company. Kubota is such a local institution that residents moved to have the garden declared a historic landmark and pushed to have the city purchase it when there was talk of building a condominium on the site. The park is filled with streams, waterfalls, bridges, and a wide range of mature plants and makes for a nice retreat.

Olympic Sculpture Park
2901 Western Ave.
(206) 654-3100
www.seattleartmuseum.org/visit/osp

There's more than grass and plants sprouting from this bluff overlooking Elliott Bay. As the name would suggest, there are plenty of sculptures, too. The nine-acre park features more than a dozen larger-than-life artworks ranging from the park's iconic painted steel Eagle by Alexander Calder to Typewriter Eraser, Scale X by Claes Oldenburg set along a Z-shaped path that runs from glass and steel Paccar Pavilion housing a lobby and a greenhouse down to the waterfront along Elliott Bay. Along the way there are four distinct landscapes with sculptures to match. Despite admission being free and all of the large-scale sculptures being out in the open, the Seattle Art Museum, which runs the park, has a strict policy prohibiting visitors from touching the artworks. The park is open every day from 30 minutes after sunrise to 30 minutes after sunset. The Paccar Pavilion is open 10 a.m. to 4 p.m. Tuesday through Sunday in winter and early spring and from 10 a.m. to 5 p.m. from May 1 to Labor Day.

South Seattle Community College Arboretum
6000 16th Ave. Southwest
(206) 764-5300
www.southseattleinternational.net/arboretum/index.html

No, not that arboretum. Although many Seattleites have at least driven through the Washington Park Arboretum, few even know this West Seattle one exists. Situated next to the Chinese Garden, the six-acre campus park was designed by students in the school's Landscape Horticulture Program and essentially serves as a living classroom where they can learn about plant

Horticultural Tourism

There was a time when garden shops and nurseries weren't considered tourist attractions. Instead, they were just places you went to buy seeds and plants and the odd bit of specialized equipment that you couldn't find in your local hardware store. All that changed when nurseries began expanding, specializing, and offering more than just the standard range of stuff. Some added furniture into the mix, others gifts, a few even opened restaurants. Before they knew it, some became so well known that people were coming from all over the region to visit, some to buy, others just to enjoy the experience. Although the area has a number of locally owned nurseries that fit the description, there are three that come up in conversation again and again.

It may be located about an hour out of town in Woodinville, but **Molbaks Garden + Home** (13625 Northeast 175th St., Woodinville; 425-483-5000) seems to be the best known. While it grows its own plants, that's only part of the attraction. Instead, the big draw here is the total package, from plants and gear to decorative touches for inside the house as well including linens, tableware, and candles. It also has free gardening seminars and a café that serves sandwiches, beer, and wine. All of which adds up to the perfect way to spend a Saturday morning or afternoon, just wandering the aisles. Be careful, though, or you just might be tempted to buy something.

identification, landscape construction, and a variety of other issues within their field of study.

Washington Park Arboretum
2300 Arboretum Dr. East
(206) 543-8800

It isn't Seattle's biggest park, but there are times when it seems like it, especially when you're driving from Montlake to Madison Park and are stuck in slow moving traffic on the two lane road that cuts through the park. Fortunately, at least the view is nice and helps calm jangled nerves, especially in a city where honking your car's horn is frowned upon. The park has 40,000 trees and shrubs, 139 endangered species of plants, and plenty of space to

Swanson's Nursery (9701 15th Ave. Northwest, Seattle; 206-782-2543) is a bit more modest. It doesn't have indoor furniture or accessories, but it does have free classes, a gift shop, café, and a koi pond where kids and adults can hang out and watch fish frolic. It's also a popular spot during the holiday season because it has reindeer and a camel. Not many people know this, but it's also where Molbaks got its start because Egon Molbak got his training here before he went off and founded his own nursery. If you're in a buying mood, the store prides itself on its deep selection of perennials and unusual varieties of plants.

Sky Nursery (18528 Aurora Ave. North, Seattle; 206-546-4851) is even more modest as its slogan, "the gardener's gardening store," might attest. Its focus is on the meat and potatoes of the business. The real attractions are its new 35,000-square-foot retail green house, its classes, and its high level of customer service. If you're in the market for gardening items, it tends to have lower prices than the other two and is quick to admit that the family-owned store isn't "a fru fru experience." Where the other destination nurseries are good places to spend the day, Sky would easily classify itself as a shorter, get-and-go type of destination.

walk among trees, flowers and shrubs. The Arboretum has a visitors' center with a gift shop and a conference room for meetings and classes. It's also a pretty place to walk during the colder months when the Winter Garden is a popular stop. Although it's not free, the park also has a Japanese Garden (admission: $5) where there's a formal tea ceremony each month.

Woodland Park Rose Garden
750 North 50th St.
www.zoo.org/visit/rose-garden

If you didn't know about this garden, you just might miss it. The 2.5-acre splash of color is located at the Woodland Park Zoo's south entrance and features 280 rose varieties on 5,000 individual plants and sees about 200,000 visitors every year. In addition to being a beautiful summertime retreat for rose lovers, it's also a popular spot for weddings. On the last Sunday of February, the park holds a free rose pruning demonstration.

GARDENING

Has seeing all those gardens got you itching to start one of your own? These organizations will help you scratch that itch.

King County Extension Master Gardeners
3501 Northeast 41st St.
(206) 685-5104
http://king.wsu.edu/gardening/mastergardener.htm

What's that you say? Your plant has developed some sort of rot and no longer looks like its happy self? You've heard that a particular shrub would look great in your backyard, but you'd like to see what it looks like in a variety of settings before you buy it? Thanks to the master gardeners' program, you're not alone and you are in luck. This cadre of trained volunteer horticulturists stand ready to diagnose problems with your favorite flora and address your concerns about other gardening related issues. And the best part is, you don't have to go all the way to their office to find them. Instead, they not only diagnose over the phone, they also host 34 plant clinics throughout the county and have six demonstration gardens. They're also happy to dispense garden-variety advice to neophytes.

Urban Garden Share
www.urbangardenshare.org

So you've finally gone out and gotten the advice, the equipment, and all the plants you need to start gardening. There's just one small problem: you live in an apartment or on a small lot and there's no place to garden. Never fear, Garden Share is here. The Web site matches up people with land who would love to have a garden on it with experienced gardeners who are willing to do just that. Instead of exchanging cash for land access, wanna-be gardeners typically end up working out some sort of swap where they give a portion of the output in exchange for the joy of getting their hands dirty.

MUSEUMS:
FREE TO SEE
IN YOUR FREE TIME

"One time I went to a museum where all the work in the museum had been done by children. They had all the paintings up on refrigerators."

—STEPHEN WRIGHT

It's amazing what people will dedicate a museum to. Over the years, the Seattle area has had museums that focus on gas stations, bananas, and even potatoes. While those are long gone, they make a museum centered on doll art, another dedicated to the weird, and a national park in the heart of Pioneer Square sound somewhat tame in comparison. Although most of the city's best museums aren't free day in and day out, many of them offer free admission at least once a month. And some of the ones that you've never heard of are free year-round.

ALWAYS **FREE**

The Center for Wooden Boats
1010 Valley St.
(206) 382-2628
www.cwb.org

Most of the exhibits here are outside, not indoors, which makes perfect sense considering that its mission is to preserve wooden boats while teaching landlubbers and new salts an appreciation of the history of the boats and the skills necessary to sail them. The facility also rents boats and offers free boat rides on Lake Union every Sunday from 10 a.m. to 2 p.m. It's also the home to the annual Wooden Boat Festival.

Coast Guard Museum of the Northwest
Pier 36
1519 Alaskan Way South
(206) 217-6993
www.rexmwess.com/cgpatchs/cogardmuseum.html

A piece of the USS *Constitution* and a Coast Guard flag that went into space on the first space shuttle are among the many artifacts at this free waterfront museum that most Seattleites have never even heard about. There are also 25 models of Coast Guard ships, displays on World War II, and a wide range of uniforms. Although security concerns now generally prevent the public from visiting whatever ships happen to be in port, if you have a group and try to set it up in advance, you might just be able to tour an ice breaker. Open from 9 a.m. to 3 p.m. Monday, Wednesday, and Friday.

Frye Art Museum
704 Terry Ave.
(206) 622-9250
www.fryeart.org

You've got to love a museum that believes that art is so important that it should always be free to the public. Much of the collection focuses on European paintings from the late 1800s and early 1900s. And did I mention that it's always free?

Hiram M. Chittenden Locks Visitors Center
3015 Northwest 54th St.
(206) 783-7059
www.nws.usace.army.mil/publicmenu/menu.cfm?sitename=lwsc&pagename=mainpage

It's always fun for kids and adults alike to watch vessels be raised or lowered as they pass between Lake Washington and Puget Sound, but the operation is even more impressive when you understand all of the effort that went into making this engineering feat an everyday experience. The Visitors' Center details the history of the project and the concepts behind the engineering that makes it work. Add to that a visit to nearby Golden Gardens Park and a stop at a nearby ice cream stand and you've got the makingss of a great day.

Klondike Goldrush National Park
319 2nd Ave. South
(206) 220-4240
www.nps.gov/klse/index.htm

Pioneer Square may not be the first place people think of as the ideal place for a national park, but this park isn't about huge tracts of land. Instead, it commemorates the turn-of-the-20th-century rush for gold in the great white north and Seattle's role as outfitter to the masses in the very area of town prospectors stopped to get their supplies. Admission is always free. The park also offers a guided walking tour of the Pioneer Square area daily at 2 p.m. year-round and has gold-panning demonstrations several times a day during the summer. Demonstrations are limited to 30 people, walking tours to 25.

I'm Not a Museum, But I Could Play One on TV

Two of Seattle's best and cheapest museums aren't really museums at all, but they should be.

While most visitors see **Ye Olde Curiosity Shop** on the waterfront as just another tacky souvenir stand, many locals know better. Of course, it sells all the standard memorabilia that you'd find at any tourist shop including Seattle key chains, snow globes, pens, and postcards, and you could run in and run out without giving the shop a second thought. If you look a little closer you'll see a collection of oddities that would easily rival those found in many small museums. There's a walrus *oosik* (penis) hanging from the ceiling, a two-headed calf, a collection of shrunken heads, a walrus skull with three tusks, fleas in dresses, a collection of Northwest native art, and even the Lord's Prayer engraved on a grain of rice. If anyone could be said to be a mascot for this strange conglomeration, it would have to be Sylvester, a mummy who was said to have been found sticking out of the sand in an Arizona desert in 1895 and who has been at the store since 1955. Or it could be Sylvia, his mummified female counterpart. Believe it or not, there's no admission fee to all this wonderful kitsch.

The other, more frequently overlooked collection is **The Giant Shoe Museum** at the Pike Place Market. Not only does it have some of the largest shoes you'll ever see, it's likely one of the world's few coin-operated museums. (Which prompted the *Seattle Post-Intelligencer* to call it a "peep shoe.") The odd accumulation features 20 ginormous brogans including a size 37 shoe that once belonged to Robert Wadlow, considered to be the world's tallest man (at 8 feet 11 inches), and the Colossus, a 90-year-old, 5-foot-long wing tip shoe. It's not free, but it's close enough. You can see the entire collection through several windows for about $1 in quarters. The whole shebang is found Down Under at the market next to Old Seattle Paperworks.

OCCASIONALLY **FREE**

Bellevue Arts Museum
510 Bellevue Way Northeast
Bellevue
(425) 519-0770
www.bellevuearts.org

This museum has the perfect location to guarantee good turnout from East-siders. It's located right across the street from a mall. The museum's focus is on art, craft, and design. Admission is free on the first Friday of the month.

Burke Museum
University of Washington Campus
Corner of 17th Ave. Northeast and Northeast 45th St.
(206) 543-5590
www.washington.edu/burkemuseum

Parents of dinosaur-loving children beware! This much-loved natural history museum has free admission on the first Thursday of the month. It also features collections of cultural artifacts from indigenous peoples of Washington state and the Pacific Rim.

Experience Music Project and Science Fiction Museum
Seattle Center
325 5th Ave. North
(877) 367-7361 (EMP-SFM1)
www.empsfm.org

Steve Martin once said, "Comedy is not pretty." If this museum dedicated to popular music is any indication, comedy isn't alone. Built by noted architect Frank Gehry, some consider this pile of stuff visible from Interstate 5 a masterpiece. Others consider it a mess. Guess where I stand. Regardless of how you feel, you can view it from the inside and see rock 'n' roll memorabilia as well as numerous relics from famous science fiction movies and television shows. Just the bridge from the original *Star Trek* series and a collection of other-worldly weapons alone should be enough to delight any sci-fi geek. Free the first Thursday of the month from 5 to 8 p.m.

Georgetown Powerplant Museum

6605 13th Ave. South
(206) 763-2542

Talk about a museum with limited hours—this National Historic Mechanical Engineering Landmark is only open on the second Saturday of the month from 10 a.m. to 2 p.m. as part of a series of events including a meeting of steam-power enthusiasts and the running of a miniature steam railroad. The museum itself is home to the steam turbines that once provided the power for streetcars that ran throughout the city. The streetcars are gone, but the turbines still work.

The Henry Art Gallery

15th Avenue Northeast and 41st Street
(206) 543-2280
www.henryart.org

One of the first art museums in the state, the institution was originally built around a collection of 19th- and early 20th-century paintings. In the years since its opening on the University of Washington campus, however, the focus has expanded to include photography from the mid-1800s to 21st-century art relying on multiple disciplines. Admission is free on the first Thursday of the month.

Kidsquest Museum

4091 Factoria Mall Southeast
Bellevue
(425) 637-8100
www.kidsquestmuseum.org

Leave it to Eastsiders to put a children's museum in a shopping center. While Factoria Mall itself is just so-so, Kidsquest is a hit with kids for its imaginative hands-on exhibits for all ages. I love the Backyard exhibit because it is a large enclosed area in the middle of the museum for toddlers to play in with plenty of room to roam. My kids enjoy putting things in the water at Central Stream and watching them head downstream. Admission is free from 5 to 9 p.m. on Fridays.

Last Resort Fire Department
301 2nd Ave. South
(206) 783-4474
www.lastresortfd.org

A self-described work in progress, this museum features a variety of fire fighting apparatus once used by the Seattle Fire Department dating back to the 1800s. There are plans to feature displays on great fires throughout the city's history. The museum has limited hours, but admission is free.

Microsoft Visitors Center
15010 Northeast 36th St.
Microsoft Campus
Building 92
Redmond
(425) 703-6214
www.microsoft.com/about/companyinformation/visitorcenter/default.aspx

The once and former Microsoft Museum has become the Microsoft Visitors' Center. Where the museum provided a look back at the early days of Microsoft and the origins of the personal computer, the center shows where the software firm is heading while showcasing its latest offerings. There's an Xbox Theater with a 13-foot screen and surround sound, a Zune station where you can learn more about the company's answer to the iPod, a gaming area, and a section detailing Microsoft research including Photo Synth and the World Wide telescope. Open 9 a.m. to 7 p.m. Monday through Friday. Call before visiting as the center does close for private events. It's also located near the Microsoft company store. The center and the store are the only two areas on campus that the public can visit.

Museum of Flight
9404 East Marginal Way South
(206) 764-5720
www.museumofflight.org

The good news is that this museum is free the first Thursday evening of the month from 5 to 9 p.m. So, you can see the Personal Courage wing and even try your hand on the flight simulator (for an additional charge). The bad news is that the Airpark is closed, so you won't get to see Air Force One or the Concorde.

Museum of Glass

1801 Dock St.
Tacoma
(866) 4-MUSEUM (468-7386)
www.museumofglass.org

It's more than just a museum featuring the works of Dale Chihuly and other great glass artists, it's also a prominent part of the Tacoma skyline. Free admission from 5 to 8 p.m. on the third Thursday of the month.

Museum of History and Industry (MOHAI)

2700 24th Ave. East
(206) 324-1126
www.seattlehistory.org

This museum is loved by kids and adults alike for the glimpse it provides into Seattle's distant and more recent past. Children also like it because of the hands-on displays and exercises that show how salmon canneries worked before automation. Free all day on the first Thursday of every month. MOHAI is slated to move to the Naval Reserve Building in South Lake Union's Lake Union Park in 2012.

Northwest African American Museum

2300 South Massachusetts St.
(206) 518-6000
www.naamnw.org

It took years of battling with the Seattle School District to prevent the destruction of the building that once housed a community school and it took even longer to get the plan off the ground, but it's finally open. And admission is free on the first and second Thursday of the month.

Seattle Art Museum

300 First Ave.
(206) 654-3100
www.seattleartmuseum.org

Most people don't realize it, but the price to get into the Seattle Art Museum is whatever you want it to be. The suggested donation is $15, but given the state of the economy, the museum itself has publicized the fact that people can donate whatever they want to get in, even if it's only $1. (You might have to pay more to see special exhibits, however.) Technically speaking, since it's a donation, you might even be able to get in for free, but most Seattleites are too polite to try. Most simply wait until one of the museum's many days when admission is free. The Permanent Collection Galleries and special exhibitions are free all day on the first Thursday of every month in conjunction with the First Thursday Gallery Walk. A discount is sometimes offered for special exhibits. The museum is also free to people 62 and over on the first Friday of the month and to teens age 13 to 19 from 5 to 9 p.m. on the second Friday of the month (ID required).

Seattle Asian Art Museum
Volunteer Park
1400 East Prospect St.
(206) 654-3100
www.seattleartmuseum.org

The sister of the Seattle Art Museum is located across town in a popular Capitol Hill park with lots of parking. It's free all day on the first Thursday of the month and in conjunction with the Capitol Hill art walk on the second Thursday of every month from 5 to 9 p.m. Seniors also get in free on the first Friday of the month and families get free admission on the first Saturday of the month.

Seattle Veterans Museum
2nd Avenue between Union and University Streets (west side of Benaroya Hall)
www.seattleveteransmuseum.org

There couldn't be a better location for this museum than right next to the Remembrance Garden, a memorial listing all of the names of Washington state members of the armed forces killed in battle since World War II. While the granite wall lists their names, the museum brings their experiences to life by displaying weapons and gear used in battle and telling the stories of the servicemen who used them. At press time, the hours were limited to Friday, Saturday, and by appointment until enough volunteers could be recruited to run the museum on weekdays.

Volunteer Park Conservatory
Volunteer Park
1400 East Galer St.
(206) 684-4743
www.seattle.gov/parks/parkspaces/volunteerpark/conservatory.htm

A plant-lover's paradise, the Victorian greenhouse harkens back to a day when the Olmstead Brothers were designing grand parks for cities throughout the country. And for good reason. The Olmsteads designed Volunteer Park, too. The building itself was inspired by London's Crystal Palace and has five rooms with distinct themes including bromeliads, palms, ferns, cacti, and seasonal plants. It also houses a collection of illegally imported plants confiscated by the U.S. Fish and Wildlife Department. Admission is free, donation suggested.

Wing Luke Asian Museum
719 South King St.
(206) 623-5124
www.wingluke.org

This International District museum details the Asian American experience in Seattle and includes a tour of a historic hotel. Admission is free all day the first Thursday and third Saturday of the month.

ADDITIONAL **RESOURCES**

One of the few frustrating things about writing a book like this is that there's no way to list every bargain because new ones pop up every day and other ones go away without warning. And any cheap bastard worth his or her salt is always looking for the latest freebies and bargains.

Here are the places I turn to keep current.

DEALS AT **LOCAL** SUPERMARKETS AND **OTHER** STORES

Centsible in Seattle
centsibleinseattle.blogspot.com

Coupon Connections Northwest
www.couponconnectionsnw.com

Seattle Mom's Deal Finder
www.seattlemomsdealfinder.com

The Coupon Project
www.thecouponproject.com

Thrifty Northwest Mom
www.thriftynorthwestmom.com

Thrifty and Thriving
www.thriftyandthriving.com

DISCOUNTED PERFORMANCES

Goldstar.com
Sports, concerts, and plays are just some of this site's offerings.

Seattle Comp Tickets
www.facebook.com

Sign up for this Facebook group and you'll get periodic notification of comp tickets that are available to performances throughout the area. Notice varies from several days before the performance to day of show.

ODDS AND ENDS

Freeattle
www.freeattle.com

A spinoff of the Fresh Picked Seattle site, which lists food events around town, Freeattle began when Fresh Picked founder Leslie Seaton began listing all of the free non-food events she stumbled across while doing research for her original site. The site lists everything from meditation classes and author readings to lectures and travel workshops. A new sister site, Seattlenaturalselection.com, lists free events that are related to the great outdoors, the environment and science.

Groupon
www.groupon.com

Couponing and social networking come together on this site that offers a different deal every day with one little catch. The only way for the deal to work is if a minimum number of people sign up and pay up. Minimums vary from deal to deal.

Living Social
www.livingsocial.com

Like Groupon, this site offers one deal a day. The only difference is, there's no minimum group requirement before the deal goes into effect.

Seattle Free School
www.seattlefreeschool.org

As the name suggests, the school offers free classes on a variety of subjects depending on the interests and passions of its instructors.

Tippr
Tippr also offers a group coupon. A certain number of people have to buy in before the deal will work. The only difference is that it offers several deals a day and that the offer is often available for purchase for more than a day.

APPENDIX B:

LIBRARY BRANCH LOCATIONS

Seattle Public Library

Ballard Branch, 5614 22nd Ave. Northwest, (206) 684-4089

Beacon Hill Branch, 2821 Beacon Ave. South, (206) 684-4711

Broadview Branch, 12755 Greenwood Ave. North, (206) 684-7519

Capitol Hill Branch, 425 Harvard Ave. East, (206) 684-4715

Central Library, 1000 Fourth Ave., (206) 386-4636

Columbia Branch, 4721 Rainier Ave. South, (206) 386-1908

Delridge Branch, 5423 Delridge Way Southwest, (206) 733-9125

Douglass-Truth Branch, 2300 East Yesler Way, (206) 684-4704

Fremont Branch, 731 North 35th St., (206) 684-4084

Green Lake Branch, 7364 East Green Lake Dr. North, (206) 684-7547

Greenwood Branch, 8016 Greenwood Ave. North, (206) 684-4086

High Point Branch, 3411 Southwest Raymond St., (206) 684-7454

International District/Chinatown Branch, 713 Eighth Ave. South, (206) 386-1300

Lake City Branch, 12501 28th Ave. Northeast, (206) 684-7518

Madrona-Sally Goldmark Branch, 1134 33rd Ave., (206) 684-4705

Magnolia Branch, 2801 34th Ave. West, (206) 386-4225

Montlake Branch, 2401 24th Ave. East, (206) 684-4720

New Holly Branch, 7058 32nd Ave. South, (206) 386-1905

Northeast Branch, 6801 35th Ave. Northeast, (206) 684-7539

Northgate Branch, 10548 Fifth Ave. Northeast, (206) 386-1980

Queen Anne Branch, 400 West Garfield St., (206) 386-4227

Rainier Beach Branch, 9125 Rainier Ave. South, (206) 386-1906

South Park Branch, 8604 Eighth Ave. South at South Cloverdale Street, (206) 615-1688

Southwest Branch, 9010 35th Ave. Southwest, (206) 684-7455

University Branch, 5009 Roosevelt Way Northeast, (206) 684-4063

Wallingford Branch, 1501 North 45th St., (206) 684-4088

West Seattle Branch, 2306 42nd Ave. Southwest, (206) 684-7444

King County Library Branches

Algona-Pacific, 255 Ellingson Road, Pacific; (253) 833-3554

Auburn Library, 1102 Auburn Way South, Auburn; (253) 931-3018

Bellevue Library, 1111 110th Avenue Northeast, Bellevue; (425) 450-1765

Black Diamond Library, 24707 Roberts Dr., Black Diamond; (360) 886-1105

Bothell Library, 18215 98th Ave. Northeast, Bothell; (425) 486-7811

Boulevard Park Library, 12015 Roseberg Ave. South, Seattle; (206) 242-8662

Burien Library, 400 Southwest 152nd St., Burien; (206) 243-3490

Carnation Library, 4804 Tolt Ave., Carnation; (425) 333-4398

Covington Library, 27100 164th Ave. Southeast, Covington; (253) 630-8761

The Library Connection at Crossroads, Inside the Crossroads Shopping Center, 15600 Northeast 8th St., (near QFC) Suite K-11, (425) 644-6203

Des Moines Library, 21620 11th Ave. South, Des Moines (206) 824-6066

Duvall Library, 15619 Main St. Northeast, Duvall; (425) 788-1173

Fairwood Library, 17009 140th Ave. Southeast, Renton; (425) 226-0522

Fall City Library, 33415 Southeast 42nd Place, Fall City; (425) 222-5951

Federal Way 320th Library, 848 South 320th St., Federal Way; (253) 839-0257

Foster Library, 4060 South 144th, Tukwila; (206) 242-1640

Greenbridge Library, 9720 8th Ave. Southwest, Seattle; (206) 762-1682

Issaquah Library, 10 West Sunset Way, Issaquah; (425) 392-5430

Kenmore Library, 18138 73rd Northeast, Kenmore; (425) 486-8747

Kent Library, 212 2nd Ave. North, Kent; (253) 859-3330

Kingsgate Library, 12315 Northeast 143rd St., Kirkland; (425) 821-7686

Kirkland Library, 308 Kirkland Ave., Kirkland; (425) 822-2459

Lake Forest Park, Lake Forest Park Towne Centre, 17171 Bothell Way Northeast, Lake Forest Park; (206) 362-8860

Lake Hills Library, 15228 Lake Hills Blvd., Bellevue; (425) 747-3350

Library Express@Redmond Ridge, 10735 Cedar Park Crescent Northeast, Redmond; (425) 885-1861

Maple Valley Library, 21844 Southeast 248th St., Maple Valley (425) 432-4620

Mercer Island Library, 4400 88th Ave. Southeast, Mercer Island; (206) 236-3537

Muckleshoot Library, 39917 Auburn Enumclaw Rd. Southeast (253) 931-6779

Newport Way Library, 14250 Southeast Newport Way, Bellevue; (425) 747-2390

North Bend Library, 115 East 4th, North Bend (425) 888-0554

Redmond Library, 15990 Northeast 85th, Redmond; (425) 885-1861

Renton Library, 100 Mill Avenue South, Renton (425) 430-6610

Renton Highlands Library, 2902 Northeast 12th St., Renton (425) 430-6790

Richmond Beach Library, 19601 21st Ave. Northwest, Shoreline; (206) 546-3522

Sammamish Library, 825 228th Ave. Southeast, Sammamish; (425) 392-3130

Shoreline Library, 345 Northeast 175th, Shoreline; (206) 362-7550

Skykomish Library, 100 5th St., Skykomish; (360) 677-2660.

Skyway Library, 7614 South 126th St., Seattle; (206) 772-5541

Snoqualmie Library, 7824 Center Blvd. Southeast, Snoqualmie; (425) 888-1223

Southcenter Library Connection @ Southcenter Westfield Shoppingtown, 1386 Southcenter Mall, Tukwila; (206) 242-6044

Valley View Library, 17850 Military Rd. South, SeaTac; (206) 242-6044

Vashon Library, 7210 Vashon Hwy. Southwest, Vashon Island; (206) 463-2069

White Center Library, 11220 16th Southwest, Seattle, (206) 243-0233

Woodinville Library, 17105 Avondale Road Northeast, Woodinville; (425) 788-0733

Woodmont Library, 26809 Pacific Highway South, Des Moines; (253) 839-0121

POOLS AND RECREATION CENTERS

This list was current at press time, but is subject to change. I did not list hours as budget cuts may lead to reductions in service. In 2010, many centers were already taking at least one furlough day every month.

SEATTLE

Community Centers

Alki Community Center, 5817 Southwest Stevens St., (206) 684-7430

Ballard Community Center, 6020 28th Ave. Northwest, (206) 684-4093

Bitter Lake Community Center, 13035 Linden Ave. North, (206) 684-7524

Delridge Community Center, 4501 Delridge Way Southwest, (206) 684-7423

Garfield Community Center, 2323 East Cherry St., (206) 684-4788

Green Lake Community Center, 7201 East Green Lake Dr. North, (206) 684-0780

Hiawatha Community Center, 2700 California Ave. Southwest, (206) 684-7441

High Point Community Center, 6920 34th Ave. Southwest, (206) 684-7422

International District/Chinatown Community Center, 719 8th Ave. South, (206) 233-0042

Jefferson Community Center, 3801 Beacon Ave. South, (206) 684-7481

Laurelhurst Community Center, 4554 Northeast 41st St., (206) 684-7529

Loyal Heights Community Center, 2101 Northwest 77th St., (206) 684-4052

Magnolia Community Center, 2550 34th Ave. West, (206) 386-4235

Magnuson Community Center, 7110 62nd Ave. Northeast, (206) 684-7026

Meadowbrook Community Center, 10517 35th Ave. Northeast, (206) 684-7522

Miller Community Center, 330 19th Ave. East, (206) 684-4753

Montlake Community Center, 1618 East Calhoun St., (206) 684-4736

Northgate Community Center, 10510 5th Ave. Northeast, (206) 386-4283

Queen Anne Community Center, 1901 First Ave. West, (206) 386-4240

Rainier Beach Community Center, 8825 Rainier Ave. South, (206) 386-1925

Rainier Community Center, 4600 38th Ave. South, (206) 386-1919

Ravenna-Eckstein Community Center, 6535 Ravenna Ave. Northeast, (206) 684-7534

South Park Community Center, 8319 8th Ave. South, (206) 684-7451

Southwest Community Center, 2801 Southwest Thistle St., (206) 684-7438

Van Asselt Community Center, 2820 South Myrtle St., (206) 386-1921

Yesler Community Center, 917 East Yesler Way, (206) 386-1245

Weight Rooms

Garfield Community Center, 2323 East Cherry St., (206) 684-4788

Loyal Heights Community Center, 2101 Northwest 77th St., (206) 684-4052

Magnuson Community Center, 7110 62nd Ave. Northeast, (206) 684-7026

Meadowbrook Community Center, 10517 35th Ave. Northeast, (206) 684-7522

Northgate Community Center, 10510 5th Ave. Northeast, (206) 386-4283

Rainier Community Center, 4600 38th Ave. South, (206) 386-1919

Indoor Swimming Pools

Ballard Pool, 1471 Northwest 67th St., Seattle; (206) 684-4094

Evans Pool, 7201 East Green Lake Dr. North, Seattle; (206) 684-5961

Helene Madison Pool, 13401 Meridian Ave. North, Seattle; (206) 684-4979

Meadowbrook Pool, 10515 35th Ave. Northeast, Seattle; (206) 684-4989

Medgar Evers Pool, 500 23rd Ave., Seattle; (206) 684-4766

Queen Anne Pool, 1920 1st Ave. West, Seattle (206) 386-4282

Rainier Beach Pool, 8825 Rainier Ave. South, Seattle; (206) 386-1944

Southwest Pool, 2801 Southwest Thistle St., (206) 684-7440

Outdoor Swimming Pools

Colman Pool, 8603 Fauntleroy Way Southwest, Seattle; (206) 684-7494

Lowery C. "Pop" Mounger Pool, 2535 32nd Ave. W, Seattle; (206) 684-4708

Wading Pools

Ballard Commons Park, 5701 22nd Ave. Northwest, Seattle; (206) 685-4075

Beacon Hill Playground Wading Pool, 1902 13th Ave. South, Seattle; (206) 684-4075

Bitter Lake Playfield, 13035 Linden Ave. North, Seattle;

Cal Anderson Park Wading Pool, 1635 11th Ave., Seattle

Dahl Playfield Wading Pool, 7700 25th Ave. Northeast, Seattle

Delridge Playfield, 4458 Delridge Way Southwest, Seattle

E.C. Hughes Playground, 2805 Southwest Holden St.

East Queen Anne Playground, 1912 Warren Ave. North

Georgetown Playfield, 750 South Homer St.

Gilman Playground, 923 Northwest 54th St.

Green Lake Park, 7201 East Green Lake Dr. North

Hiawatha Playfield, 2700 California Ave. Southwest

Highland Park Playground, 1100 Southwest Cloverdale St.

John C. Little, Sr. Park, 6961 37th Ave. South

Judkins Park and Playfield, 2150 South Norman St.

Lincoln Park, 8011 Fauntleroy Way Southwest

Miller Playfield, 330 19th Ave. East

Northacres Park, 12718 1st Ave. Northeast

Peppi's Playground, 3233 East Spruce St.

Powell Barnett Park, 352 Martin Luther King Jr. Way

Pratt Park, 1800 South Main St.

Ravenna Park, 5520 Ravenna Ave. Northeast

Sandel Playground, 9053 1st Ave. Northwest

Soundview Playfield, 1590 Northwest 90th St.

South Park Playground, 738 South Sullivan St.

Van Asselt Playground, 7200 Beacon Ave. South

View Ridge Playfield, 4408 Northeast 70th St.

Volunteer Park, 1247 15th Ave. East

Wallingford Playfield, 4219 Wallingford Ave. North

Warren G. Magnuson Park, 7400 Sand Point Way Northeast

BELLEVUE

Community Centers

Crossroads Community Center, 16000 Northeast 10th, (425) 452-4874

Highland Community Center, 14224 Bel-Red Rd., (425) 452-7686

North Bellevue Community Center, 4063 148th Ave. Northeast, (425) 452-7681

Northwest Arts Center, 9825 Northeast 24th St., (425) 452-4106

South Bellevue Community Center, 14509 Southeast Newport Way, (425) 452-4240

Fitness Center

South Bellevue Community Center, 14509 Southeast Newport Way, (425) 452-4240

Swimming Pool

Bellevue Aquatic Center, 602 143rd Ave. Northeast, (425) 452-4444

KIRKLAND

Community Centers

North Kirkland Community Center, 12421 103rd Ave. Northeast, (425) 587-3350

Peter Kirk Community Center, 352 Kirkland Ave., (425) 587-3360

Swimming Pool

Peter Kirk Pool, 340 Kirkland Ave., (425) 587-3335

REDMOND

Swimming Pool

Redmond Pool, 17535 Northeast 104 St., (425) 233-3031

APPENDIX D:

PWYC PERFORMANCES

You spend hours searching the Internet for inexpensive airfare and travel a few extra miles to save money at the outlet malls, so why pay full price to see a play when there's a chance you can spend a little less and still see the same show as everyone else? If you don't mind taking a bit of a gamble on an evening's entertainment, there are many theaters that offer reduced price tickets. Some are unsold rush tickets released just minutes before a show while others are slightly less risky **Pay What You Can (PWYC)** performances. Regardless of which you choose, remember to get there early to increase your odds of getting in and have a backup plan handy just in case you don't. After all, just getting in is half the fun. The following theaters offer a variety of discounts. If you don't see your favorite, you might want to call and ask, check its Web site or its Facebook page, or join its e-mail list to learn about unadvertised specials or receive special offers.

A Contemporary Theatre: Offers two PWYC performances during each play's run with a suggested minimum donation of $5 and day-of-show rush tickets. Full time students can get advance tickets for $10 except on Saturday nights and patrons under 25 can get advance tickets for any performance for $15, depending on availability. Who said there were no benefits to going back to school? Now, if I could just be 25 again.

Annex Theatre: Has PWYC performances during its second week of run and student tickets for $5.

Artattack: Boasts one PWYC performance during the run of each play.

ArtsWest: Presents a PWYC preview on the night before opening night, suggested donation $5. People under 25 pay $10 for all performances; seniors get a 10 percent discount on tickets.

Backwards Ensemble Theatre Company: Patrons 25 and under are eligible for PWYC prices. The company's new playwrights' series has Pay What You Can As You Leave tickets.

Balagan Theatre: PWYC performance the Monday of closing week.

Eclectic Theater Company: PWYC the Thursday before opening night, free dress rehearsals. $10 tickets for students, seniors, military, veterans, union members, Cornish College alumni.

5th Avenue Theatre: Patrons 25 and under get day-of-show tickets for $20.

Ghostlight Theatricals: Has PWYC performances on Thursday nights. Check Web site for additional discounts and PWYC shows.

Harlequin Productions: Offers PWYC shows the second Saturday of a play's run. Rush tickets for $12 to $20 half hour before show.

Intiman Theatre: Preview performance tickets and PWYC available; patrons 25 and under can get tickets for $10. Standby and rush tickets are released 15 minutes before show for $20.

Kirkland Performance Center: Check center's Web site and e-mail for PWYC performances.

Our American Theater Company: Although there is a set ticket price, all shows are PWYC for people who can't afford full price.

Phoenix Theatre Edmonds: PWYC shows on the Thursday before opening night.

Printer's Devil Theater: Offers PWYC performances the first two Thursdays of a show's run.

ReAct: Features one or two PWYC performances per run, depending on show. Call theater for details.

Redwood Theatre: Offers a PWYC performance on the first Sunday of a show's run.

Seattle Repertory Theatre: Does a PWYC preview at the Bagley Wright the Tuesday before opening night; minimum suggested donation $1. Patrons 25 and under pay $12 at all performances for best available seat. Rush tickets $22. Teen Tix are $5.

Seattle Shakespeare Company: Holds a PWYC show early in play's run, usually on Tuesday or Wednesday. Rush tickets available to a group called Groundlings on day of show for $10.

Seattle Theatre Group (the Moore and the Paramount): Some traveling shows offer student rush tickets. For more information, sign up for eNews at STGPresents.org.

Second Story Repertory: Offers a PWYC preview Thursday before opening night.

SiS Productions: Sells $5 rush tickets to Teen Tix members and has a PWYC dress rehearsal (suggested donation $5) that's only advertised on SiS listserv and its Facebook page.

Sound Theatre Company: Offers PWYC performances most Thursday nights of a play's run.

Stone Soup Theatre: All Thursday night shows are PWYC and a show's final dress rehearsal is PWYC. Stone Soup also sends two-for-one deals to members of its mailing list.

Taproot Theatre Company: Sells $10 tickets to patrons 25 and under. Holds one PWYC performance per production. Students and seniors have $4 discount on tickets, which usually sell for $20 to $35.

Theater Schmeater: If you're under 18, you can get into any show free. Save with a Thursday night PWYC performance. Some dress rehearsals are also open to the public.

UPAC Theatre Group: Offers a PWYC performance the first Thursday of the main stage show's run and a two-for-one matinee for seniors on the second Saturday.

Village Theatre: Rush tickets are available to students and members of the military 30 minutes before curtain.

WARP: Students and seniors get half price tickets to WARP productions.

Washington Ensemble Theater: PWYC shows on the Thursday before opening nights.

For detailed information on the theaters listed here, see the Theater: Free Speech chapter starting on page 2.

APPENDIX E:

ADDITIONAL SEATTLE MUSIC FESTIVALS

The musical offerings at local festivals aren't as extensive as those at the various summer concerts throughout the area, but almost all of them have a concert's worth of free live music. The list includes:

MARCH

Irish Festival
Seattle Center
www.irishclub.org/center.htm

Enjoy music, singing, stepdancing, and all things Irish at this annual festival.

APRIL

World Rhythm Festival
Seattle Center
www.swps.org

A celebration of drumming and dance with a wide range of musical workshops.

Seattle Cherry Blossom & Japanese Cultural Festival
Seattle Center

An opportunity to hear the roar of Taiko drums and all things Japanese.

MAY

Asian Pacific Islander Heritage Month Celebration
Seattle Center
www.seattleapi.com

Drill teams and dragon dances are among the highlights of this festival honoring China, Japan, the Philippines, and other South Pacific islands.

Chinese Cultural and Arts Festival
Seattle Center
www.chinaartandculture.org

Enjoy a glimpse into the traditions of one of the world's oldest cultures through a variety of arts including dance and performance.

University District Street Fair
University Way from Northeast Campus Parkway to Northeast 50th Street
www.udistrictchamber.org/StreetFair/

Neighborhood festival featuring crafts, street performers, and several music stages.

JUNE

Edmonds Art Festival
9th Avenue and Main Street
Edmonds
www.edmondsartsfestival.com

An event built around a juried art show, the gathering has something everyone can love including activities for the younger set, performers, and a wine bar that looks out over Puget Sound.

Festival Sundiata
Seattle Center
www.festivalsundiata.org.

A celebration of African-American cultural heritage featuring music from all over Africa including drumming, dance, gospel, jazz, and hip hop.

Fremont Fair
From Fremont Avenue West between North Canal and North 36th Streets
www.fremontfair.org

Seattle's only festival that comes complete with a parade featuring nude bikers. Three music stages and many buskers.

Pagdiriwang Philippine Festival
Seattle Center

Observe Filipino independence from Spanish rule at this event featuring the islands' art and culture.

Pride Fest
Seattle Center
www.seattlepridefest.org

A celebration of Seattle's gay and lesbian community.

JULY

Ballard Seafood Festival
Downtown Ballard
www.seafoodfest.org

A celebration of the Scandinavian heritage of an area Garrison Keillor once called "the only ghetto in the world with hydrangeas."

Bellevue Arts Museum Arts Fair
Bellevue Arts Museum
510 Bellevue Way Northeast
Bellevue
www.bellevuearts.org

Arts demonstrations, live music, kids events, and the opportunity to buy the works of top artists are all part of the draw at this event near the Bellevue Arts Museum.

Bite of Seattle
Seattle Center
www.comcastbiteofseattle.org

Sample food from many of the city's favorite restaurants all in one place at this annual food-focused event.

Bastille Day Celebration
Seattle Center
www.seattle-bastille.org

Recall the storming of the Bastille at this commemoration of French independence.

West Seattle Summerfest
West Seattle Junction (the corner of California Avenue Southwest and Southwest Alaska)
www.westseattlefestival.com

A community street fair complete with live music in one of Seattle's nicest out-of-the-way neighborhoods.

Seafair Indian Days Pow Wow
Discovery Park (Magnolia Hill)
Daybreak Star Indian Cultural Center
Park entrance 3801 West Government Way
www.unitedindians.org

Native American gathering featuring drum and dance contests and traditional singing.

Vashon Island Strawberry Festival
17200 Vashon Hwy SW
Vashon
www.vashonchamber.com

Strawberries may not be the king crop they once were when this festival got its start in 1909, but there are still plenty of them and that's as good a reason to celebrate as any.

AUGUST

Lake City Pioneer Days
Lake City Way
www.lakecityfestival.com/

Enjoy the city's second longest running festival in Lake City of all places. Who knew?

Tibet Fest
Seattle Center
www.washingtontibet.org/TAW/

Learn about the ancient traditions of Tibet through art, dance, and discussion during this annual event.

South Lake Union Block Party
www.slublockparty.com
101 Westlake Ave. N

Celebrate one of Seattle's newest neighborhoods with one of the city's newest festivals. Events include a wine tasting, live music, and a burger grilling challenge.

Festa Italiana
Seattle Center
www.festaseattle.com

Stomp on grapes, take in cooking demonstrations, view movies, and learn everything you wanted to know about Italian culture but were afraid to ask.

Brasilfest

Seattle Center
www.brasilfest.com

The samba and the bossa nova are just the beginning at this festival focusing on all things Brazilian ranging from soccer to Feijoada stew.

Arab Festival

Seattle Center
www.arabcenter.net

Roam a traditional bazaar, learn about all things Arab, and even dance the night away at this annual gathering.

Central Area Community Festival Association

Garfield Community Center
2323 East Cherry St.
www.cacf.com

Salute the culture and community of the city's Central District through art, food, and music.

SEPTEMBER

Seattle Fiestas Patrias

Seattle Center
www.seattlefiestaspatrias.com/festival.php

The Seattle Latin-American community's observance of Independence Day.

Korean Cultural Celebration

Seattle Center
www.koamartists.org

Korea's annual harvest day is observed through folk music, native food, and film.

Oktoberfest
Fremont
www.fremontoktoberfest.com

No one's really quite sure why Oktoberfest is traditionally held in September, but beer is just a small part of Fremont's interpretation of the celebration, which includes a Brew Ha-Ha 5K run and Texas Chainsaw Pumpkin Carving.

OCTOBER

Seattle Reverb Festival
Ballard neighborhood
www.seattleweekly.com/microsites/reverbfest

North Seattle music fans take heart. You don't have to go all the way to the Seattle Center for music when the *Weekly* sponsors this music festival in Ballard.

Croatia Fest
Seattle Center
www.croatiafest.org/

Get serenaded by the music of the tamburitza while soaking up the culture of this often overlooked corner of Europe.

Utsav—South Asian Performing Arts Festival
www.utsav-seattle.org/

A festival that shows there's more to Indian music than Bollywood and sitar, Utsav is designed to foster an appreciation of the lively arts in India and its neighboring countries.

Turkfest
Seattle Center
www.turkfest.org

Observe the creation of the Republic of Turkey with dance, music, and art.

Issaquah Salmon Days
Downtown Issaquah
www.salmondays.org

San Juan Capistrano can have its swallows, but nothing beats a festival designed to celebrate a homecoming of creatures that make for good eating.

INDEX